International Economic Indicators and Central Banks

Founded in 1807, John Wiley & Sons is the oldest independent publishing company in the United States. With offices in North America, Europe, Australia and Asia, Wiley is globally committed to developing and marketing print and electronic products and services for our customers' professional and personal knowledge and understanding.

The Wiley Finance series contains books written specifically for finance and investment professionals as well as sophisticated individual investors and their financial advisors. Book topics range from portfolio management to e-commerce, risk management, financial engineering, valuation and financial instrument analysis, as well as much more.

For a list of available titles, please visit our Web site at www.WileyFinance.com.

International Economic Indicators and Central Banks

ANNE DOLGANOS PICKER

BICENTENNIAL
1807
WILEY
2007
BICENTENNIAL

John Wiley & Sons, Inc.

Published by John Wiley & Sons, Inc., Hoboken, New Jersey.
Published simultaneously in Canada.

For general information on our other products and services or for technical support, please contact our Customer Care Department within the United States at (800) 762-2974, outside the United States at (317) 572-3993 or fax (317) 572-4002.

Wiley also publishes its books in a variety of electronic books. Some content that appears in print may not be available in electronic formats. For more information about Wiley products, visit our Web site at www.wiley.com.

Statistics Canada information is used with the permission of Statistics Canada. Users are forbidden to copy the data and redisseminate them, in an original or modified form, for commercial purposes, without permission from Statistics Canada. Information on the availability of the wide range of data from Statistics Canada can be obtained from Statistics Canada's Regional Offices, its World Wide Web site at http://www.statcan.ca, and its toll-free access number 1-800-263-1136.

Library of Congress Cataloging-in-Publication Data:

Picker, Anne Dolganos, 1936–
    International economic indicators and central banks / Anne Dolganos Picker.
        p. cm.—(Wiley finance series)
    Includes bibliographical references and index.
    ISBN-13: 978-0-471-75113-7 (cloth)
    ISBN-10: 0-471-75113-8 (cloth)
    1. Economic forecasting. 2. Economic indicators. 3. Investments—Decision making. 4. Banks and banking, Central. I. Title.
    HB3730.P515 2007
    330.01′5195—dc22

                                                    2006025756

Printed in the United States of America.

10 9 8 7 6 5 4 3 2 1

To Hope
My daughter and number one fan

Contents

List of Illustrations

List of Tables

Preface

Investors are no longer constrained for the most part by political barriers and now seek investments that diversify their portfolios geographically. The move toward globalization has presented investors with worldwide investment opportunities. Anyone interested in making an international investment is interested in the factors that may have an impact on it—be it good or bad. And the good and bad in individual global markets no matter where they are located, can affect a company's operations and that carries through to their bottom line. It is a rapidly changing world, and one needs to track economic events diligently as they occur. Why should economic growth in Europe, for example, influence a U.S. company's profits? For one thing, it could be a prime market for that company and its fortunes are tied to it.

The importance of economic data is being recognized everywhere, and vast strides have been made in data quality even over the past year since I began writing this book. Somewhat belatedly, governments are finally appreciating the value of economic data for planning purposes and attracting investment. As a result, the production of indicators is a growth industry in many nations and changes and improvements are being made continually along the way.

Investors in the United States want to know how the economy is growing, whether there is inflation, and if employment and wages are increasing. They want to know the impact of these variables on consumer spending and on the profits of companies engaged in the making and selling of consumer products. Investors are concerned about the outlook for interest rates and how they will affect the value of the dollar, and therefore of the imports that everyone wants to buy. And I could go on. It is no different in Europe, Asia, and Australia. If you are investing in Germany, you would want to know why domestic demand has been lagging other European Monetary Union countries, for example.

The overall goal is to help investors make more informed investment decisions outside of the United States. And the first stop on that road is a brief look at who watches economic data in the financial marketplace. The "watchers" and "reactors" are found in three broad markets: bonds, stocks, and foreign exchange. And because we will be talking about events that can move financial markets wherever they might be located, a brief review of the bond, stock, and currency markets follows the preface in an introduction to the financial markets.

Part I of the book is directed toward an explanation of how central banks operate and why they influence economies and your investments. Part II deals with economic indicators and how that information helps investors understand what is happening economically and why it could influence the behavior of their investments. The data can also point to new avenues of investment opportunity. And since not all indicators are created alike across geographical borders, an understanding of these differences is also important.

This book covers the major industrial countries of Canada, the United Kingdom, Germany, France, Italy, Japan, Australia, and China. The euro-zone or European Monetary Union (EMU) is also included as the umbrella organization for the three European countries covered here. I have chosen to include some brief remarks on China's central bank, the People's Bank of China, along with brief profiles of their major economic indicators and their pitfalls. Despite the rudimentary nature of their data and the information about it, it is impossible to overlook the country's ever-increasing importance in today's global economy.

Book Outline

The book begins with a brief description of the bond, stock, and foreign exchange markets. That is where investors have the opportunity to respond to the latest news on central bank actions and/or the latest data on a key economic indicator. Over time, analysts have come to expect certain reactions to these events.

Part I, Central Banks, follows this market introduction. In this section, the banks' role and how they can influence investment decisions is discussed. Part II describes economic indicators from the international perspective. I regard indicators as critical input to sound investment decisions.

Chapter 1 provides an overview of central bank functions. I have included a section on the monetary tool *du jour*, inflation targeting. In part, it explains investor fixation with price indexes. The chapter focuses on the many tasks that a central bank might perform, including currency issuance and regulatory duties. In Chapters 2 through 7, the discussion hones in on the individual central banks. In Chapter 2, the unique role of the Bank of England is discussed. In Chapter 3, the European Union (EU) and its growing pains are described. Its development and its credibility led to the founding of the European Monetary Union (EMU) and the European Central Bank (ECB). The two are inextricably linked, and it is imperative to know about the EU to understand ECB policies and problems.

Chapter 4 discusses the Bank of Japan, its difficulties in ridding the economy of deflation and the recent reintroduction of a more normalized monetary policy after years of deflation. Chapter 5 focuses on the Bank of Canada and its success with inflation targeting along with its hard-won independence from reacting to U.S. Federal Reserve policy. Chapter 6 covers the Reserve Bank of Australia. The Bank has also been successful with its inflation-targeting policies, while keeping the economy on a growth path that has lasted more than 15 years.

The People's Bank of China is the subject of Chapter 7. Not too much is known about the PBOC. It is an example of a central bank that is not independent and must have its policies approved politically before they are enacted.

Part II of the book deals with the nitty-gritty of market-moving economic indicators. It is not the purpose here to cover all indicators. Rather the goal is to focus on indicators that have proven themselves over time to be reliable gauges of economic activity and provide investors with the kind of information they need to make prudent investment decisions.

Chapter 8 provides an overall guide to major economic indicators and why they are important to the financial markets. Specifics about each country are included in the following chapters.

European economic indicators are targeted in Chapter 9. Economic indicators for the EMU are covered first. They provide the overall guidelines for the individual country members' data. However, because of the importance of Germany, France, and Italy, their national indicators are discussed as well. Despite Eurostat's (the EU statistics agency) goal of providing uniform statistics that can be compared across Member States, national idiosyncrasies are smoothed over or lost in the process. Therefore, it is important, if you want to invest in these countries, to look at their national statistics and appreciate the differences among them.

Chapter 10 describes key British indicators. The United Kingdom is a member of the EU but not the EMU. As such, they comply with Eurostat's data rules. But here, too, it is important to look at the national statistics. There are major differences here, and they could impact investment decisions.

In Chapter 11, we move to Japan. Japan's slow recovery from its asset price bubble combined with wariness about its data has taught data watchers to be very careful in their interpretations. The big debate of 2006 involving the government, the Bank of Japan, and analysts has been whether deflation has really ended. The answer—it depends on which inflation measure you use and the reason you are using it!

Canadian indicators (Chapter 12) are easy to use and straightforward. But there are indicators here that could be new to investors, such as monthly gross domestic product.

Australian indicators in Chapter 13 provide an overview of data that are quite sophisticated and reliable. Timing differences however play a role, especially for the consumer and producer price indexes.

Finally, the importance of China could not be overlooked. Chapter 14 provides a brief overview of the main Chinese indicators. While the information is sketchy, efforts are being made to improve the timeliness and quality of the data.

Acknowledgements

This book should provide the answer to the lifelong question from my family: "So what do you really do?"

There are numerous people that I would like to thank for their help and encouragement over the past year and before. I would like to thank especially:

- Drs. Lois Schwartzman, Donald Bergman, and Robert Stark, who helped me to keep mind and body together during the past year.
- Evelina Tainer, who prodded me to write this book and managed somehow to be a one-person cheerleading squad and critic at the same time.
- Maurine Haver, who provided critical comment and insights that would have been unattainable otherwise. And a special thank you to members of her staff at Haver Analytics, including Randy Gernaat and Akosua Apenteng, who patiently answered my pressing questions of the day.

Although the book is dedicated to my daughter Hope, I would be remiss if I didn't acknowledge her invaluable assistance along the way. She read the manuscript at least three times and kept me on the straight and narrow, all the while reassuring me that it was a worthwhile undertaking.

There have been many others that have helped and encouraged me along the way and they know who they are. But I should like to mention two early mentors—the late Drs. Gerhard Bry and Charlotte Boschan, who pointed me in the direction of my life's long work.

Anne Dolganos Picker
September 2006
Greenwich, Connecticut

A Brief Introduction to the Financial Markets

Throughout the book, I refer to reactions in the bond, stock, and foreign exchange markets to central bank actions and new economic information. Markets react when a central bank changes policy—or even if it stays the same. And they react to new economic news in the form of economic indicators: Did the indicator move up or down and how did the result conform with the consensus opinion prior to the release? Certain reactions are expected, but others differ from expectations. The following review outlines the workings of the three markets and spells out what type of reaction is expected to occur.

BONDS

Bond markets behave differently than stock markets—bond markets live and breathe interest rates. Therefore, central bank interest rate policies are one of the most influential factors on bond prices and returns. Other factors influence their behavior as well. In periods of political uncertainty, bonds are regarded as a safe haven. U.S. government bonds in particular have always been considered a safe haven in times of uncertainty. Just as equities and foreign currency markets respond to economic news, the bond markets do also.

When a bond is issued, whether it is a government bond or a private bond, a fixed rate of interest is attached to it. However, when these same bonds are traded in the secondary market, the bond price fluctuates inversely to the bond's yield or interest rate. That is, if the bond price increases, the yield declines. The reverse is true also. When the bond price declines, the yield increases. This allows for trading in bonds where the interest rate would otherwise no longer be an attraction to traders.

Generally, the bond market will rally (i.e., prices will go up and yield or interest rate will decline) when the news is negative. For example, when the U.S. employment report added fewer jobs than forecast, bonds rallied. That is, bond prices go up and interest rates decline. Bonds are inflation sensitive. So when the consumer price index rises more than expected, for example, bond prices will decline (interest rates increase) in anticipation of higher central bank interest rates. The opposite can happen when a "market moving indicator" beats all predictions. Then there could be a sell-off.

A bond is a contract whereby the issuer promises to pay interest and repay the principal according to specified terms. A short-term bond is often called a note. They were the outgrowth of loans that early bankers provided to finance wars beginning in the middle ages. Today, bonds are one of the most widely used of all financial instruments. Bonds are classified as fixed-income securities. However, some bonds do not guarantee a fixed income, and many have a high degree of risk such as those from an emerging market country. The principal reason for issuing bonds in the private sector is to diversify sources of funding or to take advantage of low interest rates.

Bond markets have changed dramatically in the past 25 years or so. Until the 1970s, the bond market was principally a primary market where investors purchased bonds and held them until maturity. In the late 1970s, the reasons for bond investing changed and now many investors actively trade bonds to take advantage of price differentials rather than holding them for the long term. The major reason for the change was technology. Computers made it easier to spot price differentials and trade on them. Accounting rules that required bonds be valued at their current market value under certain circumstances changed.

There are four types of entities that issue bonds: national governments; lower levels of governments, such as provinces and states; corporations; and securitization vehicles. There are also futures contracts on interest rates that are traded in many countries. Futures can give you an idea where the market thinks interest rates will be sometime in the future. Reaction to economic events primarily occurs in the government bond markets. When the media talk about a bond market reaction, they are generally referring to government bonds. For example, interest rate futures can rise or fall on the release of an economic indicator such as the CPI. A low reading is interpreted to mean that a central bank will not have to increase interest rates to fight inflation. A jump in a price index, however, could have the opposite effect.

Inflation watching is a favorite pastime of market players. Soaring energy prices and their impact on other prices (the secondary affects) are important to bond market participants as they try to gauge future central bank interest rate policies.

Because of the large amounts involved, bond market activity is dominated by institutions such as insurance companies, pension funds, and mutual funds. Nonetheless, the small individual investor is not left out. A satisfying investment experience can be had if care is taken to understand market fundamentals. Bond market transactions are almost always negotiated between buyer and seller. The trading forum is not a central physical location but is essentially a network of telephone circuits between investment dealers and dealer brokers that are augmented by closed-circuit video screens. This system brings dealers together to initiate transactions for their own accounts or to facilitate transactions for their clients. As transactions are made they are displayed on the screen, thus providing all members of the investment dealer community with instant knowledge of what transactions have occurred, their volume, and their price.

Bond funds have proven far less popular than equity funds, but are a way to get exposure to the fixed-income markets. An advantage to buying foreign bond funds is that you do not need to worry about bond quality. If you are investing domestically, you ideally have a better idea about credit quality but may not know how to do the same research for foreign bonds. The globalization of securities markets, coincident with the improved efficiency of international communications, has given investors opportunities for informed exposure to foreign currency bond issues. Although offshore markets always have been available, participation in them usually has been inappropriate for individuals because of the difficulty in acquiring detailed knowledge of a foreign market's economic environment and the forces affecting its trend in interest rates. Now, however, it is almost as easy to attain informed opinions on major foreign economies as it is to keep abreast of what's going on in one's home market.

A disadvantage to bond funds is that while the average maturity of the holdings may appeal when one makes the initial purchase, the manager might later make changes that lead to a completely different maturity and credit quality exposure than one suitable for the individual involved. In other words, when you buy into a bond fund, you have no ongoing control of the maturity or credit quality of your investments. This is being addressed by some funds. A bond fund never matures, and thus investing in a bond fund is similar to investing in a stock fund.

The chance to gain a fuller understanding of other market environments exposes investors to an increased array of investment options. Properly chosen, those options can lead to opportunities in the most attractive markets, and in the long run assure a higher investment return than attainable by restricting portfolio holdings to one particular national jurisdiction. This book should help investors by pointing the way to relevant information they would want to know for wise investment decision making.

An investor in the domestic bond market is exposed to only two components: overall investment return and income and capital value changes that result because of movements in the level of interest rates. However, buying a non-dollar-denominated bond adds a third component—foreign currency exposure. That exposure not only provides the potential for additional reward, but also increases the risk.

Traditional portfolio analysis points to the need to restrict risk as much as possible. Accordingly, participation in foreign markets was considered inappropriate for prudent investors. But the ease of communication and the constant international flow of investment capital have made currency exposure a normal and acceptable risk for those wishing to maximize their investment return opportunities. Efficient communication and more sophisticated analysis also have helped reduce the reluctance of investors to accept that the existence of currency exchange risk is a necessary part of the game. The appeal of diversifying a portfolio, by acquiring other than domestic currency bonds, lies in the fact that international economies tend to expand at differing rates and at different times.

By recognizing economies with forces at work that encourage the development of lower domestic interest rates, investors are in a position to have continuous exposure to the most attractive areas of the international market.

There are aspects of the economy that have been consistently useful barometers for bond market investors. Among them are general employment conditions, the state of the housing industry, and retail sales trends. Employment data usually has a short-term impact on bond prices, but it is the detail of the report that provides a better feel for what the longer term might look like. For example, the trend of total hours worked, overtime put in, and the level of hourly wage rates are all useful in deciding whether future employment prospects are brightening or if layoffs will occur. The health of the housing industry will often dictate the intensity of activity in durable goods manufacturing. Retail sales of home furnishings are also intimately affected by housing trends. Retail sales are among the keys to judging economic health, since they measure the real mood of the all important consumer. And in most developed economies, the consumer accounts for the largest portion of gross domestic product. Therefore, the trend in retail sales, usually can indicate general business conditions and the trend of interest rates.

STOCKS

Indicators can give clues and point to possible good stock buys. A variety of things affect their price movements other than corporate profits. Of the other events that can impact day-to-day stock movements, the most obvious of these is the status of economic growth. Is the country growing? What are the prospects for growth in the future? Central bank policies, both real and anticipated changes, can impact movements. And, of course, political and geopolitical events such as the "No" votes on the EU constitution in June 2005 is a recent example. This is discussed in Chapter 3.

FYI

Equities are a concept that go back to medieval times. During the renaissance, when groups of merchants joined to finance trading expeditions and bankers took part ownership to ensure loan repayment, equities flourished. The first shareholder-owned company might have been the Dutch East India Company, which was founded in 1602.

Equity prices have been affected by recent swings in crude oil prices in two ways: (1) Investors worried that rising crude prices would mean that consumers would cut spending; and (2) worries about inflationary prospects could hurt corporate profits. However, the higher prices were good for energy company stocks—they benefited from higher prices that in turn increased profits.

The main function of equity markets has always been to raise capital. Equity represents the owners' investment and as such attracts other investors. Bankers and bondholders are attracted because owners have put their own money at risk.

Stock prices are affected by many things, including:

- **Earnings**—simply, they are the difference between the revenue the firm has claimed to have generated during a specific period less the expenses incurred during that same time. They are influenced by both internal and external factors. Earnings are affected by economic performance (the indicators) and interest rates (central bank policies). In the late 1990s, euphoric investors, eager to get into the soaring market, thought earnings did not matter. Investors learned the hard way that they do.
- **Cash flow**—indicates whether a business is generating sufficient cash to meet its outlays.
- **Dividends**—in many countries, markets prefer shares that pay dividends because it provides returns when share prices are not appreciating.
- **Asset value**—a firm might own assets that increase (or decrease) in value because of market forces. The obvious example here is a company's mineral reserves such as crude oil. Royal Dutch Shell was forced to restate the quantity of its oil reserves downward several times. This had a negative impact on its share price.

- **Analysts' recommendations and company guidance**—both can also affect stock prices. Investors are wary of analysts' recommendations since the collapse of many dot-com companies in the late 1990s that only had analyst recommendations going for them. Analyst recommendations as well as company guidance generally depend on their individual readings of the overall economic outlook.
- **Interest rates**—higher interest rates generally depress stock prices. In May 2006, after 16 successive interest rate increases, uncertainty about Federal Reserve (Fed) policy triggered a worldwide sell-off of equities. Investors were hoping that the string of rate increases was at an end. But when a U.S. consumer price report indicated that inflation was higher than expected, equity investors sold stocks, convinced that the Fed would continue to increase rates rather than pause. And because of the Fed's dominant position in the hierarchy of central banks, international investors were upset as well and equity indexes worldwide dropped. Higher rates often (but not always) presage slower economic growth, which in turn could slow profit growth. However, higher rates often accompany higher rates of growth and are a positive signal that growth is strong. Higher interest rates could also be considered positive if they are viewed as necessary to keep inflation in check. Inflation is viewed as dangerous to asset values.
- **General economic news**—in observing the markets, it is easy to see that many indicators such as employment and retail sales move the market. But it doesn't have to be domestic economic news. Japanese exporters' stocks often fluctuate on the strength of U.S. indicators, especially those dealing with consumer spending such as autos and electronics.
- **Fads**—certainly the outrageous gains of dot-com stocks in the absence of any credible information is an example of the not-too-distant past.
- **Oil prices**—soaring energy prices have affected equities. Generally, equity indexes have moved in the opposite direction of crude oil prices. When oil prices drop, equities have tended to climb. When oil prices rise, equity prices tend to fall. The reason for this is that higher prices can put upward pressure on company costs and reduce profit margins. Higher energy costs also could leave consumers with less money to spend on other purchases.

FOREIGN EXCHANGE: THE MARKET THAT NEVER SLEEPS

Anyone who is considering an investment not in their home country has to consider an additional risk element in their decision making—foreign exchange. The relative value of their currency to other major currencies is so important to some central banks that it is a key factor in their monetary policy deliberations. In turn, currencies react to central bank actions and to movements in economic indicators.

Equities, bonds, and foreign exchange markets react differently to the same economic news. For example, what is good news for equities can be equally bad for bonds, while the foreign exchange markets totally ignore the event. Currency trading is closely linked to securities trading, especially bonds and money market instruments. An investor might want to buy a desired currency and invest in a highly liquid interest-bearing asset rather than hold cash that has no return. When a more lucrative investment opportunity presents itself, it is easy to convert the asset to cash and to the new investment.

The foreign exchange market is the largest of any financial market. In reality, there is no physical market place, but rather a worldwide network of traders connected by telephone and computers. There is no single "headquarters," either, although the dominant markets are in Tokyo, London, and New York. Transactions in Singapore, Switzerland, Hong Kong, Germany, France, and Australia account for most of the remaining transactions in the market. Trading goes on 24 hours a day. At 8 A.M. the exchange market is opening in London, at about the time the trading day is ending in Singapore and Hong Kong. At 1 P.M. in London, the New York market opens for business and later in the day the traders in San Francisco can also conduct business. As the market closes in San Francisco, the Singapore and Hong Kong markets are starting their day.

Prices for goods and services are expressed in currency units that are issued by that country's central bank or treasury. But sometimes individuals prefer to denominate transactions in an international currency such as the U.S. dollar. An example would be crude oil and other commodities that are priced in U.S. dollars. When Europeans buy oil from Saudi Arabia, they pay in U.S. dollars and not in euros or Saudi dinars, even though the United States is not involved in the transaction.

Currency markets are known for their short-term volatility as they respond to the latest news. For example, the currency markets sold the U.S. dollar when the Fed increased the fed funds target rate by only 25 basis points—they were looking for more. They also sold the U.S. dollar after the merchandise trade deficit climbed to record levels. However, in the long term, exchange rates are determined almost entirely by real interest rate expectations, defined as interest rates less inflation.

The demand for Japanese stocks also creates demand for the yen, which is needed to complete the transaction. The yen climbs in value as well. Political factors also play a role. Recently, events such as the Iraqi War, North Korea's weapons policies, and instability in the Middle East have all played a role. In Europe, the "No" votes cast by the Netherlands and France on the European Union Constitution pressured the value of the euro. National elections can affect a currency's value as well.

Traders speculate within the market about how different events will move the exchange rates. For example, news of political instability in other countries drives up demand for U.S. dollars as investors are looking for a "safe haven" for their money. A country's interest rate rises and its currency appreciates as foreign investors seek higher returns than they can get in their own countries. Developing nations undertaking successful economic reforms may experience currency appreciation as foreign investors seek new opportunities. But, ultimately, interest rates, that is, those set by central bankers, influence currency values.

Because of its volatility, risk is inherent in foreign exchange trading, and it is not for novices.

Currency Trading Has a Long History

Currency trading dates backs to ancient times. In medieval times, coins were minted from gold or silver and circulated freely across Europe's borders of that time. Foreign exchange traders provided a form of coinage to lessen worries that another currency might not contain the proper amount of a precious metal promised. And when paper money came into vogue in the eighteenth century, its value was still determined by the amount of precious metal that the government promised to pay the bearer. Even after the main industrial nations stopped linking their currencies to gold and silver in the 1920s and 1930s, governments tried to keep the rates of conversion relatively stable between currencies. The Bretton Woods system created in Bretton Woods, New Hampshire, at the end of World War II was a system of fixed rates.

But in the late 1960s, the system began to break down, and in 1972, it was decided to let market forces determine exchange rates. It was the uncertainty created by this decision that led to the growth in currency trading. In the late 1990s, currency trading volumes declined because the euro eliminated trading among the 12 European Monetary Union (EMU) countries. Bank industry consolidation on a worldwide level has reduced the number of firms with a significant presence in the market. But after the September 11, 2001, terrorist attacks in New York City and Washington, interest rates in the United States and elsewhere fell dramatically. As business normality returned but interest rates remained at historically low levels, currency traders saw an opportunity. They engaged in "carry trade"—they borrowed in a low interest rate country such as the United States (the fed funds rate was 1 percent) and invested in a higher interest rate country such as Australia (the comparable interest rate was 5.25 percent). Between December 2003 and June 2004, the spread or difference between the two countries' interest rates was 425 basis points or 4.25 percent.

Market Participants

Those participating in the foreign exchange market are a diverse and eclectic group. They include, as you would expect, exporters and importers of goods and services. An obvious example here would be Japanese companies engaged in international trade. They will benefit or suffer financially from the day-to-day fluctuations of the yen.

Investors need to have the currency in which a security is denominated in order to make a purchase on an international exchange and then again to convert earnings back into their home currency when they decide to sell. Speculators buy and sell solely to profit from the anticipated marginal changes in exchange rates without participating in any other business dealing for which a currency transaction is necessary.

Governments buy and sell at times to control the external value of their currency. An obvious example was the heavy Japanese intervention in the currency markets prior to the close of their 2003 fiscal year in March 2004. In this case, they were trying to force the value of the yen down to protect the earnings of exporters that were being repatriated back to Japan. Earlier that year, the purpose of the intervention was to lower the yen so that exporters would remain price competitive in their overseas markets.

There are four different currency markets. The spot market is where currencies are traded for immediate delivery. Examples are tourist currency purchases and an exporter cashing in receipts from overseas sales. In the futures market, participants lock in a rate for a future date by purchasing/selling a futures contract that effectively guarantees a fixed rate of conversion. Participants in international trade often use futures contracts to guarantee a fixed price. A third market is the options market. It accounts for a relatively small amount of trading. It gives the option holder the right, but not the obligation, to acquire/sell foreign exchange or futures at specified prices during a specific time period. The fourth market is the most active and deals in derivatives. Most trading occurs in this market. In common usage, it refers to instruments that are not traded on organized exchanges such as the London or New York exchanges. Briefly, they include forward contracts, swaps, forward rate agreements, and barrier options.

Exchange Rate Management

A government's decision about exchange rate management is the most important factor shaping currency markets. There are four basic categories: fixed, semifixed, floating, and fixed rate.

- **Gold standard.** The oldest is the gold standard, which was introduced by the United Kingdom in 1840 and adopted by most other countries by 1870. A country's money is directly linked to the gold reserves owned by the central bank. Gold can be exchanged at any time for notes and coins. The system was thought to be self-correcting. For example, if a country ran a trade deficit, the central bank could not eliminate the deficit via currency devaluation (which would make exports cheaper and imports more expensive). Rather, as foreigners exchanged their excess currency for gold, money in circulation would drop because there was less gold. The country would be forced into recession, which would reduce demand for imports.
- **Bretton Woods.** This system was based on foreign currencies as well as gold. Briefly the (then) newly created International Monetary Fund would lend members gold or foreign currencies to help a country deal with a short-term imbalance. It collapsed in the late 1960s and early 1970s because of the pain inflicted on several countries.
- **Pegged exchange rate.** This occurs when a country decides to hold the value of its currency in constant terms of another currency. The most notable was the peg of China's renminbi or yuan to the U.S. dollar until August 2005. At that time, China shifted to a managed float of their currency against a basket of currencies. Hong Kong's currency, the Hong Kong dollar, has kept its peg to the U.S. dollar. An interest rate increase in the U.S. is immediately passed on by the Hong Kong Monetary Authority. A peg is subject to change and could destabilize a currency. Not all pegs are successful—Argentina's peg to the U.S. dollar collapsed in January 2002 because of its inflexibility. Argentina in effect had surrendered control of monetary policy and was unable to lower interest rates to combat a depression.
- **Semifixed.** These systems are meant to provide governments with more flexibility by leaving room for currency fluctuations. There are several types. The European Exchange Rate Mechanism to which European Union members must adhere prior to joining the European Monetary Union is the most obvious example. As long as a currency stays within the band it is allowed to float.
- **Pegs and baskets.** A country pegs its currency to a basket of foreign currencies rather than just one as in the peg. The basket approach was adopted for the Chinese renminbi.

- **Floating rates.** The key difference here is that exchange rates are not the target of monetary policy. However, governments still have the option to intervene. Again, the obvious example here is Japan. The Bank of Japan executes the intervention on behalf of the Ministry of Finance.

Exchange rates respond directly to all sorts of events, both tangible and psychological. They respond to economic news including inflation expectations; merchandise trade balances and balance of payments statistics; political developments such as elections and new tax laws; stock market news; international investment flows; and government and central bank policies, among others. They also respond to exogenous events such as natural disasters.

The currency of a growing economy with relative price stability and a wide variety of competitive goods and services will be more in demand than that of a country in political turmoil, with high inflation and few marketable exports. Money will flow to wherever it can get the highest return with the least risk. If a nation's financial instruments, such as stocks and bonds, offer relatively high rates of return at relatively low risk, foreigners will demand its currency to invest in them.

About the Author

Anne Dolganos Picker is Econoday's chief economist. Econoday is an organization that provides online analysis and education for professional and nonprofessional investors. She obtained her master of business administration from New York University in economics where, during her studies, she was awarded a Ford Fellow in Economic Growth and a Lincoln Foundation Fellowship. She received a bachelor of science in business administration from Rutgers University under a full scholarship. In addition to her responsibilities at Econoday, Anne teaches an online web course for the University of Illinois at Chicago's MBA program.

Prior to joining Econoday, Anne was president of her consulting firm, Picker Associates. She provided private economic consulting services for decision makers of major corporations and financial institutions supporting their strategic and market-planning efforts in the United States and overseas. She has analyzed and forecast for industries as diverse as oil and hospitality, looking at the domestic and international long- and short-term implications for profitability. During this time, she was editor of a National Association for Business Economics periodical, *Nabe News*. Throughout her career, she has written articles for the trade press and professional journals and has frequently addressed industry groups and professional organizations.

Anne has a broad background in providing international and domestic economic analysis and forecasts. As director of economic studies at American Paper Institute, Anne prepared international reports covering socioeconomic and political environments of major industrial countries. The purpose of these reports was to provide competitive and market information that could be used by U.S. producers in their business planning. She briefed senior executives on sources of international indicators, their importance, and the outlook for the countries in question. As senior economist for business research, NYNEX Corporation, Anne wrote the long-term international outlook that required hands-on knowledge of all geographic regions of the world.

Anne is a fellow of the National Association for Business Economics, served a term as a director, and chaired numerous meetings including a national policy seminar. She also served as president of the Forecasters Club of New York and the New York Association for Business Economics.

International Economic Indicators and Central Banks

Central Banks

CHAPTER 1

An Overview of Central Banks

Central banks everywhere have several things in common regardless of where they are located. They are a banker's bank, a place where banks can seek relief in turbulent times. They usually are issuers and custodians of the currency, and protect it from everything including forgery to runs on its value. Many have regulatory powers as well. And most importantly, they make monetary policy decisions.

Financial market participants view central banks' monetary policy decisions and their timing as one of the primary inputs to the investment decision-making process. Central bank decisions impact interest rates, and interest rates have a direct effect on the cost of doing business and therefore profits. Their role in setting interest rates directly is relatively new and it is only in the last 15 to 20 years that central banks have targeted them directly. For example, the Federal Reserve (Fed) began to set the federal funds rate directly in June 1989 rather than targeting monetary aggregates (M1, M2, M3). Previously, money supply was increased/decreased to achieve the desired interest rate. And there were also periods in the 1980s and before when the Fed targeted the fed funds rate even more overtly and no announcement was made. Instead, Fed watchers would have to pore over the weekly money supply data to see if there had been a policy change.

There are many commonalities—and differences—in the business of central banking. They include the way each bank adjusts interest rates, how economic data are used to help make informed decisions, differing interpretations and uses of inflation targeting, central bank cooperation both with other central banks and financial regulators, and the list goes on. And while policies may seem similar, often terminology will differ. Some of the banks are relatively transparent in their decision making while others remain opaque. Each bank applies common central bank policies in a way that is unique to their political and social environment. A key policy tool for many—but not all—central banks is inflation targeting. But we will get to that later in this chapter.

The purpose of this chapter is to give an overview of what is common and different about the Banks but leaving until later a fuller description of each Bank's development and functions. The Banks covered are the European Central Bank (ECB), Bank of England, Bank of Japan (BoJ), Bank of Canada, Reserve Bank of Australia (RBA) and the People's Bank of China (PBOC).

A FASCINATION WITH CENTRAL BANKS

Central Bank Watching—A Major Financial Market Occupation

The U.S. Federal Reserve's (Fed's) pronouncements are sliced and diced for any hints regarding policy that would affect the economy and the financial markets. And it is no different for "other" central banks. Investors in other particular geographic areas behave in much the same way as watchers in the United States. In fact, like the Fed, these other central banks can impact financial markets worldwide. Investors everywhere watch the BoJ for assurances that deflation has ended in Japan. Investors in Europe hope that the ECB will not increase rates by too much and cut off its nascent recovery. And Canadian investors watch Bank of Canada policy as they weigh the relative merit of Canadian versus U.S. investment payoffs. Bank of England watchers are wondering if interest rates can accommodate the inflationary pressures of crude oil prices and tight labor markets while at the same time, not squashing consumer demand.

Investors care about a bank's independence from political pressures. For example, the ECB did not respond to persistent and intense political pressure to lower interest rates despite anemic growth and the stronger euro during 2004 and 2005. The ECB is the newest central bank and wanted to show how free of political interference it is—political rhetoric is bound to make it do the opposite.

The BoJ used to be part of the Ministry of Finance (MoF). Now it is fiercely independent and fends off any interference from the Ministry or, for that matter, any other part of the Japanese government. It struggled over policy especially in the late 1990s and early 2000s while the economy was in the depths of a recession. And in early 2006 when it was apparent to the central bank that deflation was ending and the economy had recovered and was out of recession, the Bank staved off an avalanche of political rhetoric and proceeded to begin the normalization of its policies. The Bank continues to act for the Ministry of Finance in the currency markets, usually selling yen for dollars to deflate the yen's value.

Central bank policies provide guidance for investors. Interest rate policies provide the broad umbrella under which business is done and the banks' announcements are broadly watched and anticipated by market players. The Bank of Canada meets about every six weeks; the Bank of England, ECB, and Reserve Bank of Australia meet monthly; and the BoJ, about every three weeks, while the PBOC meets quarterly. But all can hold emergency meetings should the situation arise. Virtually all the central banks held emergency meetings in the aftermath of the terrorist attacks on September 11, 2001, for example.

A quick word about the Fed—even though I have not included the U.S. central bank within the scope of this book. (See Evelina Tainer's marvelous description of the Federal Reserve in her third edition of *Using Economic Indicators to Improve Investment Analysis*. Hoboken, NJ: John Wiley & Sons, 2006.) I would be remiss not to mention the worldwide impact of Fed policy moves. Given the U.S. position as the world's primary engine of growth, a brief recent example of its impact on global markets should be sufficient. In the run up to the Federal Open Market Committee (FOMC) meeting in May 2004, world financial markets became transfixed as they waited for the decision on interest rate policy. When the post-meeting statement indicated that an interest rate increase would occur soon, equity markets in Europe and Asia swooned but the dollar rose on the news.

"Carry trade" became a popular form of trading in the low-interest-rate years of the early 2000s. Investors took full advantage of interest rate spreads between countries to borrow in a low-interest-rate country and then invest the funds in a higher-interest-rate country. For example, when U.S. interest rates were 1 percent, it was fashionable to borrow here and invest elsewhere—perhaps Australia, where rates were as much as 425 basis points higher at that time. As U.S. rates began to climb, the paradigm changed, investors borrowed in Europe, where rates were 2 percent and below most other countries, or in Japan, where zero interest rates prevailed.

Central Bank Tasks

Regardless of which central bank you are talking about, they all have essentially the same functions. They:

- Set monetary policy.
- Determine how the economy behaves.
- Respond to economic and financial market conditions within their jurisdiction.
- Control money supply.
- Regulate the banking system.

- Issue currency (The Federal Reserve is the exception. The U.S. Treasury prints U.S. currency while the Fed puts it into circulation.)

A Primer on How Monetary Policy Works

Setting policy by directly changing interest rates is a relatively new tool for central banks. For example, the Federal Open Market Committee (FOMC) began setting targets for the fed funds rate in June 1989. And other central banks soon followed.

When a central bank decides to change the official interest rate their goal is to eventually influence the overall level of consumer and business expenditures. Beginning in November 2003 and ending in August 2004, for example, the Bank of England increased interest rates five times with the explicit intent of slowing down the housing market, where prices were skyrocketing. At the same time, they wanted to cool torrid consumer spending. The Bank uses the interest rate at which they lend to financial institutions or "repo" as the mechanism to adjust rates. When the Bank moves the "repo" rate up or down, it triggers changes in a whole gamut of interest rates, including those set by commercial banks, building societies, and other institutions for their own savers and borrowers. Interest rate changes affect financial asset prices for bonds and equities as well. The exchange rate for a country's currency can also feel the reverberations of an interest rate change, especially when it goes against traders' expectations. In short, lowering or raising interest rates affects spending throughout the economy.

Saving is less attractive and borrowing more attractive when interest rates are reduced. This in turn stimulates spending. Recent U.S. experience with lower-than-normal interest rates is a good example of what cheap money can do. But lower interest rates can have a negative influence on both consumers' and firms' cash flow. Lower interest rates reduce savings (interest) income as well as the interest payments due on loans. Lower interest rates can boost the prices of assets such as equities and houses. Higher house prices enable existing home owners to extend their mortgages in order to finance higher consumption. Higher share prices raise households' wealth and can increase their willingness to spend. The opposite occurs when interest rates are increased.

The exchange rate can be pressured by interest rate changes. The widening (or narrowing) of the spread between interest rates in two countries impacts investment flows between the two and the consequent demand for their currencies. For example, if the United Kingdom's interest rate was higher relative to those in the U.S. it would give British investors a higher return on assets relative to their foreign currency equivalents, tending to make UK assets more attractive. This was particularly true during 2003 and 2004 when the fed funds rate rested at 1 percent and the Bank of England was in the process of increasing its key interest rate to 4.75 percent.

Fluctuations in currencies also can influence consumer and business demand in a variety of ways but usually via international trade. Again let us use the United Kingdom as an example. In theory, the wider spread in the country's favor should raise the value of the pound sterling, reduce the price of imports, and reduce demand for UK goods and services abroad. However, the impact of interest rates on the exchange rate is, unfortunately, seldom that predictable. The only thing predictable about the foreign exchange market is its unpredictability!

Some of these influences can work more quickly than others. And the overall effect of monetary policy will be more rapid if it is credible. But, in general, there are time lags before changes in interest rates work their way through to spending and saving decisions, and longer still before they affect consumer prices. It is estimated that the maximum effect on output can take up to about one year while the maximum impact of a change in interest rates on consumer price inflation takes up to about two years. So interest rates have to be set based on judgments about what inflation might be—not what it is today.

Interest Rates Come with a Variety of Names

Central banks have a variety of names for their policy-making interest rate even though they are basically similar and the goal is the same—to increase or decrease what banks must pay to borrow and thereby affect the whole gamut of interest rates available to borrowers. But regardless of what it is called, interest is payment for the use of borrowed money.

The one most familiar to investors is the federal (fed) funds rate. The fed funds rate is the interest rate charged by one depository institution on an overnight sale of immediately available funds (balances at the Federal Reserve) to another depository institution. The rate can vary from depository institution to depository institution and from day to day. The target fed funds rate is set by the FOMC. By setting a target fed funds rate and using monetary policy tools, that is, open market operations, discount window lending, and reserve requirements, to achieve that target rate, the Federal Reserve and the FOMC seek "to promote effectively the goals of maximum employment, stable prices, and moderate long-term interest rates," as required by the Federal Reserve Act.

The discount rate is the rate at which central banks lend or discount eligible paper. It is also known as the bank rate. In the United States, the discount rate is usually changed at the same time as the fed funds rate upon the request of the 12 regional Federal Reserve Banks. The Bank of Japan targets its discount rate as its policy-setting rate and uses the discount rate as its policy rate for uncollateralized loans.

One of the more common terms is *repo rate* or *repurchase rate*. It is generally used to refer to the interest rate on securities repurchase agreements used by central banks to influence domestic money markets. For example, an overnight repo is used by the Bank of England to adjust interest rates.

The overnight rate is the interest rate at which major financial institution may borrow/lend overnight or one-day funds among themselves. This is common in Canada.

The Reserve Bank of Australia uses the cash rate. The *cash rate* is the rate charged on overnight loans between financial intermediaries and exerts a powerful influence on other interest rates. It forms the base on which the structure of other interest rates is built. The cash rate is determined in the money market by the interaction of demand for and supply of overnight funds.

Looking for the Magic Formula for Monetary Policy

What is the best way to operate monetary policy in order to provide the conditions for sustainable growth? Over the years, central banks tried to find the magic combination of policies that would sustain growth. They would work for a while and then become problematic. First, central banks tried fixing exchange rates to gold and some tried fixing or pegging their exchange rates to those of other countries. Some central banks tried to target credit or the growth of monetary aggregates, while many relied solely on their own judgment. Suffice it to say that all have had their problems.

Many banks now think that the best way for monetary policy to promote sustainable economic growth is to anchor expectations in the future purchasing power of money. Bitter experience has proven that when monetary policy chases short-term goals, mistakes are made, uncertainty is increased, and fluctuations in economic activity are aggravated. Now, focusing on domestic price stability is thought to be the best contribution monetary policy can make to economic stabilization and sustainable long-term growth. But only time will tell if it is the panacea its supporters think it is.

INFLATION TARGETING

New Zealand, the first country to adopt inflation targeting, did so with strong support and fairly specific instructions from its legislature. The

Reserve Bank of New Zealand Act of 1989 established the basic framework, giving the central bank the objective of "achieving and maintaining stability in the general level of prices," with "regard for the efficiency and soundness of the financial system." The act provided that the government and Reserve Bank jointly determine the specific inflation target and other policy objectives through Policy Target Agreements. The first of these agreements defined price stability as a range of 0 percent to 2 percent in New Zealand's consumer price index, set a goal of achieving price stability in two years, and gave conditions that could justify breaching its inflation targeting range. Several changes since then have widened the price stability range and have introduced additional objectives, such as output growth stability. These modifications have made New Zealand's inflation targeting much more flexible.

Canada followed New Zealand in 1991. The United Kingdom adopted a form of targeting in 1992, while Australia and Sweden followed in 1993. Subsequently, Finland and Spain adopted inflation targeting (before becoming members of the European Monetary Union) and in the last few years several developing countries have adopted this approach. Although the European Central Bank does not identify itself as an inflation-targeting regime, the Maastricht Treaty set price stability as the ECB's primary objective, and the ECB has set an explicit numerical target for inflation.

The 1990s were a period of considerable reform and innovation in central banks around the world. Many new central banks were established, while many already established banks were given greater independence from their governments, often in exchange for a clear commitment to meet specific targets for inflation.

Governmental involvement, although important, was somewhat less explicit for Chile, Canada, and the United Kingdom. When Chile adopted inflation targeting in 1990, the move was preceded by new central bank legislation. In 1991, a joint announcement by the Canadian government and the Bank of Canada stated its target. This announcement along with the subsequent joint announcements established a target range for price stability but left the details and the responsibility for policy in the hands of the Bank. In the United Kingdom, which adopted inflation targeting in 1992, the Chancellor of the Exchequer announced the inflation goal. Though the Bank of England later gained independence, the Chancellor still sets policy goals for the Bank annually in his budget message.

There was less explicit governmental involvement in the next group of inflation targeting countries. In Sweden, which adopted inflation targeting in 1993, the government had previously announced that controlling inflation was an overriding goal for the Riksbank. At the Reserve Bank of Australia, its Governor, using broad and previously delegated authority, announced its change to inflation targeting in a speech. Norway's Norges Bank operates under a governmental mandate declaring that the long-term objective of monetary policy is to maintain the domestic and international value of its currency. The European Central Bank operates under the authority delegated to it by the Maastricht Treaty establishing the European Community with the primary goal of price stability.

What Is Inflation Targeting?

Most major central banks' primary monetary policy goal is to contain inflation. That is, a specific number or range in which inflation or price increases must remain is set. Other goals such as sustained growth are secondary in many cases. However, two major central banks have shunned inflation targeting so far—the Bank of Japan and the U.S. Federal Reserve. While they both agree that price stability is of paramount importance, they have other goals as well.

U.S. monetary policy focuses on encouraging economic growth and achieving full employment while containing inflation. It has been under pressure to consider using an inflation target as a way to make policy more transparent. Prior to being named chairman in 2006, Ben Bernanke was a leading exponent of inflation targeting during his term on the Board of Governors. The Federal Reserve Act calls on the Fed to maintain growth of credit and the money supply "commensurate with the economy's long-run potential to increase production, so as to promote effectively the goals of maximum employment, stable prices, and moderate long-term interest rates." The Fed's mandate states directly that monetary policy should aim at having the U.S. economy operate at full capacity.

The Bank of Japan has thus far spurned official inflation targeting despite pressures from the government. The suggestion implied that if the BoJ fixed an inflation target, the economy would rid itself of deflation. In the first quarter of 2006, the Bank's inflation measure, the CPI, was no longer declining—much to the consternation of government officials, who hoped for zero interest rates a while longer to finance their astronomical fiscal deficit cheaply.

Inflation targeting generally identifies price stability as the primary objective in monetary policy. An explicit numerical target for inflation is set, including a time period over which any deviation from the target is to be eliminated. Some variations do provide escape clauses related to the pace of return to price stability. While the theme is common, there are various ways in which the target can be defined. But they boil down to either a range or a specific numerical target or a combination of both. Some are dogmatic in pursuing the target, while others are more flexible and include other considerations besides inflation into their monetary policy objective.

Three Examples of Inflation Targeting

The three more prominent monetary policies that rely on inflation targeting are those of the European Central Bank and the Banks of England and Canada. The ECB is mandated by treaty to target inflation, while the Bank of England has its inflation target set annually by the Chancellor of the Exchequer in his budget message. The Bank of Canada's target range is decided jointly by the Bank and the government every five years. Both the ECB and Bank of England use a specific numerical inflation target—2 percent, but with a difference. While the ECB sets a ceiling above which inflation should not climb, the Bank of England tends toward its target but allows for symmetry around it with a range of plus or minus 1 percent around the target. Should inflation exceed/drop more than the 1 percent, the Governor is required to write a letter or remit to the Chancellor explaining why this happened. The Bank of Canada uses a range of 1 to 3 percent and tends toward the 2 percent midpoint.

Measures of Inflation for Targeting Purposes

The various central banks tend to use different measures of inflation for policy purposes. And all are calculated somewhat differently. The ECB uses the harmonized index of consumer prices (HICP), the inflation measure for the European Union. The Bank of England recently changed its inflation measure from the retail price index excluding mortgage interest payments (RPIX) to one modeled after the HICP and called the CPI. The Bank of Canada uses a consumer price index but it is formulated differently from those used by the UK and EU. Most use a core measure of consumer prices, but do not always exclude the same items. They all, however, use a year-on-year percent change measure. The United States has several consumer price measures, but former Fed Chairman Alan Greenspan preferred the personal consumption expenditure (PCE) deflator that is calculated as part of gross domestic product (GDP) rather than the CPI, believing that it better reflects the actual change in the cost of living. The Fed monitors the PCE excluding food and energy, and it is one of the variables they forecast in their annual statement. But they also keep an eye on the CPI.

In a 2005 speech, Bank of Canada Governor David Dodge provided insight to the Canadian interpretation of inflation targeting. He explained the Bank's choice of the CPI as its particular inflation measure. Among the reasons he cited was that the CPI was familiar to Canadians and choosing a well-known indicator makes it easier to be accountable to the population and provide an explanation for the Bank's actions. Because the volatility of some CPI components can cause sharp month-to-month fluctuations, the Bank uses a core inflation measure as an operational guide. The core strips out the eight most volatile components, along with the effect of changes in indirect taxes on the rest of the index to give a better understanding of inflation's trend.

He also said that the Bank uses a symmetric target and is not focused on a specific numerical target. Dodge emphasized that policy makers worry equally about inflation falling below target and about it rising above target. The symmetry provides an answer to charges that central banks target inflation at the expense of growth. Paying close attention to the deviation from target promotes timely action in response to both positive and negative demand shocks. Businesses and individuals can make long-range economic plans with increased confidence because the Bank guards against both deflation and inflation.

In the Bank's view, inflation targeting is very helpful in terms of accountability. If inflation persistently deviates from the target, it is committed to explaining the reasons why this is so, what will be done to return it to target, and how long the process should take.

The Actual Practice of Inflation Targeting

The Bank of Canada probably has the vaguest legal mandate. Its statute requires it to regulate "credit and currency in the best interests of the economic life of the nation." Despite the absence of a precise legal mandate, the details of the Bank's monetary policy objectives are reached by agreement between the Bank and the Department of Finance. The current agreement, which is renewed every five years, sets price stability as monetary policy's principal objective and sets the range for inflation as 1 percent to 3 percent, with the midpoint as the explicit target.

The Reserve Bank of Australia has a mandate most closely resembling the United States, but it is even broader and more open-ended. And although the country is considered an inflation-targeting country, it has a dual mandate rather than a hierarchical one. Their legislative mandate as stated in the Reserve Bank Act is "to [promote] stability of the currency of Australia; [maintain] full employment in Australia; and [foster] economic prosperity and welfare of the people of Australia." The explicit inflation target is 2 percent to 3 percent and is set by the central bank. It applies to the average inflation rate over a business cycle rather than a specific time horizon.

The mandate of the Bank of England is set out in Article 11 of the Bank of England Act. It sets monetary policy objectives "to maintain price stability" and "subject to that, to support the economic policy of Her Majesty's Government, including its objectives for growth and employment." The explicit target, which is set by the Chancellor of the Exchequer annually in his budget message, is currently 2 percent. The Governor of the Bank of England must write a letter to the Chancellor if inflation deviates by more than 1 percentage point from the target.

The European Central Bank was established by the Maastricht Treaty, which identifies price stability as the principal objective. Article 105 of the Maastricht Treaty states that "the primary objective of the [European System of Central Banks (ESCB)] shall be to maintain price stability." The objectives mentioned include "sustainable and non-inflationary growth," a "high level of employment," and "raising the standard of living" among member states. The ECB's Governing Council sets the explicit numerical inflation target, which is a ceiling of 2 percent.

INTER-CENTRAL BANK COOPERATION

Bank for International Settlements

Cooperation between the world's central banks is visible at times of crisis, although it certainly is not limited to only those times. Cooperation is particularly apparent through the Bank for International Settlements (BIS), an international organization that fosters international monetary and financial cooperation and serves as a bank for central banks. It was established on May 17, 1930, and is the world's oldest international financial organization. The BIS provides a forum to promote discussion and policy analysis among central banks and within the international financial community; a center for economic and monetary research; a prime counterparty for central banks in their financial transactions; and an agent or trustee in connection with international financial operations. The head office is in Basel, Switzerland, and there are two representative offices: in Hong Kong and in Mexico City.

Crisis management was apparent in the immediate aftermath of the terrorist attack on the New York World Trade Center on September 11, 2001, as central banks sought to assure global liquidity in the financial markets. In the immediate aftermath, the Bank of Canada matched the Federal Reserve's 125-basis-point interest rate reduction in September and October, while the Bank of England reduced rates by 50 basis points. The Bank of Japan had no place to go with interest rates already at near zero. The Reserve Bank of Australia also lowered rates by 50 basis points. The European Central Bank lagged the others, gradually reducing rates by 50 basis points in September and then another 25 basis points in November.

Group of Five, Then Seven

To further international cooperation, the finance ministers and central bank chairs of the major industrial countries meet periodically to discuss common economic and financial issues. The Group of Five, originally consisting of the United States, Japan, the United Kingdom, Germany, and France, met for the first time in 1975, and in 1976 were joined by Canada and Italy. The meetings expanded to include heads of state on an annual basis usually in June or July. The finance ministers and central bank chairs generally meet quarterly. Financial markets usually pay close attention to the statements that emanate from these meetings. For example, the April 2006 meeting statement saying that Asian countries should allow their currencies to rise in value was interpreted by currency traders to mean that the U.S. dollar should decline, much to the consternation of Asian governments, who prefer a lower currency value to promote their exports.

In the next several chapters, the focus will be on individual central banks. We start with the oldest, the Bank of England, and then move onto the ECB, the newest.

CHAPTER 2

Bank of England

Ⅰt is quite logical to begin the discussion of the individual central banks with the oldest. The Bank of England's history has always fascinated me, as has its continuing relevance through the centuries. Founded in 1694, the Bank's development is inextricably intertwined with the development and growth of financial markets in the United Kingdom and elsewhere. The Bank facilitated the government's use of the financial markets for its own financing needs, though not on today's scale. The oldest central bank in the world, it is sometimes known as the "Old Lady of Threadneedle Street." The Bank was nationalized after World War II on March 1, 1946, and only gained operational independence in 1997 after the Labour Party won power. Its legacy stretches over 300 years of events that influenced the workings of central banks everywhere.

THE VERY EARLY YEARS

The Bank of England was founded in 1694 explicitly to act as the Government's banker and debt manager. Since then, its role in banking and finance has developed and evolved. The Bank's primary focus is on managing the nation's currency and is the heart of the United Kingdom's financial system. To achieve its goal, it is committed to promoting and maintaining a stable and efficient monetary and financial framework.

    Much of the Bank's history is intertwined with the economic, financial, and political development of the United Kingdom (see Table 2.1 below). When the country was on the verge of a tremendous expansion in international trade, it discovered that a vital element was missing to facilitate this growth—a bank. The idea of some sort of bank gathered momentum after the 1688 Glorious Revolution when William of Orange and Queen Mary jointly ascended the throne of England. The political economist Sir William Petty recognized from the Dutch example that successful credit-based trade

TABLE 2.1 A Concise History of the Bank of England

Year	Key Person/Event	History
1688	King William & Queen Mary	When William and Mary came to the throne in 1688, public finances were weak. The system of money and credit was in disarray. A national bank was needed to mobilize the nation's resources.
	William Paterson	Proposed a loan of £1,200,000 to the Government. In return the subscribers would be incorporated as the Governor and Company of the Bank of England.
1694	The Royal Charter	The money was raised in a few weeks and the Royal Charter was sealed on July 27,1694. The Bank started life as the Government's banker and debt manager, with 17 clerks and 2 gatekeepers.
1734		Bank moved to Thread-needle Street, gradually acquiring land and premises to create the site seen today.

The Bank managed the Government's accounts and made loans to finance spending at times of war and peace. It took deposits and issued notes in its role as a commercial bank too.

18th Century		The Government borrowed more and more money. These outstanding loans were called the National Debt.
1781	Bank's Charter is renewed	Reliance on the Bank of England was such that when its charter was renewed in 1781 it was described as ' the public exchequer'.
		By now the Bank was acting as the bankers' bank too. It was liable to fail if all its depositors decided to withdraw their money at the same time. But the Bank made sure it kept enough gold to pay its notes on demand.
1797	The "Restriction Period"	By 1797 war with France had drained the gold reserves. The Government prohibited the Bank from paying its notes in gold. This Restriction Period lasted until 1821.
1844		The Bank Charter Act tied the note issue to the Bank's gold reserves. The Bank was required to keep the accounts of the note issue separate from those of its banking operations and produce a weekly summary of both accounts. The Bank Return, as it's called, is still published every week.

In the 19th century, the Bank took on the role of lender of last resort, providing stability during several financial crises.

1914-1818	World War I	National Debt jumped to £7 billion. The Bank helped manage Government borrowing and resist inflationary pressures.

(continued overleaf)

TABLE 2.1 (*continued*)

Year	Key Person/Event	History
1931	End of gold standard	United Kingdom left the gold standard; its gold and foreign exchange reserves were transferred to the Treasury. But their management was still handled by the Bank and this remains the case today.
1946	Nationalization	After World War II the bank was nationalized. It remained the Treasury's adviser, agent and debt manager.
1970s	Banking Crises	Bank played a key role during several banking crises. It was at the fore when monetary policy again became a central part of Government policy in the 1980s.
May 1997	Operational Independence	The new Labour government gave the Bank responsibility for setting interest rates to meet the Government's stated inflation target.
1998	Bank of England Act	Made changes to the Bank's governing body. The Court of Directors is now made up of the Bank's Governor and Deputy Governors, and 16 Non-Executive Directors.

Source: Bank of England.

could benefit a nation in many ways and help enlarge its sphere of influence. He wrote in 1682: "What remedy is there if we have too little money? We must erect a Bank, which well computed doth almost double the Effect of our coined Money; and we have in England Materials for a Bank which shall furnish Stock enough to drive the Trade of the whole Commercial World."

Petty looked at the Amsterdam Wisselbank, which was founded in 1609 and was credited to being pivotal in the Dutch economic success at that time. The Bank lent to the City of Amsterdam, the Province of Holland, and to the Dutch East India Company to finance trade. Amsterdam Wisselbank was also responsible for coinage and exchange. In 1683, it was empowered to lend to private customers. Payments over a certain amount were required to pass through the Bank so it was convenient for the important finance houses to hold accounts there. Thus, the Bank was in a position to oversee the Dutch financial scene and was also able to act as a stabilizing influence on it as well.

William Paterson, a London-based Scots entrepreneur proposed a plan that, after several iterations, eventually was approved by Parliament. But it was really the government's desperate need for funds that led to the Bank's creation. Public subscriptions totaling £1.2 million formed the initial capital stock of the Bank of England. The Bank received a Royal Charter in return for funds that were immediately lent to the government. The Bank remained as the government's financier for some time afterward, with no suggestion of a broader role as a central bank. But the Bank was big and it was incorporated with limited liability (extremely rare at that time), and it set out to take full advantage of this position.

One particularly significant development was in the perception of credit or, as it was then called, 'imaginary money.' It represented a fundamental and distinctive principle in the new thinking that was prevalent at this time. Some had begun to recognize the existence of an untapped source of non-metallic assets such as merchandise inventories and tax receipts, as well as land and commercial obligation revenues against which imaginary money could be raised. Credit could be, they said, the seed corn of wealth.

In the Bank's second century, the two key elements of central banking emerged—concern for monetary stability, which was born during the inflationary excesses of the Napoleonic wars, and the responsibility for financial stability, which was developed in the banking crises of the mid-nineteenth century. The 1844 Bank Charter Act gave the Bank a monopoly over note issuance, which was regarded by some as the first move toward nationalization. But the crucial clause of the Act was a monetary one. *It provided that all the Bank's notes were to be backed by gold coin or bullion above its £14 million capital. This, along with a fixed price for gold, laid the foundation for the gold standard. The gold standard spread worldwide and created a long period of price stability. Monetary policy was on auto-pilot during the nineteenth century.*

The gold standard is a monetary system under which currency issuers guarantee to redeem their notes in a fixed amount of gold. Under the gold standard, nations who redeem their notes to other nations in gold share a fixed currency relationship. The gold standard system was claimed to be resistant to credit and debt expansion, since money could not be created through government fiat currency, and would be protected against artificial inflation by currency devaluation. This was supposed to remove currency uncertainty, keep credit of the issuing monetary authority sound, and encourage lending. However, this did not prevent debt crises and depressions throughout the history of its use.

But monetary stability alone was not enough. There were, of course, crises. And in order to prevent systemic collapses the 1844 Act had to be suspended several times. Walter Bagehot, the celebrated editor of *The Economist* wrote in 1866 about the Bank's part in that crisis, stating that the Bank held, should hold, and should be responsible for holding the sole banking reserve of the country.

As with the French wars a century before, World War I led to the suspension of the gold standard along with the issuance of low denomination notes. In 1925, a vain attempt was made to return to the gold standard's discipline but it failed. And in 1931, the United Kingdom left the gold standard for good. The country's gold and foreign exchange reserves were transferred to the Treasury (or Exchequer) although their day-to-day management remained with the Bank. The note issue became entirely fiduciary—not backed by gold.

During and after World War I, internal changes began to take place. Among them were:

- The governorship, which had until then generally been a two-year term, and sometimes on a part-time basis, became a full-time professional position.
- The Bank deliberately moved away from commercial business and increasingly assumed the role of a central bank. It was an integral part of the process of returning to a peace time economy and to one which might help to rebuild war-ravaged Europe.
- The relationship with the Treasury changed. The funds that the Bank was deploying in its market operations were increasingly public funds.
- Nationalization after World War II shifted monetary policy authority to the Treasury, but that in reality had occurred years earlier. The Bank remained the Treasury's adviser, agent, and debt manager. During and for years after the war, it administered exchange control and various borrowing restrictions on the Treasury's behalf.

POST WORLD WAR II

During the 1950s and 1960s interest in monetary policy resurfaced. It was obvious that if post-war controls were to be eliminated, active monetary policy was needed to take its place. And the serious inflation of the 1970s and early 1980s proved to be the catalyst for change. First, there was a switch in macroeconomic policy from a fixed to floating exchange rate. And during the 1970s, the first signs of financial market deregulation appeared. Monetary targets were introduced in 1976 and reinforced in the early 1980s. But these proved unreliable as a sole guide to policy.

It was during this time that the following ideas about monetary policy began to be developed and eventually became part of Bank policy:

- Price stability is desirable in its own right and a necessary condition of sustainable growth.
- Inflation reduces growth and has other social costs.
- Inflation is a monetary phenomenon and without appropriate monetary measures it cannot be properly brought under control.

These tenets of monetary policy affected central banks everywhere, not just the Bank of England.

INDEPENDENCE!

After Labour's victory in the 1997 election, the new government announced that it would transfer full operational responsibility for monetary policy to the Bank of England. However, other Bank functions were transferred elsewhere—debt management on behalf of the Government was transferred to the Treasury, and the Bank's regulatory functions were passed on to the new Financial Services Authority. The 1998 Bank of England Act made the Bank independent to set interest rates.

The Bank is accountable to Parliament and the wider public. The legislation provides that if, in extreme circumstances and the national interest demands it, the Government has the power to give the Bank instructions on interest rates for a limited period of time.

The Bank's roles and functions have evolved and changed over its 300-plus-year history but certain functions have remained. Since its foundation, it has been the Government's banker and, since the late eighteenth century, it has been banker to the banking system itself. The Bank also manages foreign exchange and gold reserves and the Government's stock register. But to the general public, it now is most visible through its bank notes and interest rate decisions. The Bank has had a monopoly on the issue of bank notes in England and Wales since the early twentieth century. But only since 1997 has the Bank had statutory responsibility for setting the official interest rate.

HOW THE BANK DETERMINES MONETARY POLICY

The Bank acquired rate-setting powers after the Bank of England Act of 1998 was implemented on June 1, 1998. Control of monetary policy now resides with the Bank's Monetary Policy Committee (MPC). Figure 2.1 gives a snapshot view of interest rates since 1946.

The MPC decides what interest rates should be. The Committee is composed of the Governor, two Deputy Governors, two Bank Executive Directors, and four experts appointed by the Chancellor of the Exchequer. The Committee meets monthly (usually the first Wednesday and Thursday after the first Monday of the month) to determine interest rate policy. A rare exception was in May 2005 when the meeting had to be postponed to make way for the general election. Interest rate decisions are announced

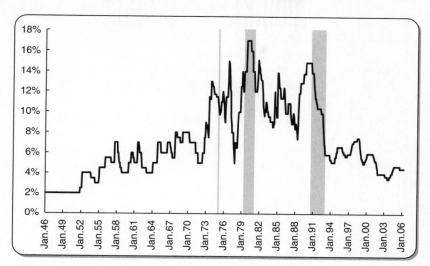

FIGURE 2.1 The Bank of England's policy interest rate has been on the low side historically of late.
Source: Bank of England and Haver Analytics.

immediately after their meetings. A statement is released at that time only if there is a change in interest rates. The following is the statement issued on August 4, 2005, after the MPC lowered its policy rate by 25 basis points to 4.5 percent:

> *The Bank of England's Monetary Policy Committee today voted to reduce the Bank's repo rate by 0.25 percentage points to 4.5%.*
>
> *In the first half of the year, output growth in the United Kingdom was subdued. Household spending and business investment growth have slowed. Although there are some signs of a pickup in consumer spending, downside risks remain in the near term. Looking further ahead, however, the rise in equity prices and the recent fall in the exchange rate should boost activity.*
>
> *CPI inflation was 2.0% in June. Higher oil prices may raise inflation further in the short term. But, in the Committee's view, the slackening in the pressure of demand on supply capacity should lead to some moderation in inflation. Against that background, the Committee judged that a decrease of 0.25 percentage points in the*

repo rate to 4.5% was necessary to keep CPI inflation on track to meet the 2% target in the medium term.

The Committee's latest inflation and output projections will appear in the Inflation Report to be published on Wednesday 10 August.

The minutes of the meeting will be published at 9.30 am on Wednesday 17 August.

The financial markets are poised to pounce on the news. Each financial market will react differently. For example, while the foreign exchange market might look on an increase in the interest rate with favor, equity markets might see things differently. Equity investors would be concerned that higher rates would cut into sales and profits while currency traders would see assets earning a better return.

The minutes, including a record of any vote, are published two weeks after the meeting. Bank watchers dissect the minutes in infinite detail as they try to determine future monetary policy moves and their potential impact on the economy and the financial markets. In contrast, the Federal Reserve began to release minutes three weeks after the Federal Open Market Committee (FOMC) meeting instead of six only in January 2005. The Bank of Japan, however, continues to wait about five or six weeks to release its minutes. Both the European Central Bank and Bank of Canada do not release minutes at all. The Bank of England publishes a quarterly *Inflation Report*, which spells out the Bank's forecasts and the thinking of committee members. Needless to say, market participants closely scrutinize the report.

Monetary Policy Objectives

The Bank's chief monetary policy objective is price stability (as defined by the government's inflation target). But at the same time, monetary policy is mandated to be supportive of the government's growth and employment objectives along with other economic policies. The inflation target is confirmed in each of the Chancellor of the Exchequer's (March) Budget statements.

In January 2004, the Monetary Policy Committee shifted their inflation measure from the retail price index excluding mortgage interest payments (RPIX) to the harmonized index of consumer prices (but called the consumer price index or CPI). The shift aligned British inflation measures with those of the European Union. At the same time, the inflation target was reduced to 2 percent from 2.5 percent. The reason for the change had to do with the spread between the two measures of inflation. This in turn can be traced to

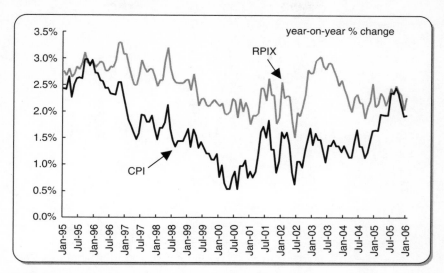

FIGURE 2.2   Historically, the retail price index less mortgage interest payments (RPIX) has increased faster because of the housing component, which is not included in the consumer price index (CPI).
Source: Office for National Statistics and Haver Analytics.

their components and the way the indexes are calculated. Among the key differences are the exclusion of council taxes and owner-occupied housing costs from the CPI. Arithmetic means are used to combine individual prices to construct the RPIX, while geometric means that allow for substitution are used in calculation of the CPI. This formula differential accounts for nearly half of the difference in the two rates. (See Chapter 10 for more on the CPI.) Figure 2.2 shows the varying differences between the two indexes.

The MPC also monitors average annual wage increases, based on a three-month moving average as another measure of inflation. The target for average annual wage increases is 4.5 percent. This enhances the Bank's view of the economy by giving it a measure of cost-push inflation that could be rooted in the labor markets. Figure 2.3 shows how average earnings have behaved in reference to the Bank's target.

The Bank is not entirely free from the Exchequer since the inflation target is assigned to it by the Chancellor. Rather, the MPC has to decide what interest rate is necessary to meet the overall inflation target. The Committee's interest rate decisions are based on what its members think are necessary to meet the target.

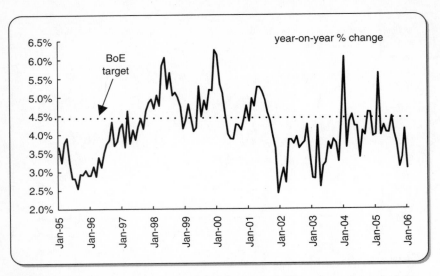

FIGURE 2.3   Average earnings growth has been much lower since the end of the dot-com boom of the late 1990s.
Source: Office for National Statistics and Haver Analytics.

The MPC sets the official "repo" rate or repurchase rate, which is the main instrument of monetary policy. The Bank implements its decisions by setting the interest rate at which the Bank lends to banks and other financial institutions through its open market operations. Obviously, the Bank has close links with financial markets and institutions. This contact is a vital link enabling it to do a great deal of its work, including collating and publishing monetary and banking statistics.

All central banks are monopoly suppliers of high-powered money and are able to determine a specific interest rate in the wholesale money markets. The operating procedure of the Bank of England is similar to that of other central banks. The Bank chooses the price (or policy-making interest rate) at which it will lend money to private-sector institutions. It then lends primarily through the use of gilt sales (fixed interest government securities named after the paper on which they were once printed) and repurchase agreements (repo) at a two-week maturity.

The Bank's monetary policy is not geared solely toward price stability like the European Central Bank, but also supports the Government's economic objectives including those for growth and employment. The Bank is guided by the philosophy that low inflation is not an end in itself. Rather, it is an important factor in helping to encourage long-term economic stability and is a precondition for achieving sustainable growth and employment. High inflation can be damaging to the economy, while low inflation can help to foster sustainable long-term economic growth.

The monthly interest rate decision requires a complex assessment of all the economic evidence. According to MPC member Rachel Lomax (in a speech to the Bristol Society at the University of the West of England, Bristol, on February 18, 2004):

[The MPC] needs to be both skeptical and open minded, if we are to avoid major error: skeptical when it comes to interpreting the data, but alert for signs that we may be getting it wrong. The decision to raise rates in February (2004), while inflation was still well below the new target, reflected a top line view that inflationary pressures were likely to build over the next couple of years. While this has been the emerging picture for some months now, we have been surprised by a number of developments pointing in different directions, which have needed careful evaluation — notably, the resilience of household spending and the strength of the exchange rate. We have also had an opportunity to reconsider earlier judgments, especially about the amount of spare capacity and the likely growth in potential supply. That is the nature of the exercise. March will be another month. There can be no foregone conclusions when it comes to setting interest rates. Every month I may have a fairly well developed view not just about this month's interest rates, but about where interest rates are likely to need to go.

Inflation Targeting

The 2 percent inflation target is expressed in terms of an annual rate of inflation based on the CPI. The inflation target is symmetrical; that is, inflation below the target is judged to be just as bad as inflation above it. If the target is missed by more than 1 percentage point in either direction, the Governor must write an open letter or remit to the Chancellor explaining why inflation has increased/decreased to such an extent and what the Bank proposes to do to ensure inflation comes back to the target.

The MPC's aim is to set interest rates so that inflation can be brought back to target within a reasonable time period without creating undue economic instability. Obviously, a 2 percent target does not mean that inflation will be held constantly at that level. That would be neither possible nor desirable and would take fine-tuning to a ludicrous degree. Interest rates would be changing all the time and by large amounts, causing unnecessary uncertainty and volatility in the economy.

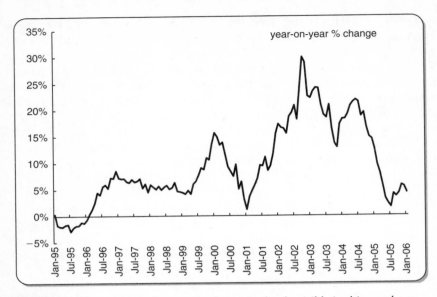

FIGURE 2.4   The end of the house price boom is clearly visible in this graph. *Source:* Halifax and Haver Analytics.

Financial markets are very sensitive to the differential between the target and the CPI. If the CPI is above the inflation target, markets worry that interest rates could rise. This, in turn, could slow growth and cut into profits because of increased costs of doing business. If inflation is tame, it is likely that interest rates could remain unchanged and could possibly be reduced. This would make it easier for consumers to borrow to buy houses. For example, the Bank raised interest rates aggressively in 2004 to nip the house-pricing bubble that had developed in the post–September 11, 2001 years of lower interest rates. Figure 2.4 shows year-on-year house price changes and illustrates why the Bank felt it was necessary to increase interest rates.

The Monetary Policy Committee

The Committee consists of nine members—five from the Bank and four external members appointed by the Chancellor. It is chaired by the Governor of the Bank of England. Each MPC member has expertise in the field of economics and monetary policy. Members do not represent individual groups or areas—they are independent. (Nor do they have to live in the United Kingdom. A May 2006 appointee to fill an external member slot teaches at Dartmouth College in Hanover, New Hampshire, and commutes to London for the monthly meetings.) Each votes to set interest rates at the level they believe is consistent with meeting the inflation target. Decisions are based on a simple majority vote and are not based on a consensus like the European Central Bank or the Bank of Canada. The Governor and two Deputy Governors serve five-year terms, while the Directors serve three years, all of which are renewable.

The MPC meetings are spread over two days. The interest rate decision is announced at 12 noon London time (7 A.M. ET in the United States) on the second day. The meeting's minutes, including a record of how each committee member voted, are published on the Wednesday of the second week after the meeting takes place. For example, for the meeting held on May 3 and 4, 2006, the minutes were released on May 17. In addition, the Bank publishes its *Inflation Report* quarterly. This provides a detailed analysis of economic conditions and the prospects for economic growth and inflation as viewed by the MPC members. The financial markets dissect these reports, looking for clues to future Bank policy.

As the MPC prepares for its monthly meeting it continually receives extensive briefings on the economy from its staff. This includes a half-day meeting—known as the pre-MPC meeting—which usually takes place on the Friday before the MPC's interest rate setting meeting. The Committee members are briefed on all of the latest economic data along with explanations of recent trends and analysis of relevant issues. The Committee is also briefed on regional business conditions by the Bank's agents. Unlike the Federal Reserve, the Bank does not have regional banks. Rather, it has twelve Agencies across the country. Their role is to assess the economy in their particular region and act as intermediaries between the business community and the Bank. The agents gain intelligence and insight to pass on to committee members about the current and future regional economic developments and prospects.

A Treasury representative attends the MPC's meetings. This is unlike the FOMC meetings, where no one save Fed employees attend. The Fed Chairman, however, meets with Treasury officials frequently. The Treasury representative is at liberty to discuss policy issues but does not have a vote. This ensures that the MPC is fully briefed on fiscal policy developments and other aspects of the Government's economic policies and that, in turn, the Chancellor is kept fully informed about monetary policy.

Other Responsibilities

While most of the focus is on monetary policy, the Bank has many other responsibilities. It maintains the stability in the financial system, analyzes and promotes initiatives to strengthen the financial system, and monitors financial developments to try to identify potential threats to financial stability. Obviously, the Bank cooperates closely with the Treasury and the Financial Services Authority (regulator of banks and other financial institutions in the United Kingdom).

The Bank is intensively involved domestically and internationally with various institutions and other central banks in order to maintain financial market stability. In this regard, the Bank is vigilant in promoting initiatives that would strengthen the financial system. And, of course, the Bank is prepared to handle any financial crisis that might arise and is the financial system's "lender of last resort." The former was apparent after the September 11, 2001, terrorist attacks when the Bank cooperated fully with the Federal Reserve and other central banks to ensure financial market stability and liquidity in the immediate aftermath. The Bank compiles and publishes monetary and banking statistics.

As a banker's bank along with its role as the Government's banker, the Bank is able to adjust the imbalances in day-to-day money flows between the Government's accounts and those of the commercial banks. The Bank supplies the cash needed by the banking system to achieve a balance by the end of each settlement day. Because the Bank is the final provider of cash to the system, it can choose the interest rate at which it will provide these funds on a daily basis. This interest rate is quickly passed throughout the financial system, influencing interest rates for the whole economy. When the Bank changes its dealing rate, it creates a ripple effect—the commercial banks change their own base rates from which deposit and lending rates are calculated.

The Bank deals in the foreign exchange market as part of its day-to-day management of the Exchange Equalization Account, which holds the United Kingdom's foreign currency and gold reserves. These may be used, subject to policy objectives, to attempt to influence the exchange rate if necessary. The Bank also operates in the foreign exchange market on its own behalf and on behalf of customers.

The Bank has been issuing banknotes for over 300 years. During that time, both the notes themselves and their role in society have undergone continual change. From today's perspective, it is easy to accept that a piece of paper that costs pennies or pence to produce is worth 5, 10, 20, or 50 pounds. This is in stark contrast to the old days of gold coins and fiat convertibility to gold on demand.

Like other central banks, the Bank produces many regular and ad hoc publications on key aspects of its work and offers a wide range of educational and research materials both in print and on their Web site. The Bank's Web site is a treasure trove in this regard. In addition, the Bank compiles and publishes a range of monetary and financial statistics including domestic banking statistics, external finance statistics, and international banking statistics.

Like every country and their institutions, the Bank has its own jargon, which could be incomprehensible to outsiders. Two such words come to mind—purdah and remit. Purdah describes what we call in the United States the blackout period—the time before and after FOMC meetings when committee members cannot comment on monetary policy. Remit is the name of the document or letter that gives the Bank its inflation target from the Chancellor. A remit would be used by the Bank's Governor to explain why the Bank has missed its inflation target if that should occur.

UNITED KINGDOM AND THE EURO

The United Kingdom has been a member of the European Union (EU) since 1973. But when it was time for the country to join the European Monetary Union (EMU), it chose not to do so, opting along with Sweden and Denmark to keep control over their monetary policy and retain the use of their currencies (the British pound sterling, the Danish krone and the Swedish krona). Rather, the United Kingdom posed five tests that must be met prior to joining the monetary union. The ramifications of this decision left the Bank of England in control of its own destiny in stark contrast with the once powerful Bundesbank that is now a regional or national bank under the ECB and has seen its influence marginalized.

When the Labour Party wrested power from the Tories in 1997, the new government sidestepped the issue of EMU membership. It said that, in principle, it favored euro entry at some stage—but only when the economic conditions were right. And that would be when five economic tests, set by Chancellor of the Exchequer Gordon Brown, had been met:

1. Can the economy demonstrate sustainable convergence with the euro-zone?
2. Is the economy flexible enough to cope with economic shocks once interest rates are set in Frankfurt (the home of the ECB)?
3. What is the impact of the euro on investment?
4. What is the impact on the City—the financial Wall Street of the United Kingdom?
5. What is the impact on employment? British unemployment is a fraction that in the eurozone.

A formal study on the viability of membership was last conducted in early 2003. At that time, Chancellor Brown concluded that economic conditions were still not right for the United Kingdom to join the EMU. He based his decision on five tests and 18 studies that were commissioned by the Treasury.

In the 2001 general election and again in 2005, Prime Minister Tony Blair said the Government, if it judged joining the EMU was in the country's interest, would hold a referendum. In announcing the decision, Brown reiterated the government's official line—euro membership is in the United Kingdom's long-term interest. But the Treasury said the tests and studies indicate that the "clear and unambiguous" case for dropping the pound in favor of the euro cannot yet be made. The government said that it would report back on progress in meeting the criteria during the prebudget announcement late that year—and then decide whether to assess the tests again. No new evaluation is in sight as this is written in 2006, nor is there any sign that it will be in the near future.

What Were the Test Results?

It was determined that the financial services industry test had been met, and that the impact on employment and investment would be favorable once sufficient convergence and flexibility have been achieved. (Many economists have pointed out that the tests were sufficiently vague to allow the government to come up with whatever answers it wanted.) Brown gave an upbeat assessment of the benefits to business from EMU membership, but did not present a detailed plan or timetable for achieving economic convergence. A national changeover plan was also published to accompany the five tests. It set out the preparations made by government and business to join the euro.

It was at that time that the Chancellor said he would be changing the then 2.5 percent inflation target and its means of measurement. The country would switch to a new Europe-wide inflation measure (to be called the CPI) rather than the old RPIX. This was sort of an anticlimax—many had been urging the Treasury to use the European measure for some time. However, this did not happen until November 2003.

Immediately after Tony Blair's reelection in 2001, the pound sterling fell in value. Financial markets anticipated that the UK membership was just around the corner given the Labour Party's bias toward entry. That clearly was not the case. Slowing the movement were polls that showed continuing reluctance on the part of the British public to join the EMU. In Europe, the British were perceived (at least until the "No" votes on the proposed constitution in June 2005) as the most euro-skeptic of all EU members. Figure 2.5 tracks the pound sterling's exchange rate over the past several years.

Historically, the United Kingdom has generally participated in Europe-wide initiatives, but only after a considerable time lag. It initially declined

FIGURE 2.5 The pound sterling is at its highest level since the early 1990s, compounding the difficulties of exporters by making British goods more expensive. *Source:* Federal Reserve Board and Haver Analytics.

to be a member of the European Economic Community (the predecessor of the current EU) in the late 1950s but joined about 20 years later. It chose not to join the exchange rate mechanism (ERM), which preceded the euro, until 11 years after its 1979 introduction. Then, in 1992, then Prime Minister John Major was forced to withdraw from ERM after the Bank of England spent £10 million in a failed attempt to defend the pound sterling's value against the then mighty deutschemark. The euro was launched across Austria, Belgium, Finland, France, Germany, Ireland, Italy, Luxembourg, the Netherlands, Portugal, and Spain for financial transactions on January 1, 1999. (Greece joined a year later.) The 12 nations started using euro coins and bills on January 1, 2002. Figure 2.6 compares EMU and the U.K. economic growth.

Monetary Policies Are a Problem

Joining the EMU isn't simply a matter of changing currencies. The euro nations have locked their economies together, submitting to the discipline of a European Central Bank that must determine a one-size-fits-all interest rate. Skeptics noted that the Bank would have difficulty in setting a rate low enough to stimulate a slumping economy yet high enough to damp inflation in the faster-growing economies. This has been amply been illustrated over the past couple of years. For example, the economic risks posed by near-term

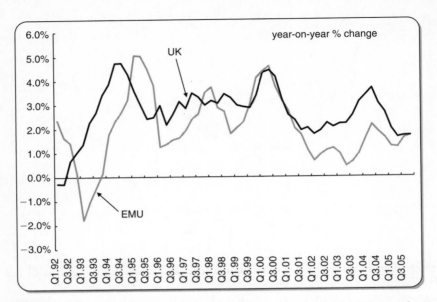

FIGURE 2.6 The British economy has grown faster than that of the EMU, making the United Kingdom's entry into the "club" even more dubious.
Source: Office for National Statistics and Haver Analytics.

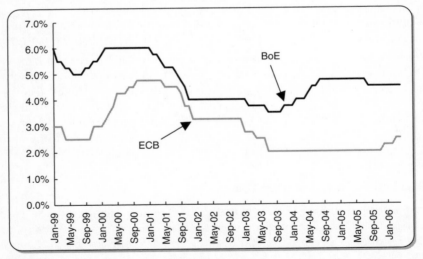

FIGURE 2.7 Despite higher interest rates, the British economy has thus far outperformed the EMU.
Source: Haver Analytics.

euro entry have been highlighted by the gap between British and eurozone interest rates. In June of 2006, the Bank's interest rate was 4.5 percent, while the ECB's was 2.75 percent (see Figure 2.7). Until the ECB increased interest rates, Germany had its lowest interest rate, at 2 percent, since records began in 1875—and it still had anemic growth. Figure 2.7 shows the interest rate differential between the United Kingdom and the EMU.

The potential for even greater divergence exists given the disparity between EMU and UK growth. But, according to Brown, the difference in short-term interest rates is not the decisive factor in the euro decision, even though the wide interest rate differential does make it more difficult for the United Kingdom. If rates dropped to bring them into line with eurozone levels, it would boost consumer spending and house prices, which at the time of the review were already high. The Bank subsequently raised interest rates to cool them down.

The British business cycle is more closely linked to the United States than to the larger members of the EMU. British consumers are more sensitive to changes in interest rates than their European counterparts because of the importance of housing as a source of wealth and the prevalence of variable rate mortgages. As a result, the British economy would suffer more than current EMU members if the single interest rate set by the ECB was not appropriate.

The ongoing public unpopularity of the euro will continue to delay any sort of referendum on EMU participation for some time. The miserable economic performance in the last few years and the muted outlook for EMU growth also precludes any action. It would be hard to explain to an already dubious public why a closer relationship with a stagnant and struggling economy would be in the country's best interests. The interest rate gap along with regulation-prone countries on the continent are further hurdles.

The government cast the euro decision as a matter of economics, not politics, although there is some question about that. The evidence presented by the studies supports the government's position of being in favor of joining in principle but against doing so until economic conditions are right. The Chancellor said it was vital that the decision—one of the "most momentous" ever taken—was made "in the British national economic interest." The British didn't reject the euro, they just said not yet—nor did they set a timetable when it might happen.

CHAPTER 3

European Union and the European Central Bank

The Past Is Prologue

Any discussion of the European Central Bank is better understood in light of how it came into existence and how it evolved from the European Union.

EUROPEAN UNION

What Is It?

The European Union (EU) is an international organization consisting of European countries or Member States committed to working together for peace and prosperity. Its members have common institutions to which they delegate some of their sovereignty so that decisions on matters of joint interest can be made at the European level. This pooling of sovereignty is also called European integration.

The historical roots of the EU lie in the rubble of World War II, when it became imperative to build international relationships to guard against any such catastrophe recurring. The French statesmen Jean Monnet and Robert Schuman are regarded as the architects of the principle that the best way to start the bonding process was by developing economic ties. This philosophy was the foundation for the Treaty of Paris, which was signed in 1951. It established the European Coal and Steel Community (ECSC), which was joined by France, Germany, Italy, the Netherlands, Belgium, and Luxembourg. Under the Treaty of Rome, which came into force in 1958, these six countries founded the European Economic Community and European Atomic Energy Community to work alongside the ECSC. In 1967 the three communities merged to become collectively known as the European Communities (EC) whose main focus was to cooperate on economic and agricultural affairs. Denmark, Ireland, and Britain became full EC members in 1973; Greece joined in 1981; Portugal and Spain in 1986; and Austria, Finland, and Sweden in 1995.

The Treaty on European Union, signed at Maastricht (in the Netherlands) in 1991, formally established the EU as the successor to the European Community. Maastricht expanded the concept of union into new areas. It introduced a common foreign and security policy and moved toward a coordinated policy on asylum, immigration, drugs, and terrorism. EU citizenship, which allowed people to move freely between Member States, was created. Crucially, it established the timetable for economic and monetary union and specified the economic and budgetary criteria that would determine when countries were ready to join.

The subsequent Stability and Growth Pact tightened up these criteria, stressing that strict fiscal discipline and coordination would be vital to the success of economic and monetary union. But this pact, which stipulated rules on fiscal deficits, was honored in the breach when economic growth deteriorated.

The euro was officially adopted by 11 members in 1999. Greece, taking longer to meet convergence criteria, joined two years later. Of the 15 original EU members, Denmark, Sweden, and the United Kingdom have chosen not to join the European Monetary Union (EMU), at least for the time being. After a transition period, the euro completely replaced the former national currencies on January 1, 2002.

Despite its difficulties, the EU has accomplished many things so far. It built a single market and launched the currency to be used within it. However, its attempts to have unified policies have faltered as members split on support for the U.S.-led Iraqi war and on the EU constitution, for example.

Organization

There are five major EU institutions, including the European Parliament (elected by the people of the Member States), Council of the European Union (representing the governments of the Member States), European Commission (driving force and executive body), Court of Justice (ensuring compliance with the law), and Court of Auditors (controlling sound and lawful management of the EU budget).

In addition, there are five other important organizations: the European Economic and Social Committee (expresses the opinions of organized civil society on economic and social issues); the Committee of the Regions (expresses the opinions of regional and local authorities); the European Central Bank (ECB, responsible for monetary policy and managing the euro);

the European Ombudsman (deals with citizens' complaints about malad-ministration by any EU institution or body), and the European Investment Bank (helps achieve EU objectives by financing investment projects).

A Singular EU Achievement — The Euro

The euro replaced the old national currencies in the 12 countries that chose to join the eurozone or European Monetary Union: Austria (schilling), Belgium/Luxembourg (franc), Finland (markka), France (franc), Germany (deutschemark), Greece (drachma), Ireland (pound), Italy (lira), the Nether-lands (guilder), Portugal (escudo), and Spain (peseta). The advantages to the single currency include easier travel, easier price comparisons with all goods and services priced in euros, and a stable environment for European business, which stimulates growth and competitiveness. These goals have proven illusive, however.

Now if you are an EU citizen, you can travel, study, and work wherever you want in all EU countries. In most of the EU, you can travel without carrying a passport and without being stopped for border checks. By creating a frontier-free single market and a single currency, the EU has already given a significant boost to trade and employment in Europe. It has agreed on a strategy for stimulating growth and generating more and better jobs. But this has faltered as the one-size-fits-all monetary policy combined with a reluctance to make needed structural changes has stymied growth, especially in the major industrial countries of Germany, France, and Italy.

EU Enlargement

Until May 2004, there were 15 EU Member States with an estimated total of 380 million citizens. Ten more countries, mainly from central and eastern Europe, joined the EU on May 1, 2004. Bulgaria and Romania will join on January 1, 2007, bringing the EU's total population to nearly 500 million. Turkey is also a candidate country and could join later, when all the conditions for membership are met.

Members of the Club

The "original" 15 members of the EU are Germany, France, Italy, Spain, Portugal, Sweden, Belgium, Denmark, Austria, Britain, Ireland, the Nether-lands, and Luxembourg. They were joined by Czech Republic, Cyprus, Estonia, Hungary, Latvia, Lithuania, Malta, Poland, Slovakia, and Slovenia to make up the EU 25.

While the EU has expanded gradually in the past, this was the most ambitious enlargement ever. It had never added so many new countries, grown so much in terms of area and population, or encompassed so many different histories and cultures. In order to become a member, a country must have a stable democracy that guarantees the rule of law, human rights, and protection of minorities; and it must have a functioning market economy as well as a civil service capable of applying and managing EU laws. The hope is that it will unite the European continent and enable its peoples to share the benefits of progress and welfare generated by European integration, and effectively bridge the gap between the old post–World War II divisions.

The EU population increased by an estimated 77 million and the number of consumers grew by 20 percent when it expanded to 25 members. But the 10 new members only added 5 percent to the EU's total gross domestic product at the time of accession. However, their economies were growing faster than the EU average and were boosted further by reduced tariffs, increased inward investment, and EU subsidies.

Enlargement has raised a lot of thorny issues, including migration, agriculture, leaky eastern borders, and the time frame for joining the euro. Expansion also highlights the need to restructure the EU itself, which was partly addressed by the Treaty of Nice in 2000 and is at the center of the EU's attempt to adopt a new constitution. The cost of enlargement worries the original 15 EU members as well. These costs were a major issue in the "No" vote cast in the Netherlands against the Constitution in 2005. (France voted "No" also, but for different reasons.)

Different Rules for the 10 New Members

Only the United Kingdom, Sweden, and Denmark of the original group were able to retain their national currency when they did not to join EMU. But unlike the original EU 15, the new members do not have a choice and cannot opt out of adopting the euro as their currency. The new countries, in order to join the EMU, must fulfill strict Maastricht criteria on inflation, budget deficits, and public debt. Several new members have already breached the mandated budget deficit ceiling of 3 percent of GDP as stipulated by the Growth and Stability Pact—but then many of the original members are currently above the mandated percentage as well.

One-size monetary policy does not necessarily fit all. The European Commission and the ECB have warned that hasty EMU entry could endanger the new members' growth prospects by depriving them of the monetary flexibility needed to cope with the pressures of the single market. Even some rich West European countries have been harmed by the single currency, with interest rates that were too high for sluggish Germany, for example, but too low for buoyant Ireland.

But several new members, namely Cyprus, Estonia, Lithuania, and Slovenia, have indicated that they want to start the process of becoming full EMU members. Estonia, Lithuania, Slovenia, Latvia, and Slovakia already have joined the Exchange Rate Mechanism 2—the waiting room for the single currency—and are candidates for eurozone membership. Estonia, Lithuania, and Slovenia had hoped to join on January 2007, while Latvia wants to join in 2008 and Slovakia in 2009. However, only Slovenia will enter the EMU on January 1, 2007. Estonia opted to wait, while Lithuania's bid was rejected. This rejection raised bitter objections to the entry criteria used to judge eligibility. The country's budget deficit is below the 3 percent of GDP limit and the country has a healthy and growing economy. However, Lithuania's inflation rate was slightly above the average of the three current EU members with the lowest inflation rate. And what particularly riled critics of this decision was that the country with the lowest inflation rate, Sweden, is not a member of the EMU. It has been pointed out that many of the current 12 members could not currently pass the tests.

In the brief time since their independence from the Union of Soviet Socialist Republics (USSR) , these countries have been very successful in changing themselves into flexible market economies. The World Bank ranks Lithuania and Estonia ahead of Germany in terms of ease of doing business. All candidate countries easily meet most of the Maastricht criteria for EMU membership. They satisfy the exchange rate and interest rate criteria, and only Slovakia narrowly missed one of the two fiscal criteria. This is in contrast to Belgium, Germany, France, Italy, and Greece, which, if they were not already eurozone members, would not be eligible to join today since they do not meet the fiscal criteria. However, according to ECB and European Commission rules, only Slovenia satisfies the inflation criterion. The rule states that the applicant cannot exceed the average of the three members having the lowest inflation rate by more than 1.5 percentage points in the year prior to examination.

The applicants also have to comply with the other membership criteria, including cutting national debt, controlling deficits and inflation, and giving full independence to their national central banks. Estonia withdrew its bid to join in 2007 but hopes to join in 2008. And Lithuania will also have to wait. Only Slovenia was slated to become an EMU member on January 1, 2007.

The three largest of the new EU members—Poland, the Czech Republic, and Hungary—are taking a slower track because of their battle to curb budget deficits. All of the new member states are bound by the EU's Stability and Growth Pact, but are being given extra time to comply with its 3 percent of GDP deficit ceiling. Once a formal application is submitted, the EU's Economic and Financial Committee of national finance officials and central bankers normally meets on a weekend to set the central parity for a national currency against the euro.

Expansion Pros and Cons

Expansion proponents view an ever-larger EU as the best way of building economic and political bonds between countries in order to end the divisions of the past. They look forward to sharing the world's largest single market and in the process to expand and consolidate stability and prosperity. Meanwhile, critics say the fact that average GDP per head for the new member states is 40 percent of the average for existing EU countries is making the new members an economic burden. Some critics contend that the EU decision-making process (which is already cumbersome) will become bogged down as the number of countries increases. Some are fearful that established EU members will see a huge influx of immigrants from former communist states seeking better job and benefit prospects.

The response from supporters of enlargement is that immigration should be welcomed—and besides, it is unlikely to occur on the large scale that many in the richer nations fear. In the short term, existing members are allowed to limit employment rights for people from new member states.

What Is Too Big?

Many of today's members view the prospect of an ever-expanding EU with a mixture of fatalism and dread. There are several reasons for this:

- The EU redistributes billions of euros from rich to poor members, and more poor members means more claimants are competing for funds. Again, this was an issue in the Dutch "No" vote on the proposed Constitution.
- One of the EU's fundamental principles is that there should be freedom of movement within its borders. But anti-immigration parties are gaining ground across western Europe, and some countries have already limited access by new member citizens because of terror concerns.
- A larger EU might be unable to function, especially if expansion continues and the Balkans, Turkey and other former Soviet Union members join. This would add up to an EU of almost 40 members.
- Farm subsidies for the new entrants will start at just 25 percent of the western levels, rising to parity only by 2013. But small farmers in the east worry that they will be wiped out by agribusiness in the west, where subsidies on average provide a quarter of the income for most current EU farmers. Farm subsidies played a major role in the collapse of the EU 2005 budget negotiations.

Among the new entrants, Poland is a particularly extreme example of dependence on small-scale agriculture and presents the biggest challenge to the system of farm subsidies that both underpins European agriculture and inspires furious arguments over global farm trade.

Some Worries

In the EU, the main concern is about the impact of the newcomers on the original 15 EU members. Some questions are purely pragmatic. How long will EU meetings take if 25 countries (and now 27) have to have their say? Can the translation system cope? But for the investor in European equities, the accession had a less dramatic impact. The combined economies of the 10 new member countries are only the size of the Netherlands and their stock markets are even smaller. If Hungary and the Czech Republic were included today in the West European indexes (including the United Kingdom), they would be a mere 0.1 percent of the total by market capitalization. The newcomers are considered to be emerging markets in the eyes of most market makers. And, clearly, risk will weigh heavily in investor decision making!

THE CONSTITUTION

A Very Brief Description

The constitution sets out the division of powers between the Member State national governments and the EU's various institutions. It also contains a charter of fundamental rights and a detailed catalog of how the union would conduct a wide range of internal and foreign policies. It includes one of the issues that was resisted by smaller nations—plans for new voting rules. While each country has an equal vote now, the proposed constitution says that measures must have the backing of at least 55 percent of EU states, representing at least 65 percent of the total population, in order to pass. However, the EU constitution does extend centralization. There will be more joint action to be decided by majority voting in immigration and asylum policies, for example. But in other areas such as defense and foreign policy as well as taxes, Member States can still go their own way.

The change in voting would also impact the ECB. Now all 12 member (13 on January 1, 2007) country central banks sit on the Governing Council. A rotating system similar to the Fed would be put in place, something the smaller members do not like.

The constitution's main aim was to replace the overlapping set of existing treaties in order to streamline EU institutions so they can cope with an enlarged bloc of countries. The treaty is about 180 pages long and has more than 260 pages of protocols and annexes. It is a compromise but is still widely seen as an improvement on treaties and texts that have governed the union until now. The treaty does not transfer any important new powers to the EU, although it does make a few more areas subject to majority voting, thus restricting the power of national vetoes and reducing the influence of Member States.

It also contains the first formal statement of the primacy of EU law over national law, a principle previously established by the jurisprudence of the European Court of Justice. While allowing majority voting in some minor areas, it retains national vetoes over direct taxation, foreign and defense policy, and financing of the EU budget. It creates several new jobs, including a president of the European Council and a foreign minister. The presidential term would be up to five years, in contrast to the current term, which rotates between members every six months. The foreign minister would combine the roles of the external affairs commissioner and the EU's high representative for foreign policy. The constitution also creates an explicit right for countries to leave the EU.

The EU is not a free trade agreement like the North American Free Trade Agreement between the United States, Canada, and Mexico. Rather, the constitution confirms that the EU is a halfway house. It has preserved some nation state rights but it also confirms that states have given up some other rights over such areas as the internal market, foreign trade, agriculture, fisheries, and the environment.

The constitution would lead to more qualified majority voting within the basic framework of the EU's institutions rather than the unanimous decisions needed now. It also would allow those states who want to get closer together to do so, as most have already done when they joined the EMU. But its opponents say it goes too far toward collective action and that Member States would eventually be forced to join in various policies rather than opt out as they might have preferred. Its supporters say that it preserves a balance, but there is yet a third group that says that it does not go far enough. To be adopted, all 25 countries must agree on the terms either in national parliaments or through public referendums. The constitution was put in doubt when both France and the Netherlands voted against it in mid-2005. But supporters of the constitution refused to give up. They hope it will still be approved at a later date. After France and the Netherlands rejected the constitution, leaders of the EU's 25 states called for a period of "reflection" for one year. This pause was originally expected to end in June 2006. But the split between those members who would like to bury the constitution and those who would like to revive it in some form continued. And the pause has been extended at least into 2008 and after the French general election.

STABILITY AND GROWTH PACT

European Union members enacted the Stability and Growth Pact as part of the Maastricht Treaty. Its purpose was to support the fledgling euro and was aimed at keeping fiscal miscreants in line. The accord was drawn up at the insistence of Germany (and the Bundesbank, the model for the ECB) in order to whip into line countries thought to be fiscally irresponsible. Since its approval by participating countries in 1997, the pact has underpinned the creation of the euro by imposing tight fiscal rules. Governments were told to balance their budget in the medium term—a feat achieved by 11 of the 15 members. A key element of the Pact was that members were forbidden to run a deficit of more than 3 percent of gross domestic product. The Pact was designed during a period of strong growth in the mid-1990s but became a problem as welfare costs soared and tax revenues fell because of faltering economic growth.

The Stability and Growth Pact implements the excessive deficit procedure included in the Treaty of Maastricht. Along with establishing the 3 percent of GDP budget deficit limit, it defines the exceptional conditions under which breaching the limit can be accepted, and establishes how and when fines can be levied against countries that display excessive deficits. The only valid concern cited to justify the Stability and Growth Pact is the danger of systemic banking and financial crises in case of debt default by a Member State. Although Germany, France, Italy, and Portugal were cited for breaching the 3 percent ceiling, they were not punished according to the rules set out in the Pact, much to the outrage of the smaller countries. Rather, the rules were changed to accommodate them.

Why a Stability Pact Was Necessary

At issue was how to maintain the stability of a single currency when the countries that use it make their own economic policy. Germany, which in the 1980s had a thriving economy and a sound budget, did not want to be dragged down by chronic debtors like Italy. If one wants a common currency, fiscal policies must harmonize somehow. The countries finally agreed at Maastricht to set out strict requirements that members had to meet before they could be admitted to the euro club.

The Stability and Growth Pact is administered by the European Commission. Countries that fail to heed the rules are supposed to be disciplined with warning letters, and then with fines equal to 0.5 percent of GDP. In its early days, the Pact seemed the perfect antidote for decades of profligate government spending.

When Italy got under the deficit ceiling, the event was hailed as an example of how the EU could bring out the best in its members. The

Pact provided a cover for leaders to cut spending for the "greater good of Europe." At this writing, seven of the 12 euro countries are running surpluses. Not surprisingly, those countries oppose changing rules with which they have complied.

So What's the Problem?

The Pact was created while European economies were basking in 2-plus percent annual GDP growth and falling unemployment amid the global economic boom of the late 1990s. Slower to nonexistent growth for several years after that exposed the limitations and fault lines between Germany, France, and Italy, on the one hand, and smaller countries, on the other, that have stuck to the Pact. Critics have derided the accord for its emphasis on stability rather than growth. Although the agreement was designed to impose financial discipline, France and Germany criticized it as too inflexible in times of economic weakness. The rules have been bent to allow Germany, Portugal, France, and Italy more time to balance their budgets. But there are many in the financial markets who, like some European finance ministers, believe that loosening was vital for coping with the downturn.

Furthermore, few believe the euro has been put at risk by the exceptions made for Germany, France, Italy, and Portugal, although they are watchful of how the Pact might be reformed in future. The problem was how to make it more flexible without creating a free-for-all of irresponsible government spending.

In March 2005, EU finance ministers weakened the Pact substantially. EU leaders concurred with the changes. Essentially, they agreed to rip up existing fiscal rules for euro members and start again. For eight years finance ministers have steadfastly insisted that the Pact was essential to the euro's health. The Pact's demands for fines on countries that persistently run budget deficits bigger than 3 percent of GDP had been defended as an essential tool to stop improvident governments from undermining the euro. But now the rules have been so loosened that they have been rendered almost entirely meaningless. A raft of possible exceptions has now been written into the Pact. Governments can now avert the threat of sanctions by pointing to any recession, however shallow, or even just to a persistent period of slow growth. And various forms of spending are to be given special consideration, including education, research, defense, foreign aid, and anything that contributes to European unification. European unification was added at the behest of Germany, who argued that its unification costs of East and West Germany has pushed its budget over the limit. Yet when the original stability pact was adopted in 1997, Germany had already been unified for six years.

EUROPEAN CENTRAL BANK

In the previous section we discussed the Euopean Union and how it came to found the Bank as a logical step toward economic integration. Now we will direct our attention to the ECB. It is truly unique among central banks.

The EU separates economic policy making into two parts, with monetary policy in the hands of a supranational organization and fiscal policy in the hands of the individual Member States. This leaves little coordination between the two. The EU's attempt at controlling fiscal policy has been honored in the breach, even within the guidelines of the revised Stability and Growth Pact that has loosened fiscal controls and gives most countries a way around fiscal discipline.

The ECB is a bank for many nations and its committees are composed of the heads of the member country central banks including the once powerful German Bundesbank. The Bank's design and focus was very much influenced by the Bundesbank and follows many of its ways of doing business.

The ECB was created by the Maastricht Treaty in 1992 at the same time that the EU was born. The statute established both the ECB and the European System of Central Banks (ESCB) on January 1, 1998. The ECB is the core of the Eurosystem and the ESCB. The ECB in conjunction with the national central banks work together on their assigned responsibilities. The ECB is a legal entity under public international law.

The ECB is empowered to set monetary policy for the members of the EMU. In 2002, the ECB oversaw the successful conversion of national currencies (deutschmark, franc, lira, drachma, etc.) to the euro for all transactions. The conversion went more smoothly than most expected, although most residents think that business took advantage of the conversion and rounded prices up, making for a higher rate of inflation.

The ECB focuses on inflation, raising questions about whether a one-size-fits-all monetary policy really works given the disparate levels of growth among EMU Member States.

Since its inception, the ECB has been trying to build its credibility. It is extremely conscious of its independence and protects it with zeal. Any attempt at political intervention in its affairs only seems to solidify its position in the opposite direction.

The ECB has adopted two policy guides or "pillars" to monetary policy:

1. A monetary target of a 4.5 percent growth rate for the M3 measure of money supply.
2. An inflation ceiling of 2 percent or less as measured by the harmonized index of consumer prices (HICP).

Organization

European System of Central Banks (ESCB) The ECB decides monetary policy, and member national central banks (NCBs) implement it. Together these banks form the European System of Central Banks (ESCB). The member banks of the ECB include Nationale Bank van België/Banque Nationale de Belgique, Deutsche Bundesbank, Banque de France, Banco de España, Banca d'Italia, Banco de Portugal, Bank of Greece, Banque centrale du Luxembourg, De Nederlandsche Bank, Central Bank and Financial Services Authority of Ireland, Oesterreichische National bank, and Suomen Pankki–Finlands Bank. They will be joined by Slovenia's central bank, the Bank of Slovenia, on January 1, 2007. The three non-ECB members are the Bank of England, Danmarks National bank, and Sveriges Riksbank.

The *Eurosystem* is the term used to refer to the ECB and the NCBs, which have adopted the euro. The nonmember banks in the United Kingdom, Denmark, and Sweden are members but with a special status—they conduct their respective national monetary policies and are excluded from the decision-making process and its implementation for the EMU.

The ECB (and the Eurosystem) is charged with maintaining price stability, while at the same time supporting the community's general economic policies and acting in accordance with open-market economy principles. Its tasks include defining and implementing monetary policy for the euro area, conducting foreign exchange operations, holding and managing the official foreign reserves of the Member States, and promoting the smooth operation of payment systems.

In addition, the Eurosystem facilitates the smooth conduct of policies relating to the supervision of credit institutions and the stability of the financial system. The ECB has an advisory role to the Community and national authorities on matters that fall within its field of competence, particularly where Community or national legislation is concerned. Finally, the ECB (assisted by the NCBs) is charged with the responsibility to collect the necessary statistical information from the national authorities or directly from economic agents.

Decision-making authority lies in the ECB's Governing Council and Executive Board. But as long as there are Member States that have not yet adopted the euro, a third decision-making body, the General Council, also exists. The Governing Council comprises all the members of the Executive Board and the governors of the NCBs of the Member States who have adopted the euro. The ECB Governing Council is charged with adopting guidelines and ensuring the performance of the tasks entrusted to the Eurosystem. It also formulates monetary policy, including decisions relating to intermediate monetary objectives, key interest rates, and the supply of reserves in the Eurosystem, and establishes the necessary guidelines for their implementation.

The Executive Board members include the President, the Vice President, and four other members of recognized standing and professional experience in monetary or banking matters. They are appointed by Member State governments on recommendation from the EU Council after consultation with the European Parliament and the ECB Governing Council. The main responsibility of the Executive Board is to implement monetary policy in accordance with the guidelines and decisions laid down by the Governing Council.

The General Council is a transitional body and includes both EMU and non-EMU member banks and will only exist as long as there are EU members who have not adopted the euro and become EMU members. The Council has a supportive role and contributes to a number of ECB functions, including the collection of statistical information; annual report preparation; establishment of standardized rules for accounting and reporting of operations undertaken by the NCBs; measures related to ECB's capital subscription other than those already laid down in the Treaty; staff employment qualifications for ECB staff; and preparations for irrevocably fixing the exchange rates of the currencies of the Member States that are not yet members.

NCB governors serve a minimum renewable term of five years, while Executive Board members serve a minimum nonrenewable term of office of eight years (it should be noted that a system of staggered appointments was used for the first Executive Board for members other than the president in order to ensure continuity).

The ECB's capital amounts to €5 billion. The NCBs are the sole subscribers to and holders of the capital. The subscription of capital is based on EU Member States' respective shares in the GDP and population of the Community. In addition, the NCBs provided the ECB with foreign reserve assets. The contributions were fixed in proportion to its share in the ECB's subscribed capital, while in return each NCB was credited by the ECB with a claim in euros equivalent to its contribution.

Basic Tasks

The ECB's basic tasks as defined by the Treaty are:

- Defining and implementing of euro area monetary policy.
- Conducting foreign exchange operations.
- Holding and management of the official euro area foreign reserves (portfolio management).

- Promoting the smooth operation of payment systems.
- Authorizing the issuance of euro area banknotes.
- Statistical data collection in cooperation with the NCBs necessary for fulfilling the tasks either from national authorities or directly from economic agents.
- Financial stability and supervision.
- International and European cooperation with relevant institutions in respect of tasks entrusted to the Eurosystem.

Like the Federal Open Market Committee (FOMC) in the United States, the Governing Council makes decisions affecting the availability and cost of money and credit. But the ECB has specific money supply growth and inflation targets. Critics complain about the ECB's lack of transparency. The ECB does not publish minutes of its meetings or report how votes were cast, but it does hold a press conference after the first meeting of the month to explain its actions. The ECB's first president was Wim Duisenberg, a former governor of the Dutch central bank. He was succeeded by Jean-Claude Trichet, who previously was governor of the Bank of France on November 1, 2003. Duisenberg oversaw many landmark ECB events, including the introduction of the euro as everyday currency.

The ECB's prime objective is to maintain price stability through interest rate policy. The Governing Council makes decisions on interest rates by consensus rather than a vote. (This is unlike the Banks of England and Japan and Federal Reserve). The Council meets every other Thursday, just as the Bundesbank does and more frequently than the FOMC. To calm markets, the ECB announced that monetary policy matters would be considered only at the first meeting of the month, rather than at all meetings. The main monetary instrument is the repo or sale and repurchase agreement. At its meetings, Council members assess monetary and economic developments and then make its monthly monetary policy decision. At its mid-month meeting, the Council discusses issues related to the ECB's and Eurosystem's other tasks and responsibilities.

Independence

The ECB was organized to be independent of political influence. This independence has been, and continues to be under attack by political leaders, who would prefer to see lower interest rates accelerate moribund growth. The ECB has been steadfast in rebuffing the verbal assaults. Financial markets prefer a monetary authority that is free from political interference, and the ECB has been organized with that in mind.

The key to the ECB's independence is specifically stated in the institutional framework for the single monetary policy (both in the Treaty and in the Statute). Neither the ECB, the NCBs, nor any decision-making body members are allowed to seek or take instructions from European Community institutions or bodies, from any EU Member State government, or from any other body. However, that has not stopped leaders of Germany, Italy, and France from trying to apply pressure on the ECB. The ECB's independence is conducive to maintaining price stability above all other considerations.

Transparency

Central bank transparency has increased worldwide. In the not-too-distant past, a policy change could be divined only by studying the Bank's operational trail in the financial markets and their (in the Fed's case) weekly money supply numbers. Now transparency is in vogue. It means that the central bank provides the general public and the markets with all relevant information on its strategy, assessments, and policy decisions, as well as its procedures in an open, clear, and timely manner. Most central banks consider transparency crucial. This is true especially for their monetary policy framework.

The ECB's transparency is argued by friend and foe. While the ECB says it gives a high priority to communicating effectively with the public, some question the Bank's motivation. The ECB says that it fosters credibility by being clear about its mandate (inflation control) and how it performs its tasks. The Bank does hold monthly press conferences to convey its latest thinking. But they are less than candid—little is known about the actual dialogue at meetings. It should be noted that invariably the press conference's opening statement is repeated virtually verbatim in its *Monthly Bulletin* released in the following week. When policy is changed, an announcement is made at the conclusion of the meeting, as in the following example:

At today's meeting the Governing Council of the ECB took the following monetary policy decisions:

1. The minimum bid rate on the main refinancing operations of the Eurosystem will be increased by 25 basis points to 2.50%, starting from the operation to be settled on March 8, 2006.

2. The interest rate on the marginal lending facility will be increased by 25 basis points to 3.50%, with effect from March 8, 2006.

3. The interest rate on the deposit facility will be increased by 25 basis points to 1.50%, with effect from March 8, 2006.

The President of the ECB will comment on the considerations underlying these decisions at a press conference starting at 2:30 P.M. today.

At the press conference, the ECB publicly announces its monetary policy strategy and communicates its assessment of economic developments that led to the decision. This helps the markets to understand the systematic response pattern of monetary policy to economic developments and shocks. But there are no minutes of the Governing Council's decisions with agreement reached by consensus rather than a vote.

Accountability

According to the Statute, the ECB is required to publish quarterly reports on the activities of the Eurosystem as well as a consolidated Weekly Financial Statement. In addition, it has to produce an Annual Report on its activities and on the monetary policy of the previous and the current year. The Annual Report is addressed to the European Parliament, the EU Council, the European Commission, and the European Council. To fulfill the requirements of the Statute, the ECB also publishes a Monthly Bulletin (in addition to a quarterly one). They also release a Weekly Financial Statement as many central banks do. Besides that, the ECB produces a range of other task-related publications.

Monetary Policy

As stated earlier, the ECB's prime objective is to maintain price stability through its interest rate policy. The main monetary instrument is the repo—short for sale and repurchase agreement. The ECB conducts open-market operations and offers standing facilities. It requires credit institutions to hold minimum reserves on accounts with the national central banks (the Bundesbank, Bank of France, etc.) Figure 3.1 shows the ECB's policy interest rate since 1999.

On October 13, 1998, the Governing Council announced the ECB's stability-oriented monetary policy strategy to guide its monetary policy decisions for the EMU. This strategy was confirmed and further clarified on May 8, 2003, following a thorough evaluation by the Governing Council.

It consists of a quantitative definition of price stability—its primary objective. It outlines an analytical framework based on two pillars—economic analysis and monetary analysis—which forms the basis of the

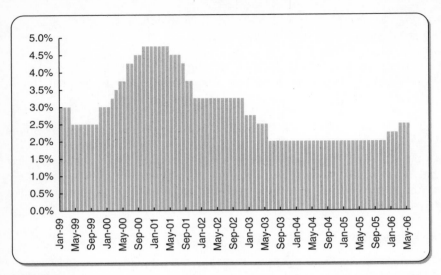

FIGURE 3.1   The ECB has kept its interest rate stable, showing little desire to be proactive to stimulate growth.
Source: European Central Bank and Haver Analytics.

Governing Council's overall assessment of the risks to price stability and its monetary policy decisions. Price stability is defined as a year-on-year increase in the harmonized index of consumer prices (HICP) for the euro area of below 2 percent. Price stability is to be maintained over the medium term. The Governing Council announced that, in the pursuit of price stability, it would aim to maintain inflation rates close to, but below, 2 percent over the medium term. Figure 3.2 shows the two pillars, the HICP and M3 money supply.

The ECB's Governing Council and the FOMC in the United States make decisions affecting the availability and cost of money and credit. But while the ECB makes decisions about both interest rate and money supply growth targets, the FOMC no longer targets money supply. The ECB decides monetary policy, and member national central banks implement it.

The two-pillar framework for the assessment of the risks to price stability include:

1. Economic analysis that focuses on an assessment of current economic developments and the associated short- to medium-term risks to price stability. It includes an analysis of possible shocks that could impact the region as well as projections of key macroeconomic variables.

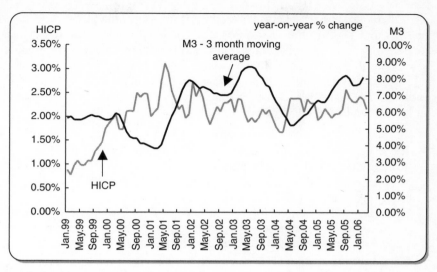

FIGURE 3.2   Both the HICP and M3 money supply growth have consistently been above the ECB's targets of 2 percent and 4.5 percent, respectively.
Source: Eurostat and Haver Analytics.

2. Monetary analysis focuses on an assessment of medium- to long-term inflation trends given the close relationship between money and prices in the long term, taking into account developments in a wide range of monetary indicators, including M3 and its components and counterparts, notably credit, and various measures of excess liquidity. The monetary analysis serves mainly as a cross-check on the medium- and long-term perspective as well as the short- to medium-term indications from the economic analysis.

The Treaty governing the ECB established a clear hierarchy of objectives. It assigned an overriding importance to price stability. The Treaty makes clear that ensuring price stability is the most important contribution that monetary policy can make to a favorable economic environment and a high level of employment. It should be noted that while the Treaty clearly establishes the maintenance of price stability as the primary objective of the ECB, it does not give a precise definition of what is meant by price stability. But the Governing Council has defined it in the context of the HICP.

Monetary Policy Instruments and Procedures   The Eurosystem conducts open market operations, offers standing facilities, and requires credit institutions to hold minimum reserves on accounts with the NCBs in the euro area. Open market operations play an important role in the ECB's monetary policy as they do for other central banks. The operations facilitate interest rate adjustments along with managing banking system liquidity and signaling monetary policy stance. Open market operations are initiated by the ECB, which also decides on the instrument to be used, along with terms and conditions for such operations. Open market operations of the Eurosystem can be divided into the following categories:

- The main refinancing operations are regular liquidity-providing reverse transactions with a weekly frequency and a maturity of two weeks. They are executed by the NCBs on the basis of standard tenders and according to a prespecified calendar.
- The longer-term refinancing operations are liquidity-providing reverse transactions with a monthly frequency and a maturity of three months. They are also executed by the NCBs on the basis of standard tenders and according to a prespecified calendar.

Fine-tuning operations can be carried out on an ad hoc basis with the aim of both managing the liquidity situation in the market and steering interest rates, in order to smooth the effects of unexpected liquidity fluctuations on rates. The Eurosystem may carry out structural operations through the issuance of debt certificates, reverse transactions, and outright transactions. Standing facilities aim to provide and absorb overnight liquidity, signal the general monetary policy stance, and bound overnight market interest rates.

Minimum reserves are an integral part of the operational framework and are intended to stabilize money market interest rates. The reserve requirement of each institution is determined in relation to elements of its balance sheet.

The monetary policy framework is formulated with a view to ensuring the participation of a broad range of counterparties. Only institutions subject to minimum reserves may have access to the standing facilities and participate in open market operations based on standard tenders.

The Treaty provisions also imply that while monetary policy decisions are aimed at maintaining price stability, the banking system should also take into account broader economic goals. Given that monetary policy can affect real activity in the shorter term, the ECB should avoid generating excessive fluctuations in output and employment if this is in line with the pursuit of its primary objective.

Price stability refers to the general level of prices in the economy and implies avoiding periods of prolonged inflation or deflation. Price stability contributes to vibrant economic activity and employment by improving price transparency. Under price stability, people make well-informed consumption and investment decisions by allowing for the efficient allocation of resources because they can differentiate changes in relative prices between different goods, without being confused by overall price-level changes. Price stability also reduces inflation risk premia in interest rates, that is, the compensation creditors ask for the risks associated with holding nominal assets. This in turn reduces real interest rates and increases incentives to invest. It helps to avoid such unproductive activities as hedging against the negative impact of inflation or deflation. It also reduces distortions that inflation or deflation can cause as it permeates the economic system.

The ECB is the sole issuer of banknotes and bank reserves. That means it is the monopoly supplier of the monetary base. By virtue of this monopoly, it can set the conditions at which banks borrow from the central bank and the conditions at which banks trade with each other in the money market. In the short run, a change in money market interest rates induced by the central bank sets in motion a number of mechanisms and actions by economic agents. Ultimately, the change will influence developments in economic variables such as output or prices.

The ECB believes that, in the long run, a central bank can contribute to raising the growth potential of the economy only by maintaining an environment of stable prices. It cannot enhance economic growth by expanding the money supply or keeping short-term interest rates at a level inconsistent with price stability. It can only influence the general level of prices. Inflation is considered a monetary phenomenon. Prolonged periods of high inflation are typically associated with high monetary growth. While other factors (such as variations in aggregate demand, technological changes, or commodity price shocks) can influence price developments over shorter horizons, over time their effects can be offset by a change in monetary policy.

CHAPTER 4

Bank of Japan

B ank of Japan's monetary policy is undergoing a profound shift from one geared solely to fighting deflation by flooding the financial markets with liquidity and a zero interest rate policy to a more conventional one. In the first quarter of 2006 they began the normalization process by curtailing liquidity. And as expected, their policy interest rate is now above zero.

AN OVERVIEW

Although the Bank of Japan (BoJ) has been around since the end of the nineteenth century, it initially fulfilled a very limited role as the Government's banker and currency issuer. It has only been "independent" since 1997, with most of the ensuing years since then spent trying to squirm out from under the Ministry of Finance's (MoF's) thumb. The Bank is zealous in protecting its independence, which was gained at the time of the Japanese big bang—a major overhaul of the financial markets and the institutions that oversee them.

There was the inevitable friction between the Bank and the MoF due to policy differences on how to tackle deflation as the BoJ tried to invoke its independence. The Bank maintained a zero interest rate policy because of poor Japanese economic performance that was exacerbated by deflation. Furthermore, it swore that it would not increase rates until its inflation measure (year-on-year percent change in the core measure of consumer prices that excludes perishable foods) was positive for a "considerable" period of time.

But as the economy finally began to grow and price declines diminished, a major difference of opinion emerged. Politicians led by then prime minister Junichiro Koizumi were concerned that an interest rate of any sort would stifle Japan's economic expansion. Government officials were also worried that any increase in borrowing costs would escalate the cost of servicing its huge fiscal deficit. Financing costs alone absorbed over 22 percent of Japan's budget in 2005, while the nation's budget deficit is forecast to swell to an estimated 151 percent of gross domestic product by the end of March 2007.

Like other central banks, the BoJ's primary objective is to maintain price stability, even though it has no official inflation target (at this time), and provide the foundations for sound economic growth. Unlike other central banks, the Bank has been fighting deflation or falling prices rather than keeping a lid on price increases or inflation. Five years ago, the BoJ launched a monetary experiment—its so-called "quantitative easing" policy, which basically meant printing lots of money in an unorthodox approach to ridding the economy of deflation. It appears to have been successful.

BoJ's Roots Intertwined with Its Mercantile Past

Shortly after its entry into world society—around 1850—Japan experienced one of the gravest financial crises of its history. Their isolationist policies that reached back to 1600 had estranged its economy from the international marketplace. And the country's isolation from the world bullion market proved to be especially disruptive and painful. Most obvious was the discrepancy in the parity of gold to silver. While Western nations' ratio of gold to silver was 1 to 15, the Japanese military government had fixed it at 1 to 5.

This discrepancy was itself a sufficient reason for severe instability. However, the immediate causes of a financial crisis were in the fundamental differences in monetary organization between Japan and the rest of the world. Internationalization, and more specifically the confrontation with the world economy at the time, was profoundly destabilizing to Japan. Political friction with the great powers of the time was followed by creeping inflation and destructive speculation. This resulted in an outflow of Japan's gold reserves. Ill-conceived attempts at financial and monetary reform further deepened the crisis. On an ideological level, these events reinforced Japan's history of traumatic encounters with foreign dependence.

As the end of the nineteenth century approached, Matsukata Masayoshi developed many of the ambitious and daring policies that laid the groundwork of Japan's economic and financial development. He also designed a modern financial infrastructure, with the Bank of Japan as "lender of last resort" and a sound system of correspondence between banks. The Bank was established under the Bank of Japan Act of June 1882 and began operating on October 10, 1882.

Japan recovered from its longtime bullion problem, adopted the gold standard in 1899, and consolidated its economic and political modernization. Roughly 50 years after it had been forced into internationalization, it defeated both China (1894 to 1895) and Russia (1904 to 1905). And prior to World War I, it already was an international power, while financially it had developed from a doubtful debtor nation into a creditworthy state.

Like most modern institutions in Japan, the Bank was born after the Meiji Restoration. Prior to the Restoration, Japan's feudal fiefs all issued their own money, hansatsu, in an array of incompatible denominations, but the New Currency Act of Meiji 4 (1871) did away with these and established the yen, the basic unit of money in Japan and equal to 100 senyen, as the new decimal currency.

The BoJ issued its first banknotes on Meiji 18 (1885), and despite some small glitches—for example, it turned out that konnyaku powder mixed in the paper to prevent counterfeiting made the bills a delicacy for rats—the run was largely successful.

The Bank has operated continually with the exception of a brief post–World War II period when the occupation forces issued military currency and restructured the Bank into a more independent entity. However, despite a major 1997 rewrite of the Bank of Japan Law intended to give it more independence, the BoJ has been criticized for its lack of independence. It should be noted that a certain degree of dependency is enshrined in the Law itself. Article 4 states that the Bank shall always maintain close contact with the government. Further, it says that there should be a continual exchange of views so that the Bank's currency and monetary control can be coordinated with the government's economic policies.

The Bubble Explodes

During the 1980s, people around the world were amazed by the inflated value of Japanese financial assets. Current account surpluses soared, the yen was strong, and asset values (land and stocks) skyrocketed. Japan became the world's largest creditor nation as they invested worldwide in virtually anything, including (and especially) golf courses. Japanese banks and securities companies expanded worldwide, and Japanese banks monopolized the upper end of the world rankings in terms of assets. Stock trading and other financial businesses were very active, and foreign banks and securities companies all wanted to do business in Japan. Tokyo indisputably became the biggest financial center in Asia and was expected to become one of the world's three major financial centers, together with New York and London.

But when the asset price bubble burst, asset prices spiraled downward and brought new woes to Japanese banks that were unlike anything they faced in the post-war growth era. In the 1990s Japanese banks, beset and overwhelmed by bad loans, were forced to undergo cataclysmic changes.

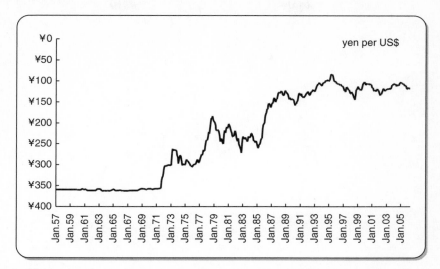

FIGURE 4.1 The yen has remained within a range of ¥105 to ¥120 to the U.S. dollar.
Source: Federal Reserve Board and Haver Analytics.

Many banks collapsed under the weight of their bad loans, even though massive amounts of public funds were injected into the banking system. Capital bank management was drastically streamlined and businesses were shed, while others merged or consolidated. And red ink ruled year-end financial results. Needless to say, these events transformed the banking industry, as did the liberalization and globalization that characterized Japanese banks in the 1980s. It eventually culminated in the Financial System Reform Law of 1992, the unveiling of the 1996 Japanese Big Bang and the ongoing reshuffling of the industry. At the same time, the Ministry of Finance was completely reorganized and the way it supervised was drastically changed. Figure 4.1 shows the impact of these events on its currency.

The economic collapse and the ensuing financial industry reforms were pivotal to the Bank of Japan. In the process of the reforms leading to the Big Bang, the Bank also gained more independence from the finance ministry.

The 1990s

During the 1990s, Japan kept its world status with respect to material things such as manufactured goods and some areas of computer software, such as game software. But financial strength, which was regarded as constituting another pillar of the Japanese economy, had suffered a serious setback. Although Japan continued to be world's largest creditor nation, asset value

FIGURE 4.2   The Nikkei has a long way to go before regaining its bubble peak.
Source: Wall Street Journal and Haver Analytics.

inflation collapsed after reaching a peak at the end of the 1980s. Since then, asset values have continued to decline. Vestiges of the collapse of stock and land prices were still apparent as recently as in 2005. The mountain of nonperforming loans that burdened Japanese financial institutions continued to weigh down the banking sector. As a result, the banking sector that had been dominant in the 1980s lost most of its international competitiveness.

The Tokyo stock market, which in the 1980s had been expected to rank alongside New York and London and to be the central market in Asia, languished as the Nikkei sank. Credit ratings of many financial institutions were downgraded, and market activity declined. At the end of 1997 and after the decision had already been made (at the end of 1996) on the basic policy for the Japanese version of London's Big Bang, Yamaichi Securities, Japan's fourth largest securities house failed and was compelled to wind up its operations voluntarily, taking several other small and medium-scale banks and securities companies along with it. This depression in the financial sector generated a mood of unease that pervaded the entire Japanese economy. Figure 4.2 shows the highs and lows of the Nikkei since 1981.

Financial System Reforms — The Big Bang

By the beginning of the 1990s the decline of Japan's financial markets and financial industry relative to the strength of the manufacturing industry, which had retained its leading global standing, had become universally clear. This was because trading volume had not risen compared with the vigorous activity in London and New York, and Tokyo's impact on the levels of market prices worldwide had diminished markedly.

The Japanese were shocked to find that, despite the relatively small size of the economies in Hong Kong and Singapore, their financial markets, which benefited from such factors as relatively little regulation, low costs (public utilities charges, taxes, office rentals, costs of running back offices), and readily available English-speaking staff, had grown rapidly in strength. In contrast, the Tokyo market had been hollowed out, so much so that these others have usurped Tokyo's status as the financial center of Asia.

During the 1990s, foreign banks and securities companies that previously had scrambled to set up operations in Tokyo shifted their Asian bases to Singapore or Hong Kong. The view was that among the world's leading markets the Tokyo market had become a local market. Furthermore, because of regulations and the time required to gain official approvals, new financial products had ceased to emerge from Japan. Compared with Japanese manufacturing, the weakness in the financial markets was very marked.

To rectify the situation, in November 1996, then prime minister Ryutaro Hashimoto laid out a basic policy of reforming Japanese financial markets and placing the Tokyo market on a par with the New York and London markets by the year 2001. This was the Japanese version of the Big Bang, under the catchwords "free, fair, and global."

Japanese Big Bang objectives were broad and were designed to reenergize the declining financial industry and its position in world markets primarily by easing regulations. The goal was to break the decline in foreign exchange business and outflows from Japan of stock-trading business and branches of foreign banks, and restore the status of the Tokyo market as Asia's leading financial market ahead of Singapore and Hong Kong.

Japan's Big Bang followed those in New York and London. The 1970s financial reform in New York and the original Big Bang in the City of London in the 1980s both brought about major changes to their respective markets. In New York, stock brokerage commissions were liberalized in May 1975, sparking fierce competition among brokers. The large-scale securities houses whose business was concentrated on wholesale business (securities businesses with large-scale investors such as companies and institutional investors) rather than individuals shifted the core of their earnings from brokerage commissions to mergers and acquisitions and profits from trading. The smaller and medium-scale brokers sought to break away from their structural dependence on stock brokerage commissions by deriving their earnings from handling investment trusts and asset-backed securities. Derivative markets were developed and focus shifted to mergers and acquisitions, the emergence of asset-backed securities, the expansion of the National Association of Securities Dealers Automated Quotation system (NASDAQ) market, and the proliferation of investment trusts.

In London, the main aspects included the complete liberalization of trading commissions, the abolition of the single-capacity system (to increase the size of and strengthen the earnings base of securities companies to enable them to cope with the liberalization of trading commissions, firms were permitted to act as both jobbers and brokers, two categories that had previously been strictly segregated), the opening up of membership of the stock exchange (City reorganization was accelerated by foreign capital), and finally, the lowering of the 1 percent tax on share transactions, the equivalent of Japan's securities transaction tax, to 0.5 percent. The financial markets were invigorated by a combination of these measures along with the increase in stock prices in 1986. Trading volume and trading value both rose, and the City reinforced its status as an international financial center.

MONETARY POLICY

According to its charter, the Bank of Japan's two main missions are the implementation of monetary policy and the issuance and management of banknotes. Other responsibilities include providing settlement services and ensuring the stability of the financial system, international activities, and compilation of data, economic analyses, and research activities.

- **BoJ responsibilities.** The Bank's goal is to pursue price stability, that is, to maintain an economic environment in which there is neither inflation nor deflation. The Bank's monetary policy is to achieve price stability that would contribute, in turn, to the stability for the entire economy. While price stability is the major goal, the BoJ does not have an explicit inflation target or policy.
- **Issuance and management of banknotes.** Banknotes (officially referred to as Bank of Japan notes) are the sole responsibility of the Bank as it is for the Banks of England and Canada, Reserve Bank of Australia, and the European Central Bank.

As with other central banks, the BoJ oversees other activities as well. Perhaps one of the BoJ's more active roles is in the foreign exchange markets, where they have actively manipulated the yen's value against the U.S. dollar to protect the country's exports and exporters. They act as an agent for the Minister of Finance when necessary. The Bank intervened extensively during the first quarter of 2004 to dampen the yen's rise as the economy improved and the stock market climbed to protect repatriated earnings at the end of the Japanese fiscal year on March 31, 2004. However, the Bank had not intervened in the last two fiscal years ending on March 31, 2005, and March 31, 2006.

The Bank provides settlement services to ensure financial system stability. It conducts various activities to facilitate the ease of transfer between financial institutions and their depositors and investors. Financial transactions between financial institutions are settled by transferring funds across the current accounts held at the BoJ. Like other central banks, the BoJ is referred to as the bankers' bank because it offers accounts to financial institutions. In order to facilitate funds transfers, the Bank operates an electronic settlement system, the Bank of Japan Financial Network System (BoJ-NET).

The Bank is responsible for the financial and managerial conditions of financial institutions and closely monitors trends in the loans and deposits of financial institutions and is the lender of last resort to financial institutions. The BoJ may provide emergency liquidity to the troubled institution should an institution become insolvent and pose a threat to the financial system. (For a vivid and unique description of the beleaguered banking sector see Gillian Tett, *Saving the Sun*, New York: Harper Business, 2003.)

As the "government's bank," the BoJ handles treasury and government securities. It also handles the receipt and disbursement of treasury funds, including acceptance of tax monies and payment of public works expenditures and public pensions. It also conducts accounting and bookkeeping for government agencies. In addition, the Bank deals with the whole gamut of activities associated with the issuance, registration, interest payment, and redemption of government securities.

The Bank plays an active role in international financial matters, including the provision of yen accounts to central banks and governmental institutions overseas. It also makes capital subscriptions and loan extensions to international organizations such as the Bank for International Settlements (BIS) and the International Monetary Fund (IMF). It participates in various international forums, such as the meetings at the BIS, the Group of Seven, and the IMF.

As with all central banks, the Bank compiles various statistics, including the highly regarded Tankan Survey, as well as the corporate goods price index and the service price index and traditional money stock data. The Bank reviews the country's economic and financial conditions based on these and a wide variety of other statistical data that are prepared by government agencies and other organizations (see Chapter 11).

Monetary Policy Board

The Monetary Policy Board was created in 1949, but it was only in conjunction with the financial sector overhaul (the Big Bang) that it achieved some measure of independence to set monetary policy. There are nine members, including the Governor and two Deputy Governors. Board members serve five year terms. Generally, the Deputy Governors are appointed at the same time as the Governor and their terms coincide with the Governor's. Unlike their overseas counterparts, the Monetary Policy Board generally meets on an irregular schedule, usually every two and a half to four weeks. The Governor holds a monthly press conference after one of its meetings.

The BoJ pursues price stability as its primary goal ideally to maintain an economic environment in which there is neither inflation nor deflation. The Bank manipulates monetary policy by means of open market operations as do other central banks. It controls the overall volume of money in the economy and interest rates on a daily basis through money market operations, that is, through its sales/purchases of money market instruments such as Japanese government securities (JGBs) to/from private financial institutions.

The official discount rate is the interest rate charged by the BoJ when extending loans to private financial institutions that have accounts at the Bank. There are two types. One is the "discount of bills" wherein the Bank purchases each bill at face value less the amount of interest to be paid by the date of maturity. The second type, "loans on bills," is extended to financial institutions and is collateralized by qualified bills or securities. A change in the official discount rate reflects changes in the Bank's basic stance on monetary policy. In managing monetary policy, the Bank conducts operations in two areas—through the supply or withdrawal of funds in the interbank money market, where financial institutions borrow and lend funds among themselves, or through the buying and selling of bills and bonds in the open market, where commercial companies can also participate. Through such operations, the Bank encourages changes in market interest rates by controlling the reserve positions of financial institutions. Figure 4.3 shows the Bank's policy interest rate since 1965.

In theory, most open market operations would function like this. If the economy (in this case, Japan's) weakened so that sales of goods declined and there was downward pressure on prices, the Bank would buy money market instruments from private financial institutions, increasing the volume of money in the economy and lowering interest rates. More money in circulation and lower rates enable firms to borrow money more easily and act as a spur to economic activity: more people purchase goods and services, and thus prices are less likely to decline. However, in 2005, despite efforts to make funds available, borrowers remain scarce.

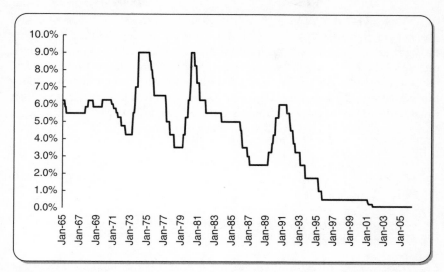

FIGURE 4.3 The Bank of Japan was awaiting definitive signs that deflation has ended before it increased its discount rate once again.
Source: Bank of Japan and Haver Analytics.

Conversely, if economic activity heated up, with sales putting upward pressure on prices, the Bank would reduce the volume of money in the economy and would raise interest rates. Accordingly, economic activity would be dampened, relieving price pressures. As noted above, the Bank conducts monetary policy to achieve price stability, thereby contributing to the stability of the economy as a whole. The Bank believes that price stability is a prerequisite for realizing sustainable and balanced economic growth.

Monetary policy until the first quarter of 2006 had been stated very simply—put an end to deflation. It has been suggested to the BoJ that they institute an inflation target, most recently in an annual Cabinet White Paper. However, the Bank has not warmed to the inflation targeting idea, even though many in the government support it.

Monetary Policy Meetings

Meetings are held once or twice a month. Most meetings are held over two days, but on occasion, a one day meeting is held. Unlike FOMC meetings where only members of the Fed staff attend, in Japan representatives from the Cabinet Office and the Ministry of Finance attend their meetings. However, they have no vote. At the conclusion of the meeting, a press release containing the results is issued at about 2 P.M. Japan time. (That translates to 1 A.M. EDT or 2 A.M. EST in the United States. Since Japan does not observe daylight savings time, the U.S. time varies depending on whether daylight savings time is being observed.) The statement below was made on March 9, 2006, when the Monetary Policy Board announced an end to its quantitative easing policy and the beginning of its move toward policy normalization. The Governor generally holds a press conference monthly, at which time he outlines the Bank's outlook and policy.

Change in the Guideline for Money Market Operations

At the Monetary Policy Meeting held today, the Bank of Japan decided to change the operating target of money market operations from the outstanding balance of current accounts at the Bank to the uncollateralized overnight call rate, and to set the following guideline for money market operations for the intermeeting period (see Attachment).

The Bank of Japan will encourage the uncollateralized overnight call rate to remain at effectively zero percent.

Measures Concerning Money Market Operations

The outstanding balance of current accounts at the Bank of Japan will be reduced towards a level in line with required reserves. Given that financial institutions have managed liquidity against the backdrop of large amounts of current account balances and extensive funds-supplying operations by the Bank for a prolonged period since the adoption of the quantitative easing policy, the reduction in current account balance is expected to be carried out over a period of a few months, taking full account of conditions in the short-term money market. The process will be managed through short-term money market operations. With respect to the outright purchases of long-term interest-bearing Japanese government bonds, purchases will continue at the current amounts and frequency for some time, with due regard for future conditions of the balance sheet of the Bank. With respect to the complementary lending facility, the loan rate will remain at the current level. The temporary waiver of add-on rates for frequent users of the facility, in effect since March 2003, will also be maintained.

The Bank's View on Economic Activity and Prices

Since March 2001, in view of preventing sustained decline in prices and preparing the basis for sustainable growth, the Bank of Japan has supplied extremely ample liquidity with current account balance at the Bank as the main operating target. The Bank also made a clear commitment to maintain the policy until the consumer price index (excluding fresh food, on a nationwide basis) registers stably zero percent or an increase year on year. The Bank has since maintained the quantitative easing policy according to this commitment.

Currently, Japan's economy continues to recover steadily. Exports have continued to increase reflecting the expansion of overseas economies. With respect to domestic private demand, business fixed investment has also continued to increase against the backdrop of high corporate profits. Robust corporate activity is positively influencing households, and private consumption has become solid. Looking ahead, the Bank expects a sustained recovery.

Concerning prices, year-on-year changes in the consumer price index turned positive. Meanwhile, the output gap is gradually narrowing. Unit labor costs generally face weakening downward pressures as wages began to rise amid productivity gains. Furthermore, firms and households are shifting up their expectations for inflation. In this environment, year-on-year changes in the consumer price index are expected to remain positive. The Bank, therefore, judged that the conditions laid out in the commitment are fulfilled.

Current View on Monetary Policy

Given that the effects of the quantitative easing policy on economic activity and prices now mainly result from short-term interest rates being zero, there will be no abrupt change as a result of today's policy decision.

Looking ahead, in considering the central scenario for economic activity and prices, there is a high probability of realizing sustainable growth under price stability. In the meantime, it should be noted that, over the medium- to long-term, there is a risk of swings in economic activity, as the stimulus from monetary policy is amplified against the backdrop of improving corporate profitability and a positive turn in price developments.

On the future path of monetary policy, there will be a period in which the overnight call rate is at effectively zero percent, followed by a gradual adjustment in the light of developments in economic activity and prices. In this process, if the risk mentioned above remains muted, in other words, if it is judged that inflationary pressures are restrained as the economy follows a balanced and sustainable growth path, an accommodative monetary environment ensuing from very low interest rates will probably be maintained for some time.

CHAPTER 5

Bank of Canada

Because of its proximity to the United States, the Bank of Canada has been trying to escape the U.S. Federal Reserve Bank's shadow for some time now, while at the same time acknowledging that it must factor U.S. monetary policy moves into its decision-making process. Unlike the Fed, the Bank has an inflation target—a 1 percent to 3 percent range with a specific focus at the 2 percent midpoint. Although the Bank monitors many economic indicators, as indeed all central banks do, the Bank converted its inflation barometer for operational purposes to a consumer price index measure that subtracts eight volatile components to better reflect core inflation. It also takes the foreign exchange rate for the Canadian dollar into its monetary policy decisions.

The Bank changed the way it announces its monetary policy decisions in late 2000. Since then, meetings and announcements have been scheduled for eight times a year along with an assessment of the Canadian economy. This effectively broke the link between Canadian and U.S. monetary policy. The Bank no longer responds directly to Fed moves, although the Bank can change policy between official announcements if it chooses.

THE BANK REFLECTS ITS GEOGRAPHY

Canada was not interested in establishing a central bank during its first 50 years of Confederation. And even up to the 1930s' depression, there was little need for one in a country whose population was scattered and mainly rural. As banks were established in the early 1800s, they issued their own notes, as did various governments and even merchants. In central Canada, the efforts of the growing financial community to solve the problem of currency were complicated by a loss of hard currency (gold and silver coins) to the United States with an increase in cross-border trade. As a result, sentiment in favor of a national currency increased.

Following Confederation in 1867, Parliament confirmed its control of currency with legislation and began to issue Dominion of Canada notes. Notes issued by both the government and the chartered banks were in common use for many years, until (and for a transitional period after) the Bank of Canada was created in 1934 and given sole responsibility for issuing paper currency within the country.

British influence also was reflected in the country's preference for a limited number of banks with multiple branches. Bank branches could be established more economically with less capital and fewer skilled officers than would have been required for independent banks at each location. The branch bank network proved to be adequate for almost a century. Chartered banks provided most of the notes in circulation, and they could meet seasonal or unexpected demands. The larger banks were able to deal with government business without strain, and the branch network gradually developed a system for clearing checks between banks.

But by the early 1930s the political climate had changed. The gathering depression and mounting criticism of the country's existing financial structure coincided with a specific concern over the lack of a direct mechanism for settling international accounts. A royal commission was set up to study the banking system in 1933. And the appendix to the resulting report became the framework for the Bank of Canada Act, which received royal approval on July 3, 1934.

In March 1935, the Bank was open for business as a privately owned institution, with shares sold to the public. But this did not last long. A new government nationalized the Bank, and in 1938 it became publicly owned and remains that way today. The Bank of Canada Act, which defines the Bank's functions, has been amended many times but the preamble has not changed. The Bank still exists "to regulate credit and currency in the best interests of the economic life of the nation."

The Bank's organization integrated new functions with those that already existed elsewhere. When the Bank opened, it became the sole issuer of Canadian currency after banknote operations were transferred from the Department of Finance. Among the many new features of the Bank was a Research Division, which was established to provide information and advice on financial developments and on general business conditions at home and abroad. The Foreign Exchange Division and the Securities Division became operative almost immediately, though the transfer of the Public Debt Division from the Department of Finance was delayed until suitable quarters were available. This did not occur until 1938, following completion of the present Bank of Canada building in Ottawa. The Bank also has regional offices in Vancouver, Calgary, Toronto, Montréal, and

Halifax in Canada and, like the Bank of Japan and the Reserve Bank of Australia, a New York City office.

The Bank is structured like many corporate entities. Overall responsibility for business affairs rests with its Board of Directors, and the Governor of the Bank is the Chief Executive Officer and Chairman of the Board. Collective responsibility for management of the Bank is in the hands of its Governing Council.

MONETARY POLICY

The Bank carries out monetary policy by influencing short-term interest rates by setting the overnight target. This in turn affects monetary conditions—that is, the impact of short-term interest rates and the Canadian dollar's exchange rate on the economy. The transmission of monetary policy occurs as changes in monetary conditions affect the demand for goods and services. Lower interest rates, for example, tend to increase spending and reduce savings, and a lower dollar can boost exports and hold back imports. Conversely, higher interest rates tend to curb domestic spending and a higher dollar tends to curb exports and encourage imports. Strong demand for Canadian goods and services puts upward pressure on prices if it exceeds the economy's capacity. Changes in monetary conditions affect inflation only indirectly and are usually felt over a period of 18 months to two years.

The overnight rate is the interest rate at which major financial institutions borrow and lend overnight or one-day funds among themselves. This key policy rate influences other interest rates charged throughout the banking system. And rate changes, in turn, impact rates systemically for consumer loans and mortgages as well as those charged to business borrowers. And they can (and do) affect the Canadian dollar's exchange rate. For example, in the aftermath of the Bank's 25-basis-point interest rate increase to 4 percent on April 25, 2006, the Canadian dollar rose above 90 U.S. cents for the first time in 28 years after the Bank hinted that rates could continue to climb.

Monetary policy goals are to aid and abet solid economic growth along with rising living standards. To achieve these goals, inflation is kept low, stable, and predictable. The inflation control target is at the heart of Canadian monetary policy that the Bank and the Government have established. The level of interest rates and the exchange rate determine the monetary environment in which the Canadian economy operates.

Inflation Targeting

Inflation targeting has been a cornerstone of monetary policy since 1991, when the government and the Bank of Canada agreed to target inflation for a five-year period. In 1991, the inflation rate was 5.9 percent as measured by the consumer price index (CPI). The initial goal was to reduce inflation to progressively lower levels to ensure a favorable climate for economic growth. By December 1993, inflation had been reduced to 2 percent. At that time, the government and the Bank agreed to extend the agreement until the end of 1998 and again in February 1998 to the end of 2001. In May 2001, the target range was renewed to the end of 2006.

Specifically, the Bank aims to keep the rate of inflation, as measured by the year-on-year percent increase in the CPI, inside the target range of 1 percent to 3 percent. The CPI was chosen as inflation's measure because it was well known to the population. The Bank aims to keep inflation near the 2 percent midpoint. Although the inflation target is stated in terms of the total CPI, the Bank uses a measure of core inflation as an operational guide. The measure, in their opinion, provides a better measure of the underlying trend of inflation and tends to be a better predictor of future changes in the total CPI. This core measure excludes eight volatile items—fruit, vegetables, gasoline, fuel oil, natural gas, mortgage interest, intercity transportation and tobacco products as well as the impact of changes in indirect taxes on the remaining components. Figure 5.1 illustrate price changes since 1993.

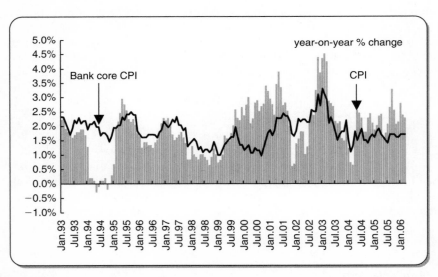

FIGURE 5.1 Inflation has remained in check since the Bank of Canada began targeting inflation as part of their monetary policy
Source: Bank of Canada, Statistics Canada, and Haver Analytics.

The inflation control target helps the Bank to determine what monetary policy actions are needed in the short and medium term to maintain relatively stable prices. To achieve this, the Bank manipulates short-term interest rates.

An advantage to monetary policy geared to an inflation control target is that it helps to make monetary policy actions more readily understandable to financial markets and the public. The target also provides a clear measuring stick for evaluating the effectiveness of monetary policy. One of the most important benefits of a clear inflation target is its role in focusing expectations of future inflation. The gap between monetary policy changes and their effects on inflation and the economy can take from 18 months to 24 months as a chain of events is set in motion that ultimately affects consumer spending, sales, production, employment, and other economic indicators.

Given the proximity to the United States, the Bank also has to factor U.S. interest rate policy into its decisions (other central banks do also). The spread between U.S. and Canadian interest rates and the relative value of their currencies dictate the direction of capital flows. In the past, the Bank was forced to respond immediately to changes in Fed policy. However, that changed when it changed the way it announces its monetary policy stance. The Bank has been proactive in both increasing and decreasing rates as required by economic events as well as inflation. Figure 5.2 shows Bank of Canada and Federal Reserve policy interest rates.

Implementing Monetary Policy — How Independent?

The Bank is responsible for the day-to-day administration of monetary policy—but in cooperation and in consultation with the Minister of Finance. If a disagreement were to occur between the Bank and the government, the Minister could issue a written directive to the Governor specifying a change in policy. The government's power to issue directives in reality means that the government assumes ultimate responsibility for monetary policy. The decision-making process itself is multilayered and follows a precise pattern.

Organization

The Board of Directors is responsible for reviewing the Bank's general policies on matters other than monetary policy and for approving the Bank's corporate objectives, plans, and annual budget. The Board of Directors includes the Governor, the Senior Deputy Governor, 12 outside directors, and the Deputy Minister of Finance (who has no vote). Monetary policy is neither formulated nor implemented by the outside directors. In this area,

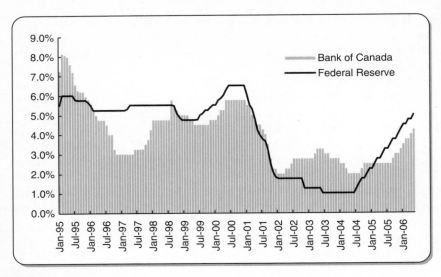

FIGURE 5.2   While the Bank of Canada continues to watch the Federal Reserve policies, it is no longer reacting to them.
Source: Bank of Canada and Haver Analytics.

the directors' job is to keep the Bank informed about prevailing economic conditions in their respective regions. The Minister of Finance appoints directors to fill vacant seats on the board for a three-year term, subject to the approval of the Governor in Council or the Cabinet.

The Governor of the Bank performs the same role as the president of a corporation. As the Bank's chief executive officer, he has control and full authority over the business of the Bank. He also presides over the Board of Directors. The Governor, like the Senior Deputy Governor, is appointed by the outside directors with the approval of the Governor in Council for a term of seven years.

There are eligibility requirements laid down in the Bank of Canada Act, which stipulate that the Governor must be a Canadian citizen; under 75 years of age; not a member of the Senate or the House of Commons, nor of a provincial legislature; not employed by the federal or provincial public service; and not a director, partner, officer, employee, or shareholder of any bank or other financial institution. The Governor cannot be relieved of his or her duties at the whim of the government. If a profound disagreement were to occur, the Minister of Finance, with the Cabinet's authorization, could issue a written directive to the governor specifying a change in policy. This would most likely result in the resignation of the governor. In the absence of a directive, the Governor has the entire responsibility for monetary policy. It is generally believed that a seven-year term gives the Governor time to adopt the medium- and long-term perspective essential to conducting effective monetary policy. This decision dates back to 1934, when the Bank of Canada Act was passed.

PREPARING FOR A POLICY ANNOUNCEMENT

A Step-by-Step Process to Decision

The Bank of Canada provides a very transparent view of how and what goes into the monetary policy decision-making process. It is very revealing in describing a procedure that most central banks, albeit with some variation, follow leading up to a monetary policy decision. It is interesting to note that each department has its special input to the process.

Staff Provides Base Case Analysis　The process begins with the Bank staff's evaluation of economic performance along with their projections. Their assessment is based on input from various departments within the Bank including the International, Monetary and Financial Analysis, and Financial Markets, as well as input from the Bank's regional representatives. The results are presented to the decision-making body, the Governing Council. At the same time, the staff recommends an appropriate interest rate that would keep inflation within its target range and near the 2 percent midpoint. The projections are organized around the national income accounts (see Chapters 8 and 12) and provide the reference point from which other sources of information are assessed.

Because of Canada's dependency on exports for growth, domestic projections begin with the International Department's assessment of developments and prospects of the global economy. Then the analysis focuses on the short-term status of and prospects for the domestic economy. Economic indicators including, for example, recent car sales, housing starts, employment, manufacturers' shipments, retail sales, and merchandise trade are evaluated and recent data revisions are factored in. Other events that could have an impact on the outlook including labor disruptions, unusual weather, and special sales and financial promotions are also surveyed.

The next step combines this new information into a structural macroeconomic model of the Canadian economy that is specifically designed to help trace the link from the interest rate target to inflation. It also highlights the very indirect nature of the Bank's influence on inflation and the fact that this influence becomes apparent only over time.

Governing Council Is Briefed   About a week before the policy announcement, the Council is briefed on four topics that could influence their decision: risks and alternatives, regional surveys and forecasts, inflationary and capacity pressures, and money and credit.

- **Risks and alternatives.** The economic model evaluates the outlook's risks and uncertainties including alternative assumptions about domestic and U.S. economic growth as well as commodity prices including crude oil. The Council is provided with alternative interest rate scenarios. One alternative illustrates the possible consequences of delaying an interest rate change proposed by the model.
- **Regional surveys and forecasts.** Regional bank representatives prepare a bottom-up forecast after surveying about 100 companies. This information provides Council members with an insight into what businesspeople are seeing and planning. The survey asks basic questions about past and expected sales growth, investment intentions, inventories, employment plans, wage growth, and prices four times a year. The survey also includes indicators of activity and capacity in the goods, labor, and real estate markets, as well as various measures of wage and price inflation, and measures of inflation expectations.
- **Money and credit.** — Information on various holdings of money and credit provide another view of what consumers and firms are doing and planning to do.

The challenge is to separate the real signals about economic activity and inflation from volatility or noise caused by other factors. The Department of Monetary and Financial Analysis provides a view from the financial side of the economy, including the outlook and risks surrounding it, and makes an interest rate recommendation as well. The evaluation includes factors such as bond market credit spreads and other changes that could affect lending conditions to businesses and households by banks.

The Financial Markets Department assesses market expectations for interest rates and what market expectations are for Bank action. Future Federal Reserve actions are also included in the discussion. The information sources include interest rate futures and expectations implicit in the term structure of interest rates, market commentary, published reports of investment banks, and the Bank's contact with dealers and investors. The market perspective acts both as a reference point against which to compare the staff's analysis and as a guide to the issues that may need to be addressed when communicating the decision.

The Final Briefing Takes Place and the Governing Council Reaches a Decision
At the final briefing, the Governing Council meets with the other members

of the Monetary Policy Review Committee, which includes six advisers, the chiefs of the four economics departments, and the directors of the Montreal and Toronto financial markets divisions. This meeting typically takes place on the Friday morning preceding a fixed announcement date (usually the following Tuesday).

The staff updates the Council on any economic or financial information that has become available since they completed their analysis. This is followed by a wide-ranging discussion on the economic outlook, the balance of risks, and the appropriate setting for interest rates. Each Committee member makes a recommendation on the appropriate interest rate setting. The Financial Markets Department chief discusses market expectations regarding the Bank's upcoming decision. This discussion highlights what market participants see as the factors weighing on the decision and how key messages should be communicated.

On the same Friday, the Governing Council begins its own deliberations and develops a consensus view on the most likely economic scenario along with its underlying inflation trend. Only after agreement is reached on the outlook do they begin deliberations on the appropriate path for the key policy rate and the related communications activities.

The Council operates on a *consensus* basis (as does the European Central Bank). There is no vote. This differs from the Fed and the Banks of England and Japan wherein a specific vote is taken and reported.

The Council reconvenes the following Monday, and by the end of the day reaches a consensus decision. With support from a senior communications staff member, they prepare the press release that outlines the reasons behind the decision. Their decision is announced the following day at 9 A.M. ET. Below is the announcement released on April 25, 2006, announcing a 25-basis-point increase in interest rates.

Bank of Canada raises overnight rate target by 1/4 percentage point to 4 percent

OTTAWA—The Bank of Canada today announced that it is raising its target for the overnight rate by one-quarter of one percentage point to 4 percent. The operating band for the overnight rate is correspondingly increased, and the Bank Rate is now 4 1/4 percent.

The global economy has been growing at a robust pace, exhibiting a little more momentum than had been anticipated. This global strength and the associated higher prices of many commodities, together with strong domestic demand in Canada, have produced solid growth in the Canadian economy at a pace consistent with the Bank's outlook in the January Monetary Policy Report Update. At the same time, global competition and the past appreciation of the Canadian dollar continue to pose challenges for a number of sectors of the economy. All factors considered, the Canadian economy is judged to be operating at, or just above, its production capacity. High energy prices have kept total CPI inflation in Canada somewhat above the Bank's 2 percent target. Core inflation has remained below 2 percent owing to persistent downward pressure from prices of imported consumer goods. Against this backdrop, the Bank decided to raise its target for the overnight rate.

Looking forward, the Bank projects that the Canadian economy will grow by 3.1 percent in 2006, 3.0 percent in 2007, and 2.9 percent in 2008. Total CPI inflation is projected to average close to 2 percent in 2007 and 2008 (excluding the effect of any changes in the GST). The Bank judges that the risks to its projection are roughly balanced, with a small tilt to the downside later in the projection period.

In line with the Bank's outlook for the Canadian economy, some modest further increase in the policy interest rate may be required to keep aggregate supply and demand in balance and inflation on target over the medium term. The Bank will closely monitor evolving developments in the Canadian economy in light of the cumulative increase in the policy interest rate since last September. A full analysis of economic developments, trends, and risks will be provided in the Monetary Policy Report, to be published on April 27, 2006.

Post-announcement Communications   Two days after an announcement and four times a year, the Bank releases either the *Monetary Policy Report* or the *Monetary Policy Report Update*. These provide details on the Governing Council's economic and inflation outlook, its risks, and the reasons for the recent rate decision. Along with background media briefings by the deputy governors and a press conference by the Governor and Senior Deputy Governor, the Report is also followed by testimony before parliamentary committees and by presentations by deputy governors and other senior staff across the country and in international financial centers. There are no minutes of the Governing Council's meeting.

THE EXCHANGE RATE

Unlike the Fed, the Bank of Canada explicitly includes the value of the Canadian dollar in its decision-making process. The Canadian dollar's value against other national currencies helps determine how much imports will cost and how much is received for exports. When the currency's value falls, imported goods become more expensive, and the volume of imports is reduced. At the same time, however, other countries pay less for Canadian products, boosting export sales. The exchange rate plays a particularly important role in the Canadian economy because merchandise trade accounts for a relatively large part of its national income. Most trade is with the United States, which is why the value of the Canadian dollar against the U.S. dollar is crucial. See Figure 5.3 for a long-term view of the Canadian dollar against the U.S. dollar.

Factors Affecting the Exchange Rate

The Canadian dollar (or the *loonie*, as it is affectionately called), like the currencies of most industrialized nations, operates on the basis of a floating exchange rate, which means that the price of a Canadian dollar fluctuates according to market conditions. A floating currency is a key component of Canada's monetary policy framework, helping the economy to adjust to shocks and playing an important part in the transmission of monetary policy. The exchange rate is affected by supply and demand for Canadian

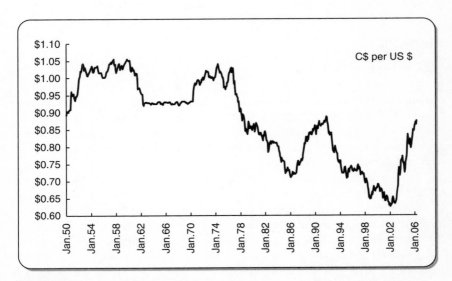

FIGURE 5.3 After being in the doldrums for many years, the Canadian dollar's value against the U.S. dolar has returned to historic levels.
Source: Bank of Canada and Haver Analytics.

dollars in international exchange markets. If the quantity demanded exceeds the quantity supplied, the value of the dollar will go up. Conversely, if the quantity of supplied exceeds the quantity demanded, its value will go down.

The supply and demand for the currency are influenced by interest rates. Investors may opt to invest in Canada should interest rates be higher there than in other countries. This would increase demand for the Canadian dollar. For example, when the Bank announced its increased interest rate on April 25, 2006, the currency increased in value against the U.S. dollar. Together, interest rates and the exchange rate determine the monetary conditions in which the Canadian economy operates. Changes in the exchange rate affect spending and demand in the economy just as changes to interest rates can either increase or decrease the level of economic activity.

The Bank can influence the exchange rate only indirectly. Neither the government nor the Bank targets any particular level for the currency, believing that this should be determined by the market. Over time, the value of the Canadian dollar is ultimately affected by economic fundamentals, such as inflation and interest rate levels, which in turn depend on Canadian monetary policy, the economic growth, and the competitiveness of its products. Since September 1998, the Bank no longer intervenes in foreign exchange markets to ensure an orderly market, but rather reserves such actions for times of major international crisis or a clear loss of confidence in the currency or in Canadian dollar–denominated securities.

Intervention

Prior to September 1998, Canada's policy was to intervene systematically in the foreign exchange market to resist significant upward or downward pressure on the Canadian dollar. The policy was changed because intervention proved to be ineffective when resisting currency movements caused by changes in fundamental factors. Current policy is to intervene in foreign exchange markets on a discretionary, rather than a systematic, basis and only in the most exceptional of circumstances.

Foreign exchange market intervention is conducted by the Bank, acting as agent for the federal government and using the government's holdings of foreign currencies. For example, if the government and the Bank decided to moderate a decline in the Canadian dollar, the Bank would buy Canadian dollars in foreign exchange markets in exchange for other currencies, mainly U.S. dollars, which come from the Exchange Fund Account. This boosts demand for Canadian dollars and helps support the currency's value. To make sure that the Bank's purchases do not take money out of circulation and create a shortage of Canadian dollars, which in turn could put upward pressure on Canadian interest rates, the Bank sterilizes its purchases by redepositing the same amount of Canadian dollar balances in the financial system.

If the goal is to slow the currency's rate of appreciation, the Bank could sell Canadian dollars and purchase other currencies. By selling Canadian dollars, the Bank increases the supply of the currency in foreign exchange markets, providing some resistance to the upward movement in the currency. To sterilize the effect of the Bank's sales (and prevent downward pressure on Canadian interest rates), the same amount of Canadian dollar balances are withdrawn from the financial system. The foreign currencies purchased when Canadian dollars are sold are added to the Exchange Fund Account.

When an intervention occurs, an announcement indicating the intervention is made on the Bank's Web site. The amount of the intervention undertaken is publicly available in the government's monthly official press release on international reserves. The last time the Bank intervened in foreign exchange markets to affect movements in the Canadian dollar was in September 1998. From time to time, Canada participates with other countries in coordinated intervention. For example, on September 22, 2000, the Bank of Canada joined the European Central Bank, the Federal Reserve Bank of New York, and the Banks of Japan and England, in a concerted intervention to support the euro.

WHAT INTEREST RATE?

The Bank of Canada recently replaced the bank rate with the overnight rate as the main lever to conduct monetary policy. The overnight rate is the rate of interest that it charges on short-term loans to financial institutions. The rate is an important tool because it is seen as the trendsetter for other short-term interest rates.

A change in the overnight rate target sends a clear signal about the direction in which it wants short-term interest rates to go. These changes usually provoke commercial banks to change their prime rate, which in turn serves as a benchmark for other loans. For example, it can indirectly affect mortgage rates as well as interest earned and paid on bank accounts and other savings.

The Bank operates a system to ensure that trading in the overnight market stays within its so-called operating band. This band, which is 50 basis points wide, always has the overnight rate target at its midpoint. Since institutions know that the central bank will always lend money at a rate equal to the top of the band and pay interest on deposits at the bottom, it gives institutions little reason to trade overnight funds at rates outside the band. The bank rate is always at the top end of the operating band. For example, if the operating band is 4.25 to 4.75 percent, the bank rate would be 4.75 percent. The overnight rate target is always at the middle of the band.

When comparing Canada's official interest rates with those of other countries, the target for the overnight rate is the best rate to use. It is directly comparable with the Fed's target for the fed funds rate, the Bank of England's two-week "repo rate," and the minimum bid rate for refinancing operations (the repo rate) at the ECB.

CHAPTER 6

Reserve Bank of Australia

RESERVE BANK OF AUSTRALIA'S ROLE

The Reserve Bank of Australia's (RBA's) main responsibility is monetary policy. Policy decisions are made by the Reserve Bank Board (RBB), with the objective of achieving low and stable inflation over the medium term. Other responsibilities include maintaining financial system stability, while at the same time promoting the safety and efficiency of the payments system. The RBA regards appropriate monetary policy as a major factor contributing to the Australian dollar's stability, which in turn leads to full employment and the economic prosperity for Australia. The Bank is accountable to the Australian Parliament and provides an annual report to them. It also briefs the Government from time to time on monetary and banking policy. The Reserve Bank Act 1959 provides the legislative foundation for the RBA's responsibilities and powers.

The Bank participates in financial markets, manages Australia's foreign reserves, issues Australian currency notes, and serves as banker to the Australian Government. It provides data on interest rates, exchange rates, and money and credit growth, along with a range of publications on its operations and research.

The RBA is unique among the banks discussed here in that it has two boards with complementary responsibilities. The Reserve Bank Board is responsible for monetary policy and overall financial system stability. The Payments System Board (PSB) has specific responsibility for the safety and efficiency of the payments system. The PSB also produces an annual report for Parliament.

Along with its policy responsibilities, the RBA provides selected banking and registry services to several Federal Government agencies and to a number of overseas central banks and official institutions. Its assets include Australia's holdings of gold and foreign exchange. The Bank is wholly owned by the Australian Government, to which its profits accrue. The

RBA's headquarters is in Sydney, with regional offices in Adelaide, Brisbane, Canberra, Melbourne, Perth, London, and New York. Note Printing Australia Limited (NPA) is a wholly owned subsidiary of the Bank and manufactures Australia's currency notes and a range of other security products for domestic and overseas markets.

RBA's Roots

In 1911, the Federation of the Australian States evolved into the Commonwealth of Australia. At that time, the Australian Parliament assumed power to make laws, including those regarding banking and currency. The first Commonwealth Bank Act authorized only the ordinary functions of commercial and savings banking. The Bank had no specific central bank authority or note issuance authority. The Governor, however, did have responsibility for bank management. The Bank opened in mid-1912. The Australian Department of the Treasury took over note issuance from private trading banks and the Queensland Government.

In 1920, however, note issuance responsibility was transferred to a Notes Board (consisting of four government-appointed members) with the Bank Governor an ex-officio member. The Bank took over the administration of note issuance even though the Bank and the Notes Board were formally independent of each other. In 1924, the Commonwealth Bank Act was amended to give the Bank control over note issue.

From this time until 1945 (when there were major changes to the legislation), the Bank's central banking activities gradually evolved. Initially, the evolution occurred because of pressures from the 1930s depression. And at the onset of World War II, its powers were expanded temporarily under wartime regulations and included exchange control along with a wide range of other controls over the banking system. They included authority to determine advance policy and interest rates and to require private banks to deposit funds in special RBA accounts.

In 1945, the new Commonwealth Bank Act along with the Banking Act formalized the Bank's powers in relation to the administration of monetary and banking policy and exchange control.

The Reserve Bank Act 1959 renamed the Commonwealth Bank as the Reserve Bank of Australia and gave it belated authority to carry on the central banking functions, many of which had already evolved over time. Other legislation separated the commercial banking and savings banking activities into the newly created Commonwealth Banking Corporation. The Reserve Bank Act 1959 took effect on January 14, 1960.

RBA functions were unchanged until the abolition of exchange control that followed the float of the Australian dollar in 1983. However, prior to that, there already had been a gradual shift to market-oriented methods of implementing monetary policy and away from a system of direct controls on banks. In the five years following a major financial system inquiry (the 1979 Campbell Committee), the Australian financial landscape was transformed to a virtually fully deregulated system. At the same time, the RBA gradually built up a specialized banking supervision function.

Another inquiry into the Australian financial system (the Wallis Committee in 1996) resulted in the transfer of banking supervision to a newly created authority, the Australian Prudential Regulation Authority, which became responsible for the supervision of all deposit-taking institutions. The Reserve Bank Act was amended to create a new Payments System Board, with a mandate to promote the safety and efficiency of the Australian payments system. New legislation—the Payment Systems (Regulation) Act 1998 and the Payment Systems and Netting Act 1998—gave the Bank relevant powers in this area. Also included in the Reserve Bank Act were the Reserve Bank Board's obligations with respect to the formulation and implementation of monetary policy. This is often referred to as the Bank's charter.

RBA Begins to Target Inflation

In 1993, then-Governor Bernie Fraser outlined price stability as a policy objective for the first time. He defined it as a rate of inflation that averaged 2 percent to 3 percent over a period of years. In August 1996, then-Governor-designate, Ian Macfarlane and the treasurer jointly issued a Statement on the Conduct of Monetary Policy. It essentially reiterated and clarified the respective roles and responsibilities of the RBA and the Australian government in relation to monetary policy and provided formal government endorsement of the RBA's inflation objective, which had been informally in place for some time.

Accountability and Independence

The RBA is an independent central bank that is accountable to Parliament for its actions. Since 1996, the Governor and senior officers have appeared twice yearly before the House of Representatives Standing Committee on Economics, Finance and Public Administration to report on monetary policy conduct. The appearances are timed to follow the publication by the RBA of its Statement on Monetary Policy and its presentation to the Treasurer and Parliament (usually in late August or early September).

The RBB is required to brief the Australian Government from time to time on monetary and banking policy. This occurs largely through frequent formal and informal contacts between the Governor and the Treasurer. If there is a policy disagreement, procedures are in place to determine whether the Bank's policy is to the greatest advantage for the people of Australia.

MONETARY POLICY

A Note about Inflation Targeting

The RBA adopted inflation targeting in mid-1993, just a few years after New Zealand. The country had pioneered inflation targeting in early 1990 as part of a fundamental change to economic management and included substantial changes to central bank legislation. Canada followed soon after. The United Kingdom started targeting inflation shortly after the pound sterling left the European Rate Mechanism (see Chapter 2) in September 1992. Early in 1993, Sweden and Finland followed a similar route. All these countries had a relatively poor inflation history, as did Australia. Figure 6.1 illustrates Australia's long-term inflation history.

Initially, people were skeptical about whether Australia actually had a meaningful target. There were reasons for this skepticism. The RBA had been trying to quell inflation for several years, but given the country's

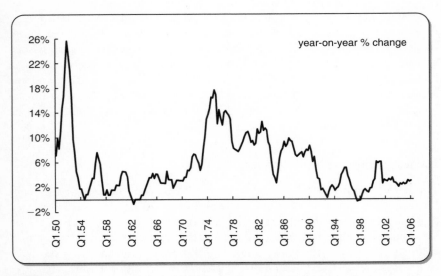

FIGURE 6.1 The Reserve Bank of Australia has cooled inflationary pressures since it began to target inflation.
Source: Australian Bureau of Statistics and Haver Analytics.

inflation history many people viewed the drop in inflation that had occurred in the early 1990s as an accident. They discounted promises and required further proof before being convinced that inflation was under control.

The RBA was, from the start, honest enough to say that inflation was not its only concern. They were leery of very strict targets because they did not think policy could be fine-tuned in the short run. Rather, they felt it was important to take a medium-term view. Ironically, while the RBA's views are now very mainstream, they tended to be seen as a sign of weakness in the early days.

The target was fairly general and flexible and there were no substantial changes in institutional arrangements. The Reserve Bank Act was not rewritten. And, unlike the United Kingdom, Canada, and New Zealand, there was no formal arrangement with the Government until much later. The Bank just started to say they wanted to keep inflation at around 2 percent to 3 percent and went about doing it in a gradual fashion. The change was evolutionary, rather than revolutionary, however, and in the early days this meant the Bank had to work hard to persuade people they were really serious about controlling inflation.

The inflation target is defined as a medium-term average rather than as a rigid target band within which inflation is to be held at all times. The reasons for this are straightforward. There are the inevitable forecasting uncertainties to deal with, and changes in monetary policy take time to permeate the economy as well. Australian experience has shown that inflation is not amenable to fine-tuning within a narrow band. The inflation target is forward looking and permits monetary policy to dampen output fluctuations over the course of the business cycle. However, when aggregate demand is weak, inflationary pressures are likely to lessen, allowing monetary policy to be eased, which in turn will give stimulus to economic activity.

Objectives

The RBA is responsible for formulating and implementing monetary policy. The duty of the Reserve Bank Board is to ensure that the monetary and banking policy is focused on improving the population's well-being. Furthermore, the Bank's powers contribute to currency stability, full employment, and the economic prosperity and welfare of the people.

The fulfillment of these objectives has been stated by means of RBA's inflation target since 1993. The target is defined as a range of 2 percent to 3 percent year-on-year percent increase in the consumer price index.

Monetary policy decisions are carried out by setting the overnight loan interest rate in the money market. Other interest rates in turn are influenced by this interest rate to varying degrees, so that the behavior of borrowers

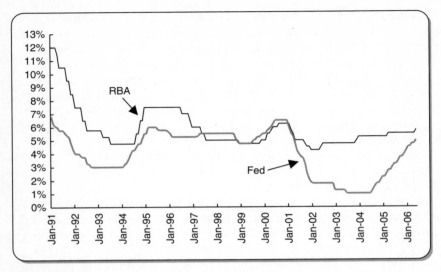

FIGURE 6.2 Over time, the Reserve Bank of Australia's policy interest rate has been above that of the Federal Reserve with the exception of a period in the late 1990s.
Source: Reserve Bank of Australias, Federal Reserve Board, and Haver Analytics.

and lenders in the financial markets is affected by monetary policy (though not only by monetary policy). See Figure 6.2 for a picture of long-run interest rates in Australia.

The Monetary Policy Decision Process

The RBB's 11 meeting dates are well known in advance. For each meeting the Bank's staff prepare a detailed account of developments in the Australian and international economies and in domestic and international financial markets. The papers contain a recommendation for the policy decision. Senior staff attends the meeting and give presentations. Decisions by the RBB to change interest rates are communicated to the public, usually on the day following the meeting. Following is the policy announcement of the May 3, 2006, increasing rates by 25 basis points to 5.75 percent.

> *STATEMENT BY THE GOVERNOR, MR IAN MACFARLANE*
> *MONETARY POLICY*
>   *Following a decision taken by the Board at its meeting yester-*
> *day, the Bank will be operating in the money market this morning*
> *to increase the cash rate by 25 basis points, to 5.75 percent.*

International developments are continuing to provide stimulus to growth in Australia. The world economy is growing at an above-average pace for the fourth successive year and, significantly, forecasts have recently been revised upwards. Commodity prices have been increasing strongly for some time, and they have risen further in the year to date. This suggests a strengthening in the outlook for Australia's export earnings, with consequent expansionary effects on incomes and spending.

In Australia, domestic spending has been growing at a solid pace recently and prevailing conditions suggest that this is likely to continue. High profitability and rising share prices are indicative of a favourable business environment in which investment growth is likely to remain strong. There are also signs that the dampening effects of household balance-sheet adjustment on consumer spending are starting to wane.

Recent trends in credit growth indicate that households and businesses have continued to find it attractive to borrow at prevailing interest rates. After touching a low point in the September quarter, the growth of household credit has picked up over the two most recent quarters. Business credit growth has continued to trend upwards. A factor that is likely to have contributed to the overall strength of credit growth has been the continuing compression of lending margins by financial intermediaries over recent years, reflecting competition among lenders. As a consequence, although the cash rate has been close to its historical average, interest rates paid by borrowers have remained below average.

These domestic and international trends have added to inflationary pressures in an economy that has been operating for some time with rather limited spare capacity and low unemployment. Wages growth, though not accelerating further recently, is higher than it was a year ago, and businesses are continuing to report that suitable labour is scarce. Raw materials costs continued to increase strongly in the March quarter, reflecting the general strength in global commodity prices. Consumer price inflation has picked up to around 3 percent in recent quarters. While this partly reflected rising fuel costs, underlying consumer price inflation also increased in the March quarter, to around 2 3/4 percent, a rate it had not been expected to reach until the second half of the year.

Taking all of these developments into account, the Board judged at its May meeting that inflationary risks had increased sufficiently to warrant an increase in the cash rate.

Monetary Policy Implementation

The Reserve Bank Board's operating target interest rate is the cash rate. The Bank's Domestic Markets Department has the task of keeping the cash rate at or near the operating target on a day-to-day basis. The cash rate is the rate charged on overnight loans between financial intermediaries. It influences other interest rates directly, forming the base rate on which the interest rate structure in the economy is built. A change in monetary policy means a change in the operating target interest rate for the cash rate and a shift in the interest rate structure prevailing in the financial system.

The RBB's decision to change interest rates is announced in a press release, which states the new target, if any, for the cash rate along with the reasons for the decision. This release is distributed through electronic news services and is posted on the Bank's Web site at the same time. Australian releases are generally available the night before on the U.S. East Coast. The RBA's announcement is usually made at 9:30 A.M. Canberra time on Wednesday. This translates to 5:30 P.M. the previous day (Tuesday) EST and 7:30 P.M EDT. (It should be noted that Australia's seasons are reverse of ours in the Northern Hemisphere. So there is a two-hour swing in time when the clocks change.) The Bank normally announces its daily dealing intentions every day at 9:30 A.M. local time.

The RBA uses its domestic market operations or open market operations to influence the cash rate. Between changes in policy, the focus of market operations is on keeping the cash rate close to the target by managing the supply of funds available to banks in the money market. The cash rate is determined in the money market by the interaction of demand for and supply of overnight funds. The Reserve Bank's ability to successfully pursue a cash rate target stems from its control over the supply of funds that banks use to settle transactions among themselves. These are called exchange settlement funds, after the accounts at the Reserve Bank in which banks hold these funds.

If the RBA supplies more funds than commercial banks want to hold, the banks will attempt to shed these funds by lending more in the cash market. The cash rate would fall under these circumstances. Conversely, if the Bank supplies less than banks want to hold, they will try to borrow more in the cash market to build up their holdings and, in the process, bid up the cash rate. Cash rate movements are passed eventually through all deposit and lending rates. However, the interest rate changes affect economic activity and inflation with a much longer lag simply because it takes time for individuals and businesses to adjust their behavior.

RESERVE BANK BOARD

The role, responsibilities and composition of the RBB were delineated in the Reserve Bank Act 1959. The RBB has the power to determine the policy about any matter except the payments system and can take the necessary action to ensure that it reaches its goal. It is also the Board's duty to ensure that the monetary and banking policy maximizes benefits for the people of Australia. It should be noted that an inflation target is not mandated by law, but, like the Federal Reserve, the RBA is mandated to maintain full employment as one of its goals.

Reserve Bank Board Meetings

The Board normally meets 11 times each year, on the first Tuesday of each month, except in January (it is midsummer in Australia and vacation time!). Each year, at least one meeting is held in Melbourne and another is held outside of Sydney. Five members form a meeting quorum. The Board has nine members: three ex-officio members—the governor (who is also chairman of the board), the deputy governor (who is deputy chairman), and the secretary to the Department of the Treasury, and six external members, who are appointed by the treasurer. The governor and deputy governor are appointed for terms of up to seven years and are eligible for reappointment. The external members are appointed for terms of up to five years.

The Reserve Bank has two boards. The Reserve Bank Act 1959 provided a clear separation of responsibilities between the Payments System Board, which has responsibility for the Bank's payments system policy, and the Reserve Bank Board, which has responsibility all other Bank policies including monetary and banking policies.

Briefly, the PSB is responsible for controlling financial system risks and promoting the system's efficiency, as well as promoting marketplace competition for payment services that is consistent with the financial system stability. The PSB's legislative responsibility and powers to promote payments system efficiency and competition are unique. This added responsibility has broadened the Bank's traditional focus on the high-value wholesale payment systems that underpin stability, to encompass the retail and commercial systems, where large transaction volumes provide scope for efficiency gains. The PSB acquired additional responsibilities for the regulation of securities clearing and settlement systems in August 2001.

INTEREST RATE DECISION SUPPORT

The Economic and Financial Markets Groups are directly involved in the process of determining what policy should be and then implementing it. They provide analytical input to both the governors and board.

The Economic Group, which is divided into the Economic Analysis and Research Departments, is responsible for domestic and international economic trend analysis as well as forecasting and research relevant to monetary policy. The Economic Analysis Department monitors and forecasts international and domestic trends, provides regular advice on these developments and monetary policy to the Governors and the Board, contributes to various outside bodies (including the Joint Economic Forecasting Group), maintains contacts with relevant analysts and institutions, undertakes applied research, and prepares reports for publication in the RBA Bulletin. The Economic Research Department undertakes longer-term research into issues relevant to monetary policy formulation and the operation of financial markets. Results are published in the *Research Discussion Paper* series. In addition, it organizes a program of internal seminars and a major annual conference and publishes research discussion papers and the Monthly Bulletin.

The Financial Markets Group, which is divided in a Domestic Markets Department and an International Department, implements the Bank's operations in domestic and foreign exchange markets and relations with major international institutions. The Domestic Markets Department is responsible for the Bank's operations in the domestic money and bond markets. The Department analyzes developments in domestic financial markets, including the cost and availability of finance through financial intermediaries and capital markets, and provides regular advice to the governors and the board on these issues. The Department also provides advice to the Treasury on the amount and maturity of securities to be issued to meet the government's domestic funding requirements and conducts the regular tenders through which these securities are issued.

The International Department is responsible for the Bank's foreign exchange operations and investment of international reserves, which comprise gold and foreign exchange, and provides regular advice on developments in international financial markets to the Governors and the Board. The Department is responsible for maintaining the Bank's relations with major international institutions. The Bank's overseas offices come under the umbrella of the Financial Markets Group.

THE AUSTRALIAN DOLLAR

The RBA has been responsible for Australia's currency since 1959. The Bank manages these responsibilities through its Note Issue Department, which arranges for note printing by Note Printing Australia Ltd, a separately incorporated wholly owned subsidiary of the RBA. The Royal Australian Mint in Canberra is responsible for the production of Australia's circulating coins.

The Australian note issue has its origins in the Australian Notes Act of 1910. Prior to this, paper currency circulating in Australia was made up of notes issued by trading banks and by one state government. The Act of 1910 vested control of note issuance with the Commonwealth Treasury and made it an offense for any bank to circulate notes issued by a state and withdrew their status as legal tender. Issuance of notes by trading banks was effectively discouraged by the 1910 Bank Notes Tax Act, which imposed a 10 percent tax per annum on all notes issued by them.

In 1920, control was transferred to a four-member board of directors appointed by the Commonwealth government, with the governor of the Commonwealth Bank an ex-officio member and chairman. At the same time the administration of note issue was taken over by a special Department of the Commonwealth Bank, although the Bank and the Notes Board were formally independent of one another. With the establishment of a Commonwealth Bank Board in 1924, control of the note issue passed from the Notes Board to the Board of Directors of the Commonwealth Bank.

The Commonwealth Bank Act in 1945 formally established the Commonwealth Bank as sole legal issuer of Australian currency notes. This role subsequently passed to the RBA in 1960, which also had assumed responsibility for the central banking. The Reserve Bank Act 1959 stipulates, among other things, that Australian notes be printed by, or under the authority of, the Reserve Bank.

Australia issued the world's first polymer note, a $10 commemorative note, in January 1988, to mark Australia's bicentenary. This note incorporated radical new technology developed in Australia and set the scene for a new era of currency notes in the world.

CHAPTER 7

People's Bank of China

BACKGROUND

Among central banks, the People's Bank of China (PBOC or PBC) has a unique history. The Bank was established in 1948 through a consolidation of the former Huabei Bank, the Beihai Bank, and the Xibei Peasant Bank on December 1, 1948, and shortly before the establishment of the People's Republic of China. After the communist victory, all Chinese banks were nationalized and incorporated into the PBOC. The headquarters was initially located in Shijiazhuang but moved to Beijing, the capital of the People's Republic of China in 1949. Between 1949 and 1978 the PBOC was the only bank in the People's Republic of China.

During the ten years of the Cultural Revolution, between 1966 and 1976, the Bank was stripped of many functions. However, in 1977, it once again regained the sole responsibility for issuing currency and controlling money supply. Finally, in September 1983, the State Council, China's ultimate decision-making body, formally designated the PBOC as the nation's central bank. Located in Beijing, the head office has 13 functional and five supporting departments. It took until March 1995 for the Bank's status as a central bank to be legally confirmed by the Law of the People's Republic of China on the People's Bank of China. Insurance and securities industries oversight was split off from the PBOC to new regulatory agencies.

Prior to the 1990s, as part of the 1980s Chinese economic reform, commercial banking functions were split off into four independent but state-owned banks, and the mission of the PBOC was refocused to undertake only the functions of a central bank. This change was reflected in the People's Bank of China Law, which was adopted in 1995. The law's goal was to complete the transformation of the PBOC into a central bank, consciously modeled after the United States Federal Reserve System. Accordingly, in 1998, the Bank underwent a major restructuring. In 1999, all provincial and local branches were abolished, and the Bank opened nine regional branches, whose boundaries did not correspond to local administrative boundaries. Like its American counterpart, this was intended to reduce the influence that local officials had on the PBOC policy-making process.

When China became a member of the World Trade Organization in 2001, the PBOC agreed to allow foreign banks to conduct local-currency business without restrictions by 2007.

The Governor of the PBOC is chosen by the National People's Congress. The current Governor is Zhou Xiaochuan. The activities of the central bank and other details are regulated by the Law of the People's Republic of China on the People's Bank of China. The Bank is managed by a governor, five deputies, a disciplinary, and three assistant governors.

The 1997 Asian financial crisis helped to shrink economic growth and inflation, as investors from Hong Kong, Taiwan, and South Korea reduced their foreign direct investment in China. It should be noted that, during that crisis, many outsiders thought the Chinese currency was overvalued and predicted China would devalue the yuan—ironically, some of the same outsiders today think the Chinese yuan is undervalued and should be revalued upward—but China resisted the pressure. By maintaining the yuan's value, China helped stabilize the economies of Hong Kong and other Asian nations, and ultimately helped to resolve the Asian financial crisis.

At present, four large state-owned banks, with 120,000 branches and 1.4 million employees, control at least 60 percent of China's $2.4 billion banking sector. The Big Four—the Bank of China, the Industrial and Commercial Bank of China, the China Construction Bank, and the Agricultural Bank of China—are faced with enormous nonloan burdens. Officially, the nonperforming loan rate is about 22 percent. Independent experts say it's probably twice that, well over $500 billion. The government directed the Big Four to lower their nonperforming loan rate to 15 percent, but that is a difficult task. In addition, there are 112 smaller state-owned commercial banks and over 30,000 rural credit cooperatives and urban cooperative banks. Many of these banks, too, have substantial bad-debt problems, yet their lending surged in 2003, and critics say credit checks are lax.

MONETARY POLICY

The current Bank structure is intentionally modeled after the Federal Reserve. But unlike the Fed and most other central banks, the PBOC is not independent. Rather, it functions under the guidance of the State Council. Although the Bank has been given responsibility for many of the same functions that other central banks have, it cannot act unilaterally.

The PBOC formulates and implements monetary policy, prevents and resolves financial risks, and safeguards financial stability. According to Chinese law, the Bank performs the following major functions: issuing and enforcing relevant orders and regulations; formulating and implementing monetary policy; issuing currency and administering its circulation; regulating the interbank lending market and interbank bond market; administering foreign exchange and regulating the interbank foreign exchange market; regulating the gold market; holding and managing official foreign exchange and gold reserves; managing the State treasury; maintaining normal operation of the payment and settlement system; guiding and organizing the anti–money laundering work of the financial sector and monitoring relevant fund flows; conducting financial statistics, surveys, analysis, and forecasts; participating in international financial activities in the capacity of the central bank; and performing other functions specified by the State Council.

Institutional Arrangements

Under the leadership of the State Council, the PBOC implements monetary policy, performs its functions, and carries out business operations independently according to laws and free from intervention by local governments, government departments at various levels, public organizations, or any individuals. At the same time, the Bank reports its decisions concerning the annual money supply and interest and exchange rates to the State Council for approval before they are put into effect. The PBOC also submits a report to the Standing Committee of the National People's Congress on the conduct of monetary policy and the performance of the financial industry. All of the PBOC's capital is invested and owned by the State.

Monetary Policy Objective

The objective of monetary policy is to maintain the stability of its currency to promote economic growth. Monetary policy tools include a reserve requirement ratio, a PBOC base interest rate, rediscounting, PBOC lending, open market operations, and other policy instruments specified by the State Council. Figure 7.1 shows PBOC interest rate history.

Monetary Policy Committee

In contrast to other monetary policy committees, the PBOC committee serves purely in an advisory role. According to Chinese law, the Bank is charged with the responsibility of establishing a Monetary Policy Committee (MPC) whose responsibilities, composition, and working procedures are prescribed

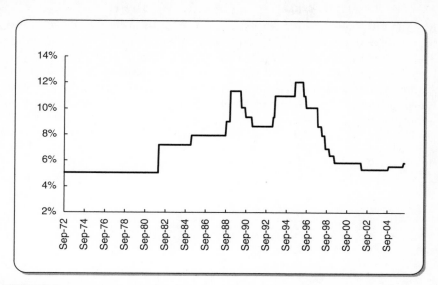

FIGURE 7.1 The China prime interest rate best shows that interest rates being charged were benign during this period of rapid growth.
Source: China Statistical Information Center and Haver Analytics.

by the State Council and filed with the Standing Committee of the National People's Congress.

The MPC plays an important role in macroeconomic management and in the making and adjustment of monetary policy. It advises on monetary policy and its targets as well as monetary policy instrument applications, major monetary policy measures, and the coordination between monetary and other macroeconomic policies. The Committee plays a purely advisory role after comprehensive research on the macroeconomic level and the government's economic targets.

The Committee is composed of the PBOC's Governor and two Deputy Governors, a Deputy Secretary-General of the State Council, a Vice Minister of the State Development and Reform Commission, a Vice Finance Minister, the Administrator of the State Administration of Foreign Exchange, the Chairman of the China Banking Regulatory Commission, the Chairman of the China Securities Regulatory Commission, the Chairman of the China Insurance Regulatory Commission, the Commissioner of National Bureau of Statistics, the President of the China Association of Banks and an expert from academia.

The Committee meets quarterly, in contrast to the monthly meetings held elsewhere. The Committee can meet more frequently if it is proposed

by the Chairman or endorsed by more than one-third of the MPC members. Unlike the European Central Bank, the MPC keeps meeting minutes.
The minutes or any resulting policy advice, if approved by more than
two-thirds of the members of the Committee, are sent to the State Council along with any proposed decisions on annual money supply, interest
rates, exchange rates, or other important monetary policy issues for their
approval.

Economic Indicators

An Overview of International Economic Indicators

This chapter, along with those that follow, unravels some of the mystery surrounding international economic indicators and provides a guide as to what is important and what is not. Indicator importance is a relatively new thing on an international basis, even though they have been important in the United States for some time. Indicators measure economic well-being, and there are special indicators to measure each segment of an economy as well as an overall measure that tries to incorporate virtually every part of the economy. For example, there are many employment measures to keep track of the labor force. Retail sales and expenditures contribute to knowledge about consumers. Industrial production or output measures try to get a handle on the "real" segment of an economy. So it stands to reason that while some indicators have universal importance, others will be more important in some countries than in others. And then there are the indicators *du jour*—those that catch the fancy of the financial markets and, at least for a while, are followed avidly. An example here would be the bright spotlight on anything that measured crude oil and its availability in 2005 and 2006. Another example was the intense focus on U.K. house prices from the end of 2002 through 2004 when higher Bank of England interest rates punctured the bubble.

It is not my intent to cover all indicators. Indeed, new measures are created almost monthly. Rather, the focus is on those indicators that have proven themselves over time and that analysts and the financial markets believe are keys to economic performance.

WHAT IS AN ECONOMIC INDICATOR AND WHY IS IT IMPORTANT?

An economic indicator provides information about the way the economy and its component parts are performing. Some indicators cover a specific industry, such as retail sales, while others cover the aggregate of many industries, such as manufacturers' orders or industrial production. Investors need this information on performance so they can make more knowledgeable and prudent decisions, especially if they are risk averse. While all indicators are watched by market players, some have more of a punch for one market than the others. When released, an indicator potentially can have a different impact on the bond, stock, and foreign exchange markets. For example, currency traders watch merchandise trade and current account balances carefully so they can estimate the supply and demand for a specific currency, while bond traders might watch employment numbers because of their possible impact on monetary policy. Equity investors might look at gross domestic product (GDP) carefully to make sure the economy is growing.

If you have a basic idea of what U.S. indicators are, then you are on your way to understanding indicators abroad. But each country has developed its own set of indicators and sometimes calculates them differently. If you follow business news—and even if you don't—economic indicators are headline news in the United States and elsewhere. But there are data problems overseas that users of U.S. data are not aware of or that rarely occur in U.S. data, including:

- Advance knowledge of when indicators will be released (although this has improved).
- Limited history when data are revised. This makes interpretation difficult if the data are not carried back in history to make a continuous series. For example, in April 2004 the Bank of Japan released what is considered its most important set of data—the Tankan Survey. (We will talk about this series in Chapter 11 when we discuss Japanese indicators.) The method of collection and aggregation had been revised and as a result there were only two data points in the new series!
- Some indicators have different names than in the United States but essentially measure the same thing. For example, the United Kingdom issues two producer price series—one for input prices and another for output prices. In the United States, the major categories include prices for finished goods, intermediate materials, supplies and components, and crude materials for further processing.

- Some European indicators take a summer vacation in August. This is particularly true in France, when so many businesses close that data cannot be collected.
- What time is it? The investor needs to be aware of time differences between the United States and Europe and Asia. This will be an even more vexing problem when the United States changes its starting and ending dates for daylight savings time in 2007.
- Until recently there were few international rules to make cross-country comparisons easy, nor is the quality of the data uniform despite the efforts of international organizations such as the International Monetary Fund (IMF), the United Nations (UN), and the Organisation for Economic Co-operation and Development (OECD)!

Who Collects the Data

Some countries such as Japan, and to a lesser extent, Germany have a host of official data collectors and issuers. In addition, there are private data issuers just as there are in the United States. But, in many cases, the private surveys are more important to the financial markets than government data primarily because of timeliness. Examples include the monthly purchasing managers' surveys (PMIs) that are published for many countries worldwide by NTC Research in the United Kingdom, usually on the first and third business days of the month. But distribution restrictions have made these data hard to come by and they are less useful as a result. In Germany, the Ifo and ZEW sentiment surveys are available in the third week of the month and are watched very closely by all financial markets. The European Union survey of business and consumer sentiment is eagerly awaited by the financial markets as well. There are also surveys conducted by many of the government statistical agencies, such as those in Japan, Italy, and France. Many of the agencies also issue forecasts for various indicators and economic growth for the following month. This is a common practice in Japan.

The major issuers of economic indicators for the Group of Seven countries (excluding the United States), Australia, and China are listed in Table 8.1.

Despite the creation of Eurostat (a suprastatistical agency for the European Union) that aggregates indicators for a European Union (EU) members and the 12 European Monetary Union (EMU) members (the number increases to 13 on January 1, 2007, when Slovenia becomes a member), the statistical agencies for the individual member nations still flourish. In fact, Eurostat relies on them for the raw data that provide the

TABLE 8.1   International Statistics Agencies

Country	Issuing Agency
Canada	Statistics Canada (StatCan)
UK	Office of National Statistics (ONS)
EMU	Eurostat
France	INSEE (Institut National de la Statistique et des Etudes Economique)
Germany	Deutsche Bundesbank Statistisches Bundesamt Labour Office Federal Economics Ministry
Italy	ISTAT (Istituto Nazionale di Statistica)
Japan	METI (Ministry of Economy, Trade and Industry) Ministry of Finance Ministry of Health, Labour and Welfare Bank of Japan Cabinet Office
Australia	Australian Bureau of Statistics
China	National Bureau of Statistics

basis of their calculations. The information is made comparable so that it can be aggregated across countries. National estimates of key data series such as employment differ from those used as input to the aggregated data because Eurostat reconfigures the data in its harmonization process. The changes could include anything from excluding of some components to different weights for the component parts. The ramifications of the differences in definition are illustrated below.

In January 2004, the unemployment rate as calculated by the German Bundesbank was 10.2 percent but the rate used in calculating the EMU harmonized unemployment rate was 9.2 percent. But for France in that same month, the Eurostat rate was closer to the INSEE calculation—9.6 versus 9.5. (The answer is in the definition of unemployment, but more about that later!) See Figure 8.1.

Another example is the harmonized index of consumer prices. The treatment of the medical and housing components can make for vastly different outcomes when compared with the national indexes. The difference was all too apparent when the Bank of England shifted its inflation

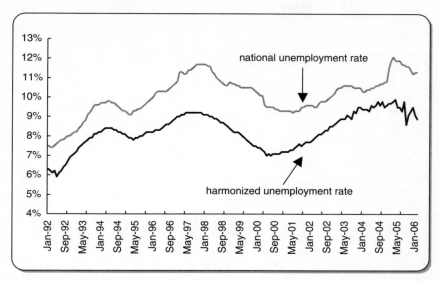

FIGURE 8.1 The definition of unemployment accounts for the differential between the German national unemployment number and that of Eurostat.
Source: Eurostat, Deutsche Bundesbank, and Haver Analytics.

target to the consumer price index that is calculated using Eurostat's harmonized methodology. The new measure has been consistently below its predecessor—the retail price index less mortgage payments. The investor should be aware of intracountry data differences when trying to balance relative performance. Figure 8.2 on page 104 illustrates this difference.

Observers of U.S. economic data have been spoiled. They are accustomed to having the calendar for the next year's releases available as early as mid-September in the preceding fall. What is more, the dates do not change during the year, except in rare circumstances. That is not so in most other countries. While not available as early as in the United States, Canadian and Italian statistics agencies publish event calendars in December that are usually available for the calendar year ahead. The United Kingdom publishes a rolling 12-month calendar with the later months in skeleton outline form. Date changes are not frequent for Canada and the United Kingdom. Eurostat also publishes an annual event calendar that is available in mid-November of the preceding year. But changes in release dates are frequently made at the last minute, so one needs to be vigilant and check for changes on Friday of each week. France releases its calendar for a rolling four-month period. And in Australia, a six-month calendar is available.

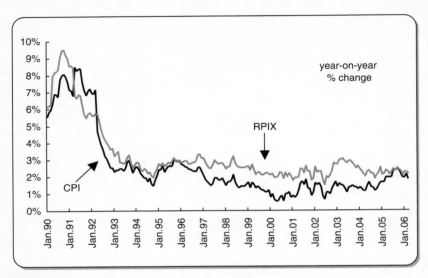

FIGURE 8.2   The weighting and inclusion of components plus a differing methodology account for the spread between the United Kingdom's retail price index excluding mortgage interest payments and the consumer price index, which follows Eurostat's harmonized index of consumer prices.
Source: Office for National Statistics and Haver Analytics.

Germany is probably the most equivocal. The Statistical Office confirms or announces its release dates on Fridays only for the following week. Release dates for certain series such as manufacturers' orders and industrial production are known in advance, but they don't originate with the Statistical Office. Another complication here is that most of the same data are also released by the Bundesbank, generally a couple of hours later—and the data sometimes differ. The Statistical Office and the Bundesbank use different seasonal adjustment programs, which sometimes can come up with very different results! But progress is being made. The Statistical Office now uses the U.S. Census Bureau Arima X12 method, in addition to the Berlin method for seasonally adjusting data, and puts the data in line with the Bundesbank.

Japan differs from all of the above. Event release availability is dependent on the indicator and is generally contained within the most recent release. And for merchandise trade data, dates are estimated for the months ahead but are confirmed about a week before the estimated release date. Release calendars generally conform to the Japanese fiscal year that begins April 1 rather than the calendar year. For example, the release schedule for the CPI and unemployment become available only around the last week in March.

Most estimates are subject to seasonal variation, that is, annually recurring fluctuations attributable to climate and regular institutional events such as vacations and holiday seasons. Seasonal adjustment programs such as the U.S. Census Arima X12 are used to remove seasonal variations in order to facilitate analysis of short-term changes. Consideration of whether the data are adjusted for seasonal factors is vividly illustrated by the example below for Japan.

January 2006 unadjusted merchandise trade balance registered the third deficit in 20 years as the Chinese Lunar New Year holiday curbed export growth to Asia and rising demand at home fueled imports. The trade deficit was ¥348.9 billion, the first since 2001, compared with a surplus the same month a year earlier. Two days of the Chinese Lunar New Year holiday, which is typically observed in the first week of February, fell in January. The holiday is observed in China, Hong Kong, Taiwan, South Korea, Singapore, and Malaysia, which together buy about 60 percent of Japanese goods shipped overseas. However, on a seasonally adjusted basis, the merchandise trade balance recorded a surplus of ¥572.3 billion, down slightly from December's surplus of ¥587.9 billion. Not only did the results differ, but they differed in direction as well.

More Differences

Data for a given month or quarter generally are available later than in the United States. Only recently have European and Japanese agencies made an effort to improve on their timing. For example, France, Germany, EMU and other EU countries issue "flash" GDP numbers in an effort to make growth information available at an earlier date. Japan has also pushed up its first GDP release as well. Although these data lack the detail that is found in the U.S. advance report, they serve as a broad indicator of the most recent past quarter's performance.

Another feature of international data is the release of scheduled mid-month revisions. This practice is prevalent in Germany and Italy and for Japanese industrial production and retail sales data in contrast to the United States, where revisions are generally incorporated in the next month's release. CPIs in Germany and Italy have set revision dates. German man-ufacturing orders and industrial production also are revised, but now are incorporated in the next month's release rather than the midmonth revisions that were never announced in advance.

Revisions are viewed stoically by most analysts, even when methodology is not the issue. Often, growth estimates can change direction from one release to the next, usually because of incomplete data for the earlier releases. For example, U.S. GDP figures in 2001 caused the National Bureau of Economic Research (NBER), the official arbiter of U.S. business cycles, to say the United States was in a recession. Subsequent data revisions now show only one negative quarter of growth (the third) belying the two-quarter decline rule of thumb for defining a recession. By the way, the NBER denies there is such a rule.

Why Indicators Are Important Even if the Data Are "Old"

The reasons indicators are important are numerous:

- The data are carefully monitored by central banks as part of their considerations when setting monetary policy.
- The data are carefully monitored by financial market players when evaluating investment opportunities.
- The data indicate which industries are growing and which are not.
- The data tell whether the macroeconomy is soaring or sinking.
- Monthly data can give advance indications long before quarterly data are available. For example, monthly retail sales data will tell you if consumers are buying rather than waiting for the quarterly consumer spending numbers in the GDP reports. (There are always exceptions! Italian retail sales data are generally ignored because they bear little relation to the consumer spending component of GDP.) These data can give you leads on what is hot and what is not in your investment analysis.

Another example is manufacturing orders. These data tell you what components and products are being ordered for sale. In Germany the orders are aggregated by domestic and foreign sales, an important clue to the economy's performance. The detail can give you investment tips on growth sectors and those that are declining. By studying the components that make up the overall number, one could track a segment that looks appealing.

Even though investors may be located elsewhere geographically, U.S. indicators sometimes are watched more intently than those closer to home simply because U.S. data are issued in a more timely manner and are important to exporters. Many overseas economies rely on exports to grow, and the United States is their biggest market. Overseas markets also have a tendency to follow U.S. markets simply because they are the largest in the world. International exporters such as those in Japan and Germany eagerly await U.S. retail sales data—and any other spending report, for that matter—that would indicate that the United States continues to absorb imports at a healthy pace.

Countries Have Their Own Idiosyncratic Way of Looking at the Data

The important or market-moving numbers differ between countries. For example, some prefer year-on-year percent change comparisons, while others only care about monthly or quarterly percent changes. Still others prefer moving averages that smooth month-to-month variations. Italy pays attention to year-on-year changes in things like retail sales, while monthly changes are more important in the United States and Canada. In the United Kingdom a moving average is important for series such as retail sales and industrial output.

The United States usually opts for seasonally adjusted data. This isn't so in many countries overseas. It depends on the indicator. Canadians, for example, prefer to look at the unadjusted CPI, while analysts prefer the seasonally adjusted index in the United States.

It helps if you can read the native language, because many times the detail will be in Italian, Japanese, or German, for example, although information available in English has been improving. In Japan, initial retail sales data are available in English but the revised numbers, available about two weeks later, are available only in Japanese. Professional data watchers will generally subscribe to a data service such as Haver Analytics so they do not have to worry about such problems!

Everyone has a favorite set of indicators and what number might be special. Annualized rates for GDP are common in the United States but are not used overseas for the most part, except in Japan and now in Canada. Some data are quarterly, some monthly. Italy is unique, as it issues only quarterly unemployment statistics with a huge lag. And Australia offers quarterly producer and consumer price data only.

Data Classification Schemes Present Another Hurdle

An important factor in data comparability for investment purposes on an international level is the manner in which the data are classified below the overall total. Standards have been developed to classify business establishments for the collection, analysis, and publication of statistical data. Attempts to create consistent data have been a combined effort of the UN Statistical Division, the IMF, and the OECD, along with many of the national statistics offices worldwide. Accounting standards for national accounting and international trade were developed as part of their efforts to make data more comparable.

Another formidable project deals with industrial classification systems. An international classification system, ISIC, was developed for that purpose. Eurostat has established a classification for European Union members (NACE), while in North America, the United States, Canada, and Mexico have established the North American Industry Classification System (NAICS). Australia and New Zealand have combined their individual systems to create the Australian and New Zealand Standard Industrial Classification (ANZSIC). And there are others besides. Japan stands alone with its Japanese Standard Industrial Classification (JSIC).

NAICS is the first North American industry classification system. The system was developed by the Economic Classification Policy Committee, on behalf of the U.S. Office of Management and Budget, in cooperation with Canada's Statistics Canada and Mexico's Instituto Nacional de Estadística, Geografía e Informática to provide comparable statistics across the three countries after the North American Free Trade Agreement (NAFTA) was signed. Government and business analysts can now compare industrial production statistics collected and published in the three NAFTA countries. NAICS also provides for increased comparability with the International Standard Industrial Classification System (ISIC, Revision 3), developed and maintained by the United Nations. In 1997, NAICS was adopted by the United States replacing the old Standard Industrial Classification (SIC) system that was considered obsolete by most. A goal of NAICS was to respond to increasing and serious criticism about the standard industrial codes on the grounds that they did not reflect the economy's evolving structure. The new codes reflect the structure of today's economy in the United States, Canada, and Mexico, including the emergence and growth of the service sector and new and advanced technologies. It is a flexible system that allows each country to recognize important industries below the level at which comparable data would be shown for all three countries.

Typically, the level at which comparable data is available for the three countries is at the five-digit NAICS industry level. But for some sectors (or subsectors or industry groups) an even a higher level of detail is available. Canada and the United States agreed on an industry structure and hierarchy to ensure comparability of statistics between those two countries. Canada and the United States also established the same national detail (six-digit) where possible, and used the same codes to describe comparable industries.

International Standard Industrial Classification of All Economic Activities (ISIC), Revision 4, is a standard classification of economic activities. Many countries have used ISIC as the model for their own classification systems. By using the system, like entities can be classified according to their primary activity. ISIC categories, at the most detailed level, echo what is, in most countries, the customary combination of activities described in statistical units and considers the relative importance of the activities included in these classes.

ISIC is a basic tool for studying economic phenomena and enabling data comparability, as well as providing guidance for national classification development and the promotion of sound national statistical systems. The ISIC is used widely both nationally and internationally. Data are classified according to the kind of economic activity for production, employment, national accounts, and other statistical areas.

NACE is the common statistical classification of economic activities within the European Union in order to ensure comparability among national and Community classifications and therefore among their statistics. The classification was originally established in the European Communities between 1961 and 1963 and became know by its acronym NICE. In 1965, the classification of trade and commerce in the European Communities was compiled to cover all commercial activities (known as NCE) followed by similar classifications for services and agriculture. Finally in 1970, the General Industrial Classification of Economic Activities within the European Communities was compiled and is known as NACE.

ANZSIC was produced by the Australian Bureau of Statistics and the New Zealand Department of Statistics for use in the collection and publication of statistics in the two countries. It replaced their original national classification systems. They have aligned ANZSIC with the ISIC, Revision 3, wherever possible.

INTERNATIONAL DATA PROVIDERS

Besides the national statistical agencies, there are international organizations that collect data and shape it to meet their particular specifications. These include the United Nations, the International Monetary Fund, and the Organisation for Economic Cooperation and Development. However, all rely on the same national data collection agencies for their source data. Their main role has been to establish international standards and guidelines for basic information contained in the national accounts and in balance of payments. This in theory should make international comparisons easier.

Aside from international organizations, the U.S. Bureau of Labor Statistics (BLS) has a Foreign Labor Statistics (FLS) program that provides international comparisons primarily with other industrialized nations of selected employment data including hourly compensation costs, productivity and unit labor costs, labor force, employment and unemployment rates as well as consumer prices. But BLS acknowledges that statistical methods and concepts differ among countries, thus making international comparisons misleading. Rather, BLS attempts to derive meaningful comparisons by selecting a conceptual framework for comparative purposes; analyzing foreign statistical series and selecting those which most nearly match the desired concepts; and adjusting statistical series, where necessary and feasible, for greater intercountry comparability.

Plan of Attack

This chapter will cover the basic market-moving indicators that are produced by government statistics offices everywhere—GDP, employment, consumer and producer prices, international trade, and production measures. First, we will discuss the intent of the overall indicator, beginning with a definition and why it is important. In the ensuing chapters, on a country-by-country basis, we will delve into the variations and indicators unique to that country. In this chapter the focus is on general concepts and in the country chapters, the details. Remember, all countries have variations in weights and calculations that are unique to their economies.

STANDARD NATIONAL ACCOUNTS

National accounting systems are the backbone and resource for gross domestic product data. They were developed slowly over time. A historical perspective of where they came from and how they were developed can help give a better understanding to the uses of these data and in particular to GDP and other relevant data.

National Accounting Is Not a Recent Development

Attempts to measure national income go back as far as the mid-seventeenth century and Sir William Petty. There were two reasons: the need to raise revenue and to assess England's war potential. The eighteenth-century French economists, the Physiocrats, restricted the concept of national income by arguing that only agriculture and the extractive industries were productive. But Physiocrat François Quesnay set out the interrelationships among various economic activities in his 1758 *Tableau Économique*, which was the forerunner of the twentieth-century work on input-output statistics.

In *An Inquiry into the Nature and Causes of the Wealth of Nations* (New York: Random House, 1937), Adam Smith rejected agriculture's preeminent position and recognized manufacturing as another productive activity. However, Smith along with the early classical school did not recognize the rendering of services as a productive activity. Some English economists, in particular David Ricardo and Alfred Marshall, further refined the concept of production and in the 1920s, welfare economists led by Arthur C. Pigou undertook the first effective measurement of national income.

The Great Depression, along with the attempts by John Maynard Keynes and others to explain what was happening to the world economy, led economists away from their preoccupation with national income as a single measure of economic welfare. Instead, they turned to the development of a statistical model to describe the workings of the economy that in turn could be used by government to develop policy prescriptions to encourage a high and stable level of economic activity. By the end of the 1930s, the elements of a national accounting system were in place in several countries.

In the 1940s, economic modeling was given further impetus because of the need to efficiently run wartime economies and by the 1941 publication of Wassily Leontief's classic input-output study, *The Structure of the American Economy*. After the war, governments accepted the full responsibility for national and international economic management. And by the end of the decade, integrated statistical reporting systems and formal national accounting structures were in place in Australia, the United States, the United Kingdom, Canada, the Scandinavian countries, the Netherlands, and France.

The Development of the System of National Accounts

The need for comparable data for member countries by the new international organizations prompted development of international standards for national accounting in the late 1940s and early 1950s. The OECD sponsored Richard Stone's work at Cambridge University's National Accounts Research Unit from which emerged the summary accounts.

In 1968, the UN Statistical Office published a fully revised version of the System of National Account (SNA), which pulled together the various threads of economic accounting including estimates of national income and expenditure both at current and constant prices; input-output production analysis; flow-of-funds financial analysis; and balance sheets of national wealth. And in 1977 they published detailed international guidelines on the compilation of balance sheet and reconciliation accounts within an SNA framework.

Updating and revising the SNA was coordinated from the mid-1980s by the Inter-secretariat Working Group on National Accounts. They worked with the assistance of international organizations and experts from national statistical offices around the world. The Working Group consisted of Eurostat, the IMF, OECD, the UN, and the World Bank. The resulting

MORE ON THE SYSTEM OF NATIONAL ACCOUNTS (SNA93)

The 1993 System of National Accounts (SNA93) is a conceptual framework that sets the international statistical standard for market economy measurement. It is published jointly by the UN, the Commission of the European Communities, the IMF, the OECD, and the World Bank.

SNA93 consists of an integrated set of macroeconomic accounts, balance sheets, and tables based on internationally agreed concepts, definitions, classifications, and accounting rules. Together, these provide a comprehensive accounting framework within which economic data can be compiled and presented. The format is designed specifically for economic analysis, decision taking, and policy making. It also serves as the main reference point for statistical standards for the balance of payments along with financial and government finance statistics.

Since the SNA is a conceptual framework, it does not attempt to provide guidance on making estimates, nor does it describe how to set priorities. And there are no specific instructions on which accounts and tables should be developed nor on the frequency and presentation format. For practical compilation guidance, international agencies have developed separate handbooks. An example would be the handbooks of national accounting prepared by the United Nations Statistics Division.

Updates through 2002 have been incorporated in the electronic version of the 1993 SNA (blue book). The Table of Contents of the 1993 SNA provides easy reference to the complete and updated text. A search facility allows users to search words or word groups in the entire 1993 SNA. The glossary of terms shows definitions used in national accounts as well as references to where they are to be found in the 1993 SNA.

System of National Accounts 1993 (SNA93) was released under the auspices of those five organizations.

SNA93 tried to clarify and simplify the 1968 system, while at the same time updating it to reflect new circumstances. It fully integrated national income, expenditure and product accounts, input-output tables, financial flow accounts, and national balance sheets to enable the examination of production relationships and their interaction with countries' net worth and financial positions. SNA93 also introduced the concept of satellite accounts to extend the analytical capacity of national accounts in areas such as tourism, health, and the environment.

GROSS DOMESTIC PRODUCT—A SNAPSHOT OF ECONOMIC ACTIVITY

Among the most familiar of the economic indicators is gross domestic product (GDP). It is the broadest measure of aggregate economic activity and encompasses every sector of the economy. In many respects, these data provide the framework for central bank analysis of the economy.

Although the data are very important, they are available with a considerable time lag. For example, GDP data for Canada and Australia are not available until two full months after a quarter's end, while for the European countries it is at least a six-week wait, and then there is no detail. The United Kingdom offers minimal data within a month of a quarter's end, while the United States provides full preliminary estimates for all components. However, they could be subject to extensive revisions in the following month.

But despite the time delay, these data give the most complete picture of the relative strength of different sectors of the economy. For example, the data will tell you if the consumer sector is growing and how investment is stoking growth. This could be a clue of where to look for growth companies for your investment portfolio. And since central banks include GDP in their arsenal of data while wrestling with policy decisions, they can be an important input for potential changes in monetary policy.

Stock, Bond, and Currency Markets React Differently

Each financial market reacts differently to GDP data because of their focus. Equity market participants cheer healthy economic growth because it improves the corporate profit outlook, while weak growth generally means anemic earnings. Equities generally drop on disappointing growth and climb on good growth prospects. In 2004 and 2005, there appears to have been a disconnect in the relationship. While growth withered in Germany and France in 2005, the DAX and CAC stock indexes continued their rallies and were up 27.1 percent and 23.4 percent respectively that year.

Bond or fixed-income markets are contrarians. They prefer weak growth so that there is less of a chance of higher central bank interest rates and inflation. GDP growth that is poor or negative indicates anemic or negative economic activity. Bond prices will rise and interest rates will fall. When growth is positive and good, interest rates will be higher and bond prices lower.

Currency traders prefer healthy growth and higher interest rates. Both lead to increased demand for a local currency. However, inflationary pressures put pressure on a currency regardless of growth. For example, if the United Kingdom reports that the consumer price index has risen more than the Bank of England's 2 percent inflation target, demand for sterling could decline. Similarly, when the Bank lowered interest rates in 2005, the pound sterling weakened. (Currency traders also watch the interest rate spread between countries. But that is a topic for another day.)

What Is GDP and How Is It Measured?

GDP measures aggregate economic activity that represents the unduplicated value of production. It is measured two ways—by incomes arising from production and by final expenditures on production. The first is the sum of factor incomes generated by productive activity or the incomes representing returns to the labor and capital employed. The second is the sum of all sales to final users (consumers, governments, business on capital account, and exports less imports). In theory, the two estimates should be equal, but are not. Therefore, the statistical discrepancy is used to measure the difference between the income and expenditure estimates.

Growth estimates for GDP components can be split into two parts. The first are estimates of current price values in different periods. The second separates changes in current prices into a price change and a quantity change. Values are expressed in a common currency unit and are additive across different products. While measuring the change in aggregate value is conceptually straightforward, dividing the change into a price change and a quantity change is not. This is because aggregate price changes and aggregate quantity changes must be estimated because they cannot be observed directly in economic terms.

In order to measure volume growth, price change effects are eliminated. Until recently, a common practice was to keep prices constant by choosing a base year and then aggregating volume changes in subsequent periods using the price structures and weights of the fixed base year. Most recently, the year 2000 has been the base year of choice. Thus, the value of the aggregates in subsequent periods were said to be expressed in constant 2000 prices. Cross-country comparisons have stumbled in part because of varying base years.

Over time, base year relative prices were found to be progressively less relevant the farther away from the base year the growth estimate period became. To adjust, the base year was updated about every five years. However, such updating, even at shorter intervals, had its shortcomings. For example, the information, communication, and technology goods sectors have demonstrated how dramatic price changes can be.

As a result, GDP measurement has been going through methodological overhaul over the past 10 years worldwide. Most countries now have changed over to the chain-link method of calculating growth from base year or are in the process of doing so. Indeed, all the countries included here, with the exception of China, have adopted chain methodology.

The basic idea of chain linking is to update the base year more frequently and to link short-term movements. In Europe and elsewhere, updates are on an annual basis. In this case, period-to-period changes of volumes (the links in the chain) are calculated using the prices (i.e., weights) of the previous year. That way the use of up-to-date price structures is ensured. (This was why Japan's GDP was subject to such large revisions when the new methodology was introduced, given the country's recent chronic deflation.)

All of the countries included here (except China) use chain methodology, which should make comparisons easier, except—and there always seems to be an exception—the base years differ. And different base years harm comparability. Japan uses 2000 as a base year, while Canada uses 1997 and the United Kingdom uses 2002. Australia does not use the calendar year; rather, its base year spans the third quarter of 2002 to the second quarter of 2003. However, Germany, France, Italy, and the EMU all use chained 2000 euros. Eurostat converted to chain methodology for third quarter 2005 GDP data. But France was the laggard and only converted to chain methodology with its release of first-quarter 2006 data. For a discussion of the European conversion to chained methodology, see Chapter 9. China's data differ from everyone's—they provide only year-on-year percent change on a quarterly basis.

While most countries have switched to the international classification system (SNA93), the United States continues to use the National Income and Product Accounts (NIPA). Both are systems of national accounts of which GDP is a subset. See Appendix B for a comparison of the two systems.

When the data are released, there are several ways to measure overall growth. The United States uses annualized quarterly growth rates—that is, what growth would be if the economy performed in the same way for all four quarters. However, in most other countries, growth—or the lack of it—is measured by a simple quarter-on-quarter percent change (fourth quarter over third quarter) and simple year-on-year percent change (fourth quarter compared with the same quarter in the previous year). Japan has been moving toward using the annualized growth rate. For example, in the first quarter of 2006, the preliminary estimate of GDP was up 0.5

MORE ON CHAIN MEASURES

Without getting overly technical, the new chain measures are an average of two distinct measures of change in volume—one calculated as if prices were constant in the first of two adjacent periods (Laspeyres volume) and the other calculated as if prices were constant in the second of the two adjacent periods (Paasche volume). A disadvantage to this is that the values are now in index form. GDP in currency values now are the result of a conversion from the chain index, and the categories no longer add up without adjustment.

Chain indexes attempt to address one of the more basic problems in measuring real output and prices—choosing the base period with which all others are compared. Quantity and price indexes are analytical devices for decomposing changes in nominal GDP into that part due to changes in prices and that part due to changes in quantity. Thus, real GDP is an expression of the changes in output that are associated with changes in quantity and not with changes in prices. This is especially important for Japan because falling prices inflated actual growth.

The easiest way to calculate real GDP is to specify a single base period or constant set of prices and then value the output in all periods in those prices. Unfortunately, because relative prices and associated patterns of purchases change over time, this measure of real GDP growth will be quite sensitive to the choice of the base year, and a shift in the base year often has a significant impact on the measured growth rates. Normally, changing the base period does not reverse the direction of change in GDP, but the effect is still quite important. When the base year for real GDP was updated, the size of the revisions to the rates of growth in real GDP and its components due solely to updating the base year became topics of debate in discussions of budget projections and monetary policy.

However, the recalculations provide less accurate measures of growth for earlier periods because the price weights are farther away from the prices appropriate to those periods. For later periods, even the new weights eventually get out of date, and measures of growth in output become increasingly overstated.

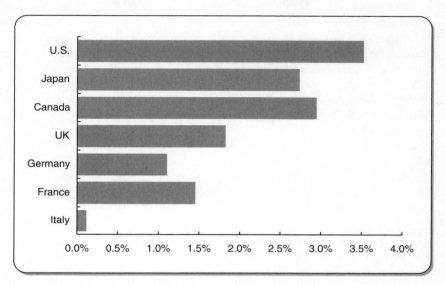

FIGURE 8.3   The graph shows the differing levels of growth achieved during 2005 by the Group of Seven countries.
Source: Eurostat and Haver Analytics.

percent on a quarterly basis, 3 percent when compared with the same quarter a year ago, and 1.9 percent at an annualized pace. For intercountry comparisons, it is critical to use the same measure. Accurately describing a country's performance has ramifications that go beyond national borders. Economic growth impacts exchange rates, interest rates, and stock prices, along with government policies and the political environment. Figure 8.3 shows comparative Group of Seven GDP 2005 rates for the United States, Japan, Canada, the United Kingdom, Germany, France, and Italy.

GDP Components

The GDP accounts, regardless of the system used to calculate them, provide a wealth of information on consumption and investment to a varying degree of detail. While the detail varies from country to country the following sectors are always included in any GDP analysis. They are private and government consumption, private gross fixed capital formation by structure and equipment type, public gross fixed capital formation by government source and defense, inventory change, and international trade (exports and imports).

With most industrialized economies reliant on consumer spending for over 60 percent of GDP, the data in the consumption sector focuses in on the main growth driver. Germany's GDP growth suffered in 2005 because domestic consumption was almost nonexistent. In the SNAs, consumption includes both government spending and the private sector, while in the U.S., government is a separate category. The gross capital formation sector in the SNAs includes data by major industries such as agriculture, transport, metal products and machinery, and so on. This differs from the U.S. GDP. For example, the United States counts capital spending on military hardware such as nuclear missiles as investment that contributes to its GDP, while other countries include only military investment that has possible civilian uses, such as army hospitals.

Data Revisions

Revisions are handled quite differently geographically. There are usually three releases of GDP data. In the United States, they are referred to as the advance, preliminary, and final. In the EMU, the first release is the flash estimate, which is one number: year-on-year percent change. The flash is followed by a preliminary and final release that include detail. In the United Kingdom, there are three releases, each containing more detail and, of course, revisions to prior GDP releases. Japan follows a similar pattern. However, in Canada and Australia, there is only one quarterly release. Revisions come into play only in the next quarter's release. Finally, in China, the GDP release consists of only a year-on-year percent change and is subject to revision. For example, December 2005's huge reestimation of the size of China's economy had a profound impact on GDP measurement.

But the end result for analysts is that history has to be relearned again and again, especially when there is a change in methodology and/or a change in the base year. This was particularly true in Japan when they converted to chain methodology primarily because of the way price changes are computed.

PRICE MEASURES

Although price levels were always a concern in the financial markets and elsewhere, price index watching has risen to new heights now that most central banks are targeting the rate of inflation. Markets will move on the direction of price reports. If prices go up more than expected, currency traders might bid up that currency on the thinking that interest rates will also go up. However, equity markets may drop because higher interest rates could mean lower profits and reduced growth. The bond market will also drop because higher prices could mean higher interest rates.

In those economies where the central bank uses inflation targeting as a policy determinant, price movements obviously are very important. And even in non-price-targeting Japan, price changes loom large. Japan had been suffering the scourge of deflation—that is, falling prices—since 1999. But the signs of price stability and even some inflation that occurred in early 2006 were a welcome signal that the economy had finally recovered from the bursting of the asset price bubble of the late 1990s.

What Are Price Indexes?

A price index reflects the changes in the prices of a specified set of goods and services. And price measurements—whether they are up or down—are important to all economies. Most price indexes are weighted averages of prices, where the weights are assigned to components based on spending of the mythical average family. Base-weighted indexes measure changes over any time period. With the weights held constant, changes reflect price movements only. However, implicit deflators show both price and spending pattern changes. For example, the GDP price deflator reflects the differences between current and constant price GDP, thereby measuring price changes as well as changes in the composition of GDP.

Inflation is an increase in prices or wages. Deflation is an absolute decline in prices. Many times disinflation, which is a slowing of the rate of inflation, is confused with deflation, the drop in prices. Inflation can either be demand pull or cost push. When demand is stronger than the supply of goods and services available, usually because of vibrant growth, prices increase. This in turn, could eventually lead to a reallocation of resources. Cost push inflation occurs when prices are pushed up by more expensive inputs such as higher wages and raw material costs. Cost push inflationary fears dominated discussions in 2006 as the European Central Bank fretted about secondary inflationary effects of soaring energy prices.

There are three major adverse effects from inflation: (1) It creates uncertainty because it is unpredictable and discourages investment; (2) it redistributes income from creditors to borrowers and from those on fixed incomes to wage earners; and (3) it makes it difficult to distinguish between relative prices and changes in the general price level. The classic example of hyperinflation occurred in Germany between 1919 and 1923, when wholesale prices rose by about 1.5 trillion percent. However, when deflation grips an economy, consumers stop buying and wait for still lower prices as they did in Japan in the early 2000s. Debts soar as borrowers are unable to pay off loans and default as prices fall. This is what happened during the Great Depression of the 1930s. But one can look to modern-day Japan for a more recent example of deflation and its debilitating effect on the banking industry.

The CPI, which in some form is used by inflation targeters to measure inflation, is but one of many price measures. The CPI is considered the most important because it measures price changes that impact consumers and is used for a variety of public and private purposes. For example, wage increases can be tied to increases in the CPI, and in the United States it is used to measure the annual cost-of-living adjustment for Social Security recipients. It is also used as a focus for monetary policy.

Other price measures include the GDP price deflator, producer price indexes, import and export price indexes, commodity price indexes, and the price components of various surveys, including the purchasing manager surveys.

Consumer Price Index

The consumer price index (CPI) is a measure of the average price level of a fixed basket of goods and services purchased by consumers. Usually issued on a monthly basis, changes in the CPI represent the rate of inflation or, in the case of Japan until recently, deflation. Most countries, with the exception of Australia, release these data on a monthly schedule. Australia issues both its CPI and PPI quarterly.

The CPI is one indicator that all central banks watch closely. Since the Banks of England and Canada, the European Central Bank, and the Reserve Bank of Australia have inflation targets, these data also are watched closely by investors for potential interest rate policy changes. For the most part, the nonseasonally adjusted data are preferred, in contrast to the United States, where analysts prefer seasonally adjusted data. All have a core CPI that excludes food and/or energy and sometimes alcoholic beverages and/or tobacco. But it is important to note that most CPIs are not intended to be cost-of-living indexes but rather representative of "average" expenditures by an "average" family.

Weights for components that make up the overall index vary across countries, so it is difficult to compare inflation rates among them. The variations are in part due to cultural and social differences. For example, home ownership in the United Kingdom is more important than in other EU countries; therefore, the housing component carries a different weight. Climate affects energy usage and its weighting. And health care prices carry vastly different weights, depending on whether there is a national health scheme that pays for doctors and medications. Another problem

A PERSONAL ASSESSMENT OF WHETHER THERE IS INFLATION

Sometimes local prices jump dramatically and affect consumers within a limited area. But these price increases are unlikely to make it into the national numbers unless it happens in a lot of places. For example, on January 1, 2006, my local electric company increased rates by over 20 percent for a section of Connecticut. This translated to an average household bill rising by over $20. Small businesses were affected even more. Increases like this are not likely to be reflected in the national numbers, although the local perception is quite different.

is the changing composition of the index, as new components are added and absorb a larger portion of expenditures. New products or innovations usually are incorporated into the indexes only after a lag of several years. For example, it took some time before computers were included in the various indexes. And they still produce additional problems for compilers as their prices continue to decline.

Another example occurred in August 2006 when Japan introduced their updated consumer price index. The recomposition of the basket of items included showed that many old standbys were tossed out while new ones were added to it. Sewing machines were no longer included, while doughnuts and flat-screen TV sets were added for the first time. The base year was updated at the same time. The result was to lower recent increases in the index, and for some months, convert index increases into declines.

For the European Union, Eurostat has created a harmonized index of consumer prices that irons out these differentials to calculate a meaningful number for its Member Countries. This is imperative since the ECB is virtually myopic in its focus on prices as the primary determinant of monetary policy for the EMU. But making a consistent comparison across countries can lead to a distortion of the facts. The marginalization of housing, and in particular the missing owner's equivalent rent component in the HICP is an apt illustration. Housing, which is very important in countries such as the United Kingdom, is less important elsewhere and leads to an index that does not reflect consumer costs evenly across countries.

Virtually all industrial countries use some form of the Laspeyres index to compute their CPIs. A Laspeyres index is calculated from a set basket of fixed quantities of a finite list of goods for two different time periods. Assuming that the price index from period one is the base, then the value of the index in the second period is equal to the total price of the basket of goods in period two divided by the total price of exactly the same basket in period one.

Investors pay close attention to core measures of the CPI that omit volatile items such as food and energy to get a snapshot of underlying inflation. These are also under close scrutiny by the central banks. But there are variations here as well. In Japan, only fresh food was omitted for the core measure. However, when the newly configured CPI was released in August 2006, new core measures were added. Now there is a core that also excludes energy besides fresh food. In many European countries, tobacco is also excluded for the core measure in addition to food and energy. Eurostat calculates several core measures of the HICP, among them a core that excludes food, energy, alcohol, and tobacco and another that excludes only energy and unprocessed food. The ECB prefers the latter. And the Bank of Canada has constructed a core CPI that excludes eight volatile components (fruit, vegetables, gasoline, fuel oil, natural gas, mortgage interest, intercity transportation, and tobacco products) that is their operational measure of inflation. The Bank's inflation target however, is stated in terms of the CPI.

Producer Price Index

The producer price index (PPI) was particularly affected by soaring oil prices over the past several years, so it is not surprising that many investors look here to see if there are any underlying signs for consumer inflation brewing. For example, investors would want to see the impact of rising energy prices on producers' costs. If producers have pricing power, they are able to pass increased costs on to consumers. But profits could be hurt if they have to absorb these price increases because of an inability to pass these costs on. One reason for the prolonged deflation in Japan has been the inability of domestic goods producers especially to pass on increased costs to consumers. This is a hot topic because of the huge increase in crude oil prices. West Texas intermediate crude oil has soared from a low of $12.33 in January 1999 to over $77 in the summer of 2006.

The PPI is a measure of the average price level paid by producers for a fixed basket of capital and consumer goods. The name of the index varies across countries. In Canada, it is called the industrial product price index (IPPI) and the raw materials price index (RMPI). In Japan, it is called the corporate goods price index (CGPI). In the United Kingdom, it is the producer output index and the producer input index.

A producer's price is the amount received by a producer from the purchaser of a unit of goods or services produced as output less any value added tax (VAT) or similar deductible tax, invoiced to the purchaser. It excludes any transportation charges invoiced separately by the producer.

Those accustomed to U.S. data will generally look at finished-goods data, although there are two other categories: crude material prices and intermediate prices. Commodity prices got a good deal of attention in 2005 and 2006 when these prices soared. In Australia, where the economy is commodity oriented, the central bank compiles an index only for commodity prices, and unlike the PPI and CPI, it is available on a monthly basis.

The United Kingdom and Canada look at input and output prices separately, while Japan reconfigured its index into a corporate goods price index a few years ago. It should be noted that in Japan the CGPI also was monitored to see if deflation had finally ended. Although the CGPI began to increase in 2005, the increases only began to trickle through to consumer prices in 2006. The CPI remained stubbornly in a deflationary mode because producers were unable to pass along input price increases to consumers.

The component breakdown differs from the United States. While the United States uses finished, intermediate, and crude materials, the European PPI is categorized by capital, intermediate, and consumer goods. There are three major industrial categories—manufacturing; mining and quarrying; and electricity, gas, and water. However, not only the names but the categories of the indexes differ. These are discussed in the chapters on each country.

GDP Deflator

As stated above, deflators, which are a product of the GDP accounts, measure both price and composition of spending from period to period. The implicit price deflator is the ratio of the current-dollar value of a series to its corresponding chained-dollar value, multiplied by 100. Deflators are constructed for various components of GDP. While deflators are important to U.S. investors, they are less so elsewhere for the most part. In Japan, the deflator is but one of several price measures monitored in the search to find the end of deflation. In early 2006, it was suggested by members of the Japanese government that the Bank of Japan watch the deflator rather than the CPI as they awaited firm signals that deflation had ended. They were trying to persuade the Bank not to change its monetary policy, which was helping to ease the pain of financing Japan's huge fiscal deficit.

LABOR MARKET INDICATORS

One of the most important indicators in world markets is the U.S. employment situation report usually issued on the first Friday of the month for the preceding month. Given the U.S. position as the engine of growth, not to mention the main market for exporters, the data are evaluated closely everywhere. The data will move currency, bond, and stock markets, although in Asia the reaction generally occurs on the following Monday. (Asian markets are closed when the report is released.) The report is all encompassing, including information on employment, unemployment, hours worked, and earnings. While all this information is not necessarily contained in other countries' reports, you can be certain that whatever the data, they have the capability to move markets just as the U.S. data do!

Unemployment

Unemployment data are watched everywhere and by all financial markets. Seasonally adjusted data are a must for unemployment data. Most major monthly unemployment rate changes are usually due to seasonal variations. School terms, holidays, and religious festivals all can lead to large changes in the unemployment rate, and can hide important underlying trends. The seasonal variations are well known from historical data and statistical adjustments are made to remove these effects. Seasonal variations can account for as much as 95 percent of the change in the numbers from month to month. For example, the sudden impact of those who are no longer in school and are entering the labor market each summer can skew the data so a statistical adjustment is made for them as well. Figure 8.4 on page 125 shows the wide variation in unemployment rates between countries.

Most countries base their unemployment statistics calculations on the unemployment definition as developed by the International Labour Organisation (ILO), which excludes job seekers who did any work during the month and covers only those people who are looking for and are available for work. The ILO unemployment rate is the number of people who are unemployed as a proportion of the resident economically active population of the area concerned. A rising (falling) unemployment rate usually means that consumers are less (more) likely to spend and is negative (positive) for the economy. But many countries vary from a strict interpretation. For example, in Germany, one can work for a few hours during the measurement period and still be counted as unemployed. This has led to large differences in the unemployment rate as calculated by Eurostat and the national rate.

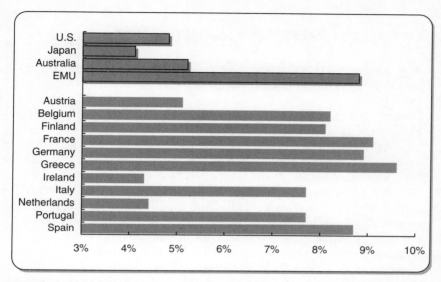

FIGURE 8.4 Unemployment rates vary from country to country within the EMU. The United States, Japan, and Australia are shown for comparative purposes *Source:* Eurostat and Haver Analytics.

Employment

Employment data are viewed as the more important indicator by most investors. Employment means that consumers will have money to spend. And since consumers make up the largest segment of most economies, it is important (obviously) that they earn wages so that they can purchase goods and services.

Employment data count the number of paid employees working part time or full time in a nation's business and government establishments. Employment gains or losses are relevant only when considered alongside population and labor force numbers. Employment is one of the most watched of the economic indicators. Employment means income, which leads to spending, which boosts overall economic performance.

Data availability varies widely among the industrialized countries. For example, Canada issues a separate earnings report about two weeks after employment and unemployment data become available. Australia also issues a combined employment and unemployment report, but separate wage information. In Germany, the emphasis is on the number of unemployed, and employment data until recently lagged by two months.

THE INTERNATIONAL LABOUR ORGANISATION

The International Labour Organisation (ILO) is based in Geneva and is part of the United Nations. The role of the ILO is to improve conditions for working people and to prevent unemployment worldwide. The ILO definition provides the basis for all other definitions of unemployment. It is quite long and complicated.

The unemployed comprise all persons above a specified age who, during the reference period, were without work (were not in paid employment or self-employment); currently available for work (were available for employment or self-employment during the reference period); and seeking work (had taken specific steps in a specified time period to seek paid employment or self-employment). In short, the unemployed are those who are out of work, available for work, and seeking work. The specific steps taken to find a job may include registration at a public or private employment exchange; application to employers; checking at worksites, farms, factory gates, markets, or other assembly places; placing or answering newspaper advertisements; seeking assistance of friends or relatives; looking for land, building, machinery, or equipment to establish one's own enterprise; arranging for financial resources; and applying for permits and licenses.

The list goes on. In Japan, employment and unemployment data are released in their Labour Force Survey, but earnings data are found in another report entirely. In France, unemployment data are monthly, but employment is a quarterly series. Hourly earnings are available monthly but at a later date than unemployment. In Italy, employment and unemployment data are available only on a quarterly basis with a very long lag. For example, third-quarter 2005 data were released on December 22, 2005. However, earnings data are available monthly.

Other than in the United States, the most complete report is in the United Kingdom. Released midmonth, the report contains both monthly claimant unemployment, which is similar to the U.S. weekly job claims data, and average earnings. However, the employment and unemployment data are provided as a three-month moving average in accordance with ILO definitions. Generally, the claimant unemployment number is preferred by market watchers because it is more current, but the government labels the ILO numbers for employment and unemployment as the "official" ones.

MERCHANDISE TRADE AND BALANCE OF PAYMENTS

Economic interrelationships are characterized by transactions between countries and measured by the balance of payments (BOP) and merchandise trade. Financial markets, and especially the currency markets, usually pay more attention to monthly merchandise trade data.

The value of a currency is of critical importance when evaluating the trade balance. The data are available in local currency, making it difficult to compare trade performance across national borders other than comparing those with surpluses and deficits. (In the EMU, unique issues exist and are discussed in Chapter 9.) Merchandise trade data are especially important to foreign exchange traders. The U.S. dollar, for example, has been pulled down in value in part due to its huge merchandise trade and current account deficits. The data can tell investors which sectors rely on exports and would be more vulnerable to changes in the world outlook. A good example here has been the reliance of the Japanese economy to grow through exports, especially to the United States. This also puts U.S. data, including the trade report, in the "must follow" category for investors in Japan. Trade is a major reason that U.S. data are so important to those overseas who rely on exports to the United States for growth.

Merchandise Trade Balance

Merchandise trade data measures both the imports and exports of goods and services (or just goods), while the balance of payments records all cross-border currency flows regardless of the source of the transaction. Data usually record the value of trade at the point of customs clearance. Exports are typically free on board (FOB), while imports generally include cost, insurance, and freight (CIF). These data are generally available on a monthly basis.

The trade balance reflects the difference between exports and imports of tangible (or visible) goods and intangible (or invisible) goods and services. A trade deficit can be interpreted as either as a constraint on supply or a loss of competitiveness, especially if they are accompanied by high inflation. For an industrial country, a trade imbalance could reflect choice as much as necessity and is not necessarily a problem. For example, the UK's visible trade deficits have been more than offset by trade on invisibles such as insurance and so on. However, countries such as Japan and Germany typically run visible trade surpluses and invisible deficits.

Imports

Merchandise or visible imports relate to physical goods, while service or invisible imports are payments to foreigners for items such as shipping; travel and tourism; and financial services of all sorts, along with things like advertising, education, health, commissions, and royalties. Visible trade data are more prominent because they are among the more reliable and rapidly available figures. Price changes can reflect genuine price changes and exchange rates fluctuations or increasing or decreasing volumes. Imports tend to move cyclically and can act as a drag on domestic growth and can also increase competitive pressures among domestic producers. For example, import increases can occur when domestic capacity is stretched to its limits and can help remove otherwise inflationary pressures from the economy. And higher consumer goods imports can also imply the strength of consumer demand for all things foreign made.

Exports

Exports earn foreign exchange and boost domestic production (and GDP). This is an important indicator for many countries, such as Japan and Germany, that rely on exports for growth. Demand for a country's exports depends on foreign economic health and prices, which reflect competitiveness and relative foreign exchange levels.

Balance of Payments

The Balance of Payments (BOP) is an accounting record of international transactions. It measures the financial flows usually within a calendar year. Inflows in accounting terms are considered as credits or positive entries, while outflows are debits or negative entries. Inflows include payments for services or goods imports or the purchase price of a share of stock on the domestic market. Outflows are payments for imports or the purchase price of a share on an international stock market. It is a double-entry bookkeeping system, with each item entered on both sides of the ledger. In the end, debits should equal credits.

To keep track of these payments, most countries have adopted the IMF methodology outlined in the Balance of Payments Manual since the late 1990s. In practice, it is virtually impossible to keep track of all transactions, especially invisibles and speculative flows, where there is no physical evidence. And the entries on both sides of the ledger do not always occur within the same reporting period. To cover the disparities, a balance is forced through the use of the statistical discrepancy. BOP data are generally used to analyze the value of trade and match the trade components in GDP.

The balance of trade in goods and services plus income and current transfer payments is referred to as the current account balance. These data are generally available on a quarterly basis. A visible trade deficit can be covered by exports of services or new inflows of income and transfers, but the overall current account cannot remain in deficit indefinitely. It has to be financed by any or all of inward investment, loans from overseas, sales of overseas assets, and depletion of official currency reserves.

OUTPUT

Even though manufacturing accounts for a smaller portion of GDP in the major industrialized countries, the ripple effect on other important segments of the economy make it a much watched number, especially in countries like Japan, Germany, and Italy. These data are usually very detailed and, as such, can provide industry information that is not always available elsewhere. The data are usually available within a reasonably short time following the reference month. And, of course, they feed directly into GDP data. German and Japanese output data always get a market response. Output from manufacturing is particularly important to these two economies because of their dependence on exports to grow.

Industrial Production

The index of industrial production or output measures the physical output of a nation's factories, mines, and utilities. The preferred measure differs. Japan includes mining and manufacturing in its press release number, for example, and you would be hard pressed to find a total output number. In the United Kingdom, manufacturing gets precedence over the total industrial output number. But not all countries publish separate industrial production indexes and reports. In Canada, output is part of its monthly GDP report, and in Australia, there is no corresponding series. As noted above, the data are especially important to export-dependent economies.

Production is a critical component of an economy's structure that is needed to satisfy domestic demand as well as a country's exports, so a timely and detailed report is necessary. Asian economies have used their output to grow by exporting to more industrialized countries rather than for developing domestic demand at home. Their exports are used as inputs to manufacturing elsewhere. Their main markets are where the economic focus has shifted to services. Indeed, the United States' virtually insatiable appetite has kept the world economy afloat by purchasing imports from developing as well as developed countries. And Japan has pulled itself out of its economic funk by aggressively exporting. But sooner or later, domestic demand is needed to grow. And by monitoring the subcategories, one can discern whether the economy is reviving domestically and might provide a good investment opportunity.

Besides international trade, the industrial output data are a link to the employment situation. Employment data can give an early sign as to industries that are growing and those that are having a reversal of fortune. These trends can be confirmed by comparisons with the industrial output data, which are generally available about a month later than the employment data.

Industries are classified by the international classification systems— NAICS in Canada and NACE in Europe and the United Kingdom. Japan however, does not use one of these systems, but uses a different method of categorizing output (Japanese Standard Industrial Classification). Base years vary from 2000 to 2002 and are updated about every five years.

RETAIL SALES

For investors, retail sales are another tool to help evaluate consumer spending, especially since the data are a direct input into GDP growth. Many retailers' securities trade on the stock and bond markets, and the data could be a guide to evaluating investments in these stocks. While usually not providing the detail of an industrial production report, the subcategories are useful in evaluating investment possibilities within overall consumer goods.

Retail sales measure the total receipts at stores that sell durable and nondurable goods. Measures here vary wildly in quality despite their importance to overall growth. Consumer spending accounts for a hefty chunk of GDP (60 percent and higher in most developed countries) and is therefore a key contributor to economic growth.

Methodology varies widely, with some countries using currency measures of retail sales, while others use an index or volume measure. The use of seasonal smoothing varies between countries as well. Like the price indexes, analysts look at retail sales less its more volatile components—autos and sometimes gasoline station sales. Revisions can change the outlook significantly. And while for most countries the data are input to GDP, in Italy, the series is generally ignored because it has no relationship to GDP and is not used even by its compiler (Istituto Nazionale di Statistica or ISTAT) in its GDP calculations.

PURCHASING MANAGERS' INDEXES

The purchasing managers' indexes (PMIs) have grown in importance and popularity over the last several years. These data have filled a vacuum left by official data because of their timeliness. They are available immediately after the end of the reference month (the manufacturing index is available on the first working day of the month, and the services index is available on the third working day). They give an up-to-date reading while the official data lag by a considerable margin. The PMI data are not subject to revision, while official data usually go through several iterations. An advantage to the PMIs is that they are comparable across countries because the same methodology is used to compile each index.

The data for the United Kingdom, Germany, France, Italy, the EMU, Japan, and China are compiled by NTC Research in the UK and are monitored closely as a gauge of manufacturing and services health. The index for Australia is compiled by PricewaterhouseCoopers and is called the Australian Performance of Manufacturing Index, while in Canada, the index is compiled by the Richard Ivey School of Business and the Purchasing Management Association of Canada and is available about a week after the others.

All the PMIs are diffusion indexes that are calculated differently than measures such as the CPI, PPI, and industrial output indexes, where a base year is equal to 100 and the change is calculated from there. Rather, the diffusion index measures those respondents who say business is increasing and those that are decreasing, with 50 as the breakeven point—that is, neither rising nor falling. If business is increasing more than decreasing, the number would be above 50—the higher the value, the more robust the growth. Conversely, if the reading is below 50, business is declining. The lower the reading, the more business is contracting.

Unfortunately, the producer of the PMIs for Europe and many other countries, NTC Research, has chosen to make the data available only to subscribers and at a steep price. As a result, a valuable early indicator has been lost to most investors.

CHAPTER 9

European Indicators: Eurostat and National Statistics

This chapter covers a lot of ground. While it focuses on indicators for the entire European Monetary Union, it also looks at the data released nationally by the statistics offices of the big three—Germany, France, and Italy. The European Union's statistics are produced by Eurostat. While most data releases lag those in the United States, Eurostat data lag by an even longer time period. And when combining the individual country series, features that are unique to a particular country can be lost in the translation. For this reason, I have included sections that cover important national releases in Germany, France, and Italy. The chapter includes the following indicators: gross domestic product; harmonized index of consumer prices; producer price indexes; employment and unemployment; industrial production; merchandise trade and the balance of payments; retail sales; M3 money supply; and government and selected private sentiment surveys.

The EMU, despite its relatively short existence, is considered one of the world economy's engines of growth along with the United States and Japan. But the region has fallen behind in fulfilling this role. Nevertheless, market analysts follow developments here closely. Although the euro has only been around since 1999, its relationship with the U.S. dollar is one of the more critical pairings in currency markets, along with the dollar-yen and dollar–pound sterling or cable. The euro has replaced the once invulnerable German deutsche mark as the European currency to watch. For example, the euro will go up/down in value if the U.S. merchandise trade deficit increases/decreases. And other indicators will influence their relative values as well. When the dollar was weakening in 2006, talk pervaded the currency market that central banks that were awash in dollars such as those in Russia, the Middle East oil countries, and China (among others) would diversify their reserves into euros.

EUROSTAT

The responsibility for compiling European Union (EU) economic data lies with Eurostat, the statistical agency created by the Maastricht Treaty. They are saddled with the task of providing comparable data across all EU members (and possible new entrants to the EU) while relying on diverse national statistical agencies that vary in sophistication for their raw data. The data are generally reported for the individual Member States as well as aggregated for the 12 members (13 on January 1, 2007) of the EMU and the 25 EU members (27 on January 1, 2007). The Eurostat web site is multilingual, so everything is readily accessible in almost any language.

Despite Eurostat's usage of the same data as the national statistical agencies, there are differences between Eurostat's statistics and those published by the individual countries. For example, there are disparities between the EMU consumer price measure and those of the national statistics offices. Differences occur for unemployment as well. Both content and computational methodology play a role in explaining why they differ. Because of its reliance on national data, Eurostat lags with most of its data releases. Therefore, many market watchers rely on surveys because they are timelier than data from Eurostat despite the agency's effort to speed things up. And published data may not include all members because of delays on the national level in providing the basic information.

Eurostat is unique among statistical agencies—it does not collect data at the grassroots level. This is done in Member States by their statistical authorities. Eurostat compiles the data and is the only provider of statistics at the European level. Its role is to process and publish comparable statistical information at the European level by using a common statistical language that embraces concepts, methods, structures, and technical standards.

Eurostat was established in 1953 to meet the requirements of the Coal and Steel Community. Over the years its tasks have expanded, and when the European Community (EC) was founded in 1958 it became a directorate-general of the European Commission. Eurostat supplies statistics to other directorates as well as to the Commission and other European institutions so they can define, implement, and analyze their policies.

As EC policies developed, Eurostat's role changed. Now, for example, collecting data for the EMU and developing statistical systems in EU candidate countries are more important than they were 10 years ago.

In 1997, the Council of the European Union adopted a Statistical Law that defines the division of responsibility between national statistical authorities and Eurostat. That same year, Eurostat's role was also clarified and made part of the Amsterdam Treaty. It reaffirmed the need for Community statistics to follow fundamental principles to ensure that the statistics are scientifically independent, transparent, impartial, reliable, pertinent, and cost effective.

Since the early days of the Community, it was recognized that decisions must be based on reliable and comparable statistics. So the European Statistical System (ESS) was developed gradually, with the objective of providing comparable statistics at EU level. The ESS includes Eurostat and the statistical offices, ministries, agencies, and central banks that collect official statistics in Member States (along with Iceland, Norway, and Liechtenstein). The ESS functions as a statistics network. With Eurostat leading the way in the harmonization of statistics ESS concentrates mainly on EU policy areas. But as the scope of EU policies has grown, harmonization has been extended to nearly all statistical fields. The ESS also coordinates its work with international organizations such as the Organisation for Economic Co-operation and Development, the United Nations, the International Monetary Fund, and the World Bank.

At the heart of the ESS is the Statistical Programme Committee, which is chaired by Eurostat and brings together the heads of Member States' national statistical offices. They focus on issues involved in making member data compatible including the development of common classifications, methodology, and definitions; implementation of common statistical surveys based on harmonized methods; and collection, analysis and dissemination of statistical data for the EU, including comparisons between countries and regions.

Key programs include the European System of Accounts (which defines the accounting rules and concepts for Member States); Intrastat (a way to measure trade within the EU after the abolition of customs formalities); the Prodcom classification of industrial statistics (the harmonized system for product classification); a Community Labour Force Survey; and the harmonised indexes of consumer prices (used to measure EU inflation and one of the convergence criteria for countries participating in EMU).

Located in Luxembourg, Eurostat publishes an annual release calendar, which usually is available in mid-November of the preceding year. However, changes are frequently made with relatively short notice. It is imperative to check each Friday to see if the release dates for the coming week have been confirmed. Data are usually released at 11 A.M. local time, which translates to 5 A.M. ET. Eurostat has an e-mail service that notifies participants of key statistics and research paper releases. However, they arrive late in the day, usually about 12 hours after the data are released. That is about 4:30 P.M. ET and later. In contrast, one can receive e-mails from U.S. statistical agencies within a few minutes of the indicator's release.

GROSS DOMESTIC PRODUCT

GDP is calculated using the European System of Accounts 1995 (ESA95), which were derived from and are wholly compatible with the Standard National Accounts (SNAs). Eurostat publishes a flash estimate of the year-on-year percent change of aggregate GDP about six weeks after the end of the quarter, generally based on flash estimates from Germany, France, Spain, Italy, the Netherlands, Finland, Belgium, Austria, and Greece. For example, first quarter 2006 GDP flash was released on May 11, 2006. The first estimates, which contained detailed information, were released on June 1, and the second estimate was available on July 12. In contrast, U.S. GDP advance for the same quarter, and with most detail, was available on March 30, the preliminary on April 28, and the final on June 29. Figure 9.1 tracks EMU GDP performance.

A Change in Methodology

Eurostat changed to chain-weighted calculations with the release of third-quarter 2005 GDP data. This is something that analysts have long been

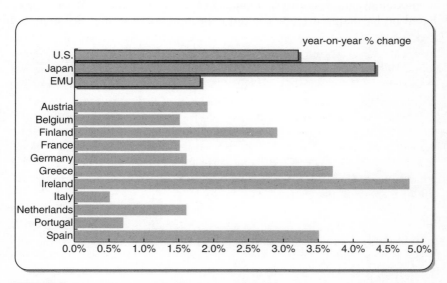

FIGURE 9.1 A comparison of growth rates for the fourth quarter of 2005 shows that only EMU members Ireland and Spain matched or exceeded the United States and Japan.
Source: Eurostat and Haver Analytics.

seeking—comparability of statistics across country borders. The United Kingdom, Japan, the United States, Canada, and Australia are among the nations that now use chain-link methodology. The United States has been using it since 1996, while Canada has since 2001 and the United Kingdom since 2003. Japan switched methodologies only at the end of 2004, while Germany changed with first-quarter 2005 GDP. And slowly but surely, other EU members are changing as well. The downside, as with any change, is that analysts are forced to relearn history yet again.

When Eurostat changed to chain weights for its third-quarter 2005 GDP release, they also combined it with another important step that helped bring EU data more in line with international standards—the allocation of financial intermediation services indirectly measured (FISIM) to user sectors or industries. Most EU members, with the notable exceptions of Italy and France, implemented both new methods in 2005. Italy changed methodology in March 2006. The differing implementation dates has had an impact on data comparability and on the availability of time series data during the transition. To confuse things further, France did not implement the FISIM and chain-weighted methodology at the same time. The country waited until May 2006 to adapt quarterly chain GDP—but did not make the FISIM changes at that time.

Financial intermediaries provide services for which customers may or may not be charged explicitly. The latter are known in national accounts lingo as the financial intermediation services indirectly measured (FISIM). In this case, service income is generated by paying or charging different rates of interest to borrowers and lenders. Until recently, FISIM was not allocated to the sectors/industries that consumed the service, neither as final nor as intermediate consumption. Instead, using a simplifying assumption, all FISIM was recorded as intermediate consumption of a notional industry.

EU legislation required the change in order to improve GDP measurement. FISIM must be allocated to user sectors/industries. Studies indicate that GDP levels are expected to increase by as much as 1 percent to 1.5 percent, but will vary across Member States. No systematic effect on growth rates is expected, however.

During 2005 and 2006, most EU members will have converted to chain linking for their national accounts statistics. Chained volume measures are expressed as index numbers with a reference year of 2000. Analysts should be aware that chain linking results in the loss of additivity of volume data (except for the data relating to the reference year). This means that in chained-level series GDP components do not add up to total GDP. The chained level of an aggregate is not equal to the sum of the chained parts. Nonadditivity is also relevant for geographical aggregations such as those for the EMU and EU.

For the more recent years, the changeover to chain linking is expected to reduce volume growth for GDP and most of its components marginally. This is because fast-growing product groups such as information and communication technology tend to be those where prices increase less than average or decline. Therefore, when GDP volume growth is calculated using more recent weights, the product groups with strong output growth get a lower weight, resulting in a lower GDP volume growth of about 0.2 percentage points for annual GDP growth rates compared to a system with a fixed base year. The effect for GDP components may, however, be larger, albeit canceling out to a large extent at aggregate level.

To those with a precision bias, even the eventual release of the EU's reconfigured data still will not give 100 percent comparability due to definitional differences between countries in and out of the EU and variations in the methodology itself. And the staggered introduction of the new FISIM and chain methodologies in the various Member States only postpones the day of true data comparability. Investors will just have to wait a little longer for the day when they can compare opportunities without regard to geographical divisions! After the changeover, historic data will be limited. The reason is simply the limited availability of back data at the national level.

In the EMU press release, data are available on a level basis in euros, a quarter-on-quarter percent change and a year–on–year percent change for one year. Eurostat does not provide annualized growth data. U.S. GDP is also available in this format, but the preferred measure is on an annualized percent change basis. Historical data in the U.S. press release go back four years; for the EMU, one year. Table 9.1 shows the major categories of GDP.

TABLE 9.1　Gross Domestic Product

Gross domestic product
Final consumption expenditure
Private final consumption
Government final consumption
Gross capital formation
Gross fixed capital formation
Agriculture, fishing, and forestry
Metal products and machinery
Transport equipment
Housing
Other construction
Other products
Change in business inventories and acquisitions less disposals of valuables
Net exports of goods and services
Exports of goods and services
Imports of goods and services

Source: Eurostat.

Data availablity in the Eurostat GDP press release nowhere approaches what U.S. data watchers are accustomed to reviewing in the Bureau of Economic Analysis (BEA) GDP press release. Eurostat has built a framework based on the SNA reporting system discussed in the previous chapter. The BEA does not use SNAs in building GDP data—it uses National Income and Product Account methodology—but does present U.S. GDP data annually on an SNA basis for the OECD. Eurostat is more intent on presenting geographical growth rates. Therefore, the data are aggregated in several ways, including for the EU as well as the EMU. Data are presented for each Member State as well.

PRICES

Harmonized Index of Consumer Prices

One of the most important indicators produced by Eurostat is the harmonized index of consumer prices. The HICP, which is available monthly, is an internationally comparable measure of inflation calculated by each Member State using a specific formula. Since January 1999, the European Central Bank (ECB) has used the HICP as its target measure of inflation and one of its two pillars of monetary policy (the second is money supply). As discussed earlier, the ECB adheres strictly to its inflation target of under 2 percent as measured by the HICP, much to the chagrin of some policy makers over the last few years.

Consumer price indexes are constructed to measure the changes over time in the prices of consumer goods and services acquired, used, or paid for by households. HICPs are specifically designed for international comparisons of consumer price inflation. They are used in the assessment of inflation convergence as required by the Treaty of Amsterdam for prospective EU members. The coverage of the HICPs is defined in terms of "household final monetary consumption expenditure," which refers to the European System of Accounts (ESA 1995) national accounts concepts.

Each Member State has its own HICP, and at European level there are aggregate indexes with different geographical coverage. For example, the Monetary Union Index of Consumer Prices has the narrowest coverage of only eurozone countries. The European Economic Area Index of Consumer Prices has the widest coverage of all Member States plus Iceland and Norway. The European Index of Consumer Prices measures the annual inflation in the EU. However, the key market-moving inflation measure is the HICP for EMU members only.

In addition to the geographic breakdowns, which are available in the press release, there are also special aggregate indexes for goods, services, and energy in addition to various core HICP measures available elsewhere. The most common core measure excludes energy, alcohol, food, and tobacco. A flash report is issued at the end of the month based on preliminary data from Germany, France, and Italy plus energy prices. This report consists of one number—the year-on-year percent change. For example, the flash report for March 2006 was available on March 31. A final report is issued about three weeks later. The final report for March 2006 was published on April 20.

Historically, HICPs have been published since March 1997. However, interim indexes, (which were based on existing CPIs and adjusted to reduce differences in coverage of goods and services between the various national indexes) are available back to 1995 or 1996. Historical series, also based on national CPI series but with a limited number of indexes, are available back to the early 1990s for a number of Member States. Figure 9.2 shows the variation in the rate of inflation in the EMU countries.

It should be noted that all of the countries maintain their national CPI for domestic purposes. Many cost-of-living adjustments and union contracts are pegged to these national indexes. In the United Kingdom, for example,

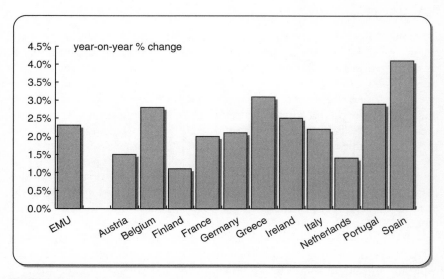

FIGURE 9.2 Despite the huge increase in crude oil prices, inflation in the EMU remained relatively tame in February 2006.
Source: Eurostat and Haver Analytics.

the CPI as calculated using HICP methodology is used solely for monetary policy purposes. It was one of the criteria laid out by the Labour government for joining the EMU.

In March 2006, the Bureau of Labor Statistics introduced an experimental HICP for the United States for international comparison purposes. The index follows European methodology. The HICP differs in scope and coverage from the U.S. CPI. For example, the U.S. CPI covers only urban areas, while the HICP includes rural areas as well. But most importantly, the U.S. CPI includes owner-occupied housing (and carries an impressive weight of 23.4 percent in the index), while it is not included in the HICP. This element has made an important difference in the UK calculations of the HICP as well, and therefore an index reading lower for both countries than they would be otherwise. And the series produces data that really is not reflective of either economy. This is one of the ongoing issues in trying to make international comparisons and a reason why EU members have not discarded their national indexes. The HICP calculation is a geometric rather than an arithmetic formula, but both methods are still used in the EU. Eurostat has confirmed that they are working on adding "owners' equivalent rent" to their housing component. They said they hope to incorporate this change by June 2007.

Producer Price Index

Like the CPI, Eurostat's producer price index (PPI) is also harmonized across the EMU and the larger EU membership. PPIs provide another layer of information on inflation and can be an early warning of inflationary pressures building in the economy. They also record the evolution of prices over longer periods of time. PPIs report on input prices or commodity prices and can tell whether producers are able to pass through increases in costs to their customers. For example, at the end of 2005, many producers found that they were unable to pass through soaring fuel costs and were forced in many cases to absorb these costs at the expense of profits. This was particularly true in many of the EMU countries where consumption was weak and producers could not increase prices. PPIs are business-cycle indicators, showing the monthly development of transaction prices of economic activities. As with CPIs, Member States publish PPI estimates on a national basis.

The output price index measures the average prices of all goods and related services. The indicators of domestic and nondomestic prices require separate output price indexes to be compiled according to the destination of the product. The destination is determined by the residency of the third party that has ordered or purchased the product. The domestic market is defined as third parties resident in the same national territory as the observation unit. The PPI excludes construction. A core index excluding construction and energy is also available, as are indexes for capital goods, intermediate goods, consumer goods, and intermediate and capital goods Separate indexes are also available for energy and mining, quarrying and manufacturing. Figure 9.3 below shows the wide disparity of producer price changes between EMU members.

The price indexes are calculated as a weighted average with the base year of 2000. The price measured is the ex-factory price that includes all duties and taxes on the goods and services invoiced but excludes the value added tax (VAT) invoiced and other similar deductible taxes directly linked to turnover. Transport costs are included in order to show the true evolution of price movements. In addition, the price is the actual transaction price, not a list price, and takes into account product quality changes. Prices are classified using NACE Revision 1 (EU classification system).

Data are published for the EMU, the EU and for each country separately, if available. Data are collected by the Member States and sent to Eurostat for the reference calendar month in raw, unadjusted form. Data are revised when additional information from national statistical authorities becomes available. PPI data become available about five weeks after the end of the

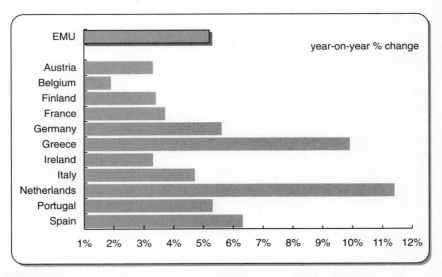

FIGURE 9.3 Producer output prices also for February 2006 give another perspective on EMU inflation. These data show that crude oil price increases were not necessarily passed on to consumers, but were absorbed by producers. *Source:* Eurostat and Haver Analytics.

TABLE 9.2   Producer Price Index

Industry total and market groups
   Mining and quarrying
   Manufacturing
      Food products, beverages and tobacco
      Textile and textile products
      Leather and leather products
      Wood and wood products
      Pulp, paper, publishing and printing
      Coke, refined petroleum products and nuclear fuel
      Chemicals and manmade fibers
      Rubber and plastic products
      Other nonmetallic mineral products
      Basic metals and fabricated metal products
      Machinery and equipment (not elsewhere classified)
      Electrical and optical equipment
      Transport equipment
      Manufacturing (not elsewhere classified)
      Electricity, gas and water supply

Source: Eurostat.

reference month. For example, March 2006 data were released on May 3. Table 9.2 illustrates the typical industrial breakdowns for which PPI data are available.

LABOUR FORCE

Labour force data encompass several critical components—employment, unemployment, and sometimes, earnings. Because these data usually are available sooner than most other economic data, they are coveted by investors looking for the latest information. Eurostat data are available about five weeks after the reference month and much later than the country data. The monthly press release focuses only on the unemployment rate, even though employment data are produced for both a monthly and a quarterly report.

Unemployment

Unemployment data are expressed both as a numerical value and as a percent. Generally, the definition of those unemployed follows that of the International Labour Organisation (ILO). It states that an unemployed person is one between the ages of 15 and 74 years of age who was not employed during the reference week, had actively sought work during the past four weeks, and was ready to begin working immediately or within two weeks. The unemployment rate measures the number of unemployed as a percentage of the total number of active persons in the labor market. Active persons are those who are either employed or unemployed. Data are broken down by sex and age. Figure 9.4 shows the large variation in unemployment rates among EMU members.

Eurostat provides an unemployment rate for each EU country as well as for the EMU and EU as a whole. It should be noted that the unemployment rate for a country will frequently differ with that reported by the national statistics agency. That is because of the varying interpretations of the ILO definition by Member States and Eurostat. Data are revised when additional information becomes available. Eurostat data are available about five weeks after the reference month. For example, March 2006 data were released on May 3. The lag between EU data and national data can be substantial. For example, German national labor force data for March 2006 were available on March 30.

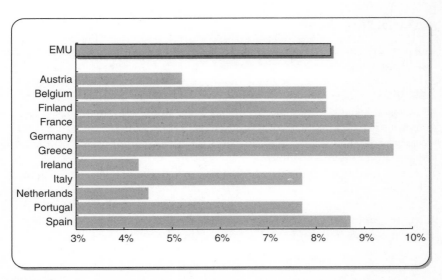

FIGURE 9.4 Unemployment remains a problem in most of the EMU. The stickiness in unemployment rates as illustrated by January 2006 data, is usually blamed on the reluctance of the respective member governments to initiate structural reforms in the labour market.
Source: Eurostat and Haver Analytics.

Labour Cost Index

The Labour Cost Index is a quarterly indicator that measures cost pressures arising from labor input to the production process. These data are available about 12 weeks after the end of the reference quarter. The data covered relate to total average hourly labor costs (with and without bonuses) along with wages and salaries and employers' social security contributions plus taxes paid minus subsidies received by the employer. Data are broken down by cost items and by economic activity.

OUTPUT

Output data are important for those countries that are especially dependent on exports to grow. Therefore, analysts watch these data closely for industry trends as well as overall macroeconomic growth. Production statistics measure the quantity and/or value of goods and their related industrial services. The goal is to show in a representative manner the short-term development of individual industries and of industry as a whole.

Industrial Production

Industrial production (IP) measures changes in the volume of output. The industrial production index provides a measure of the volume trend in value added at factor cost over a given reference period, excluding VAT and other similar deductible taxes. The preferred number is industrial production excluding construction. As with other Eurostat statistics, the data are provided by the national statistics offices. NACE Revision 1 is used to classify the data. Figure 9.5 shows the divergence of industrial production growth among EMU members.

Data are published for the eurozone, the EU and for each country separately, if data are available. It should be noted that EMU data up to the end of 2000 cover 11 Member States and then 12 with Greece's entry at the beginning of 2001. The eurozone is treated as an entity regardless of its composition. For analytical purposes, and for the convenience of users, there is a series that covers historic time series for the 11 Member States plus Greece, starting before the year 2001. On January 1, 2007, when Slovenia becomes a member of the EMU, the number will increase to 13. Data are released approximately six weeks after the reference month. For example, March 2006 data were available on May 17. Table 9.3 illustrates the industries for which IP data are available.

Data collection is carried out by Member States through statistical questionnaires and is sent to Eurostat no later than one month and 15

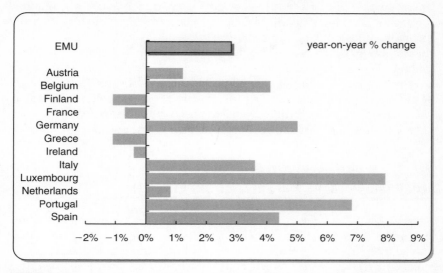

FIGURE 9.5   Improvements in industrial output excluding construction (Eurostat's favored measure) proved spotty despite the improving overall outlook in December 2005.
Source: Eurostat and Haver Analytics.

TABLE 9.3   Industrial Production

Industry totals
    Mining and quarrying
    Electricity, gas and water supply
    Construction
    Manufacturing
        Food products, beverages and tobacco
        Textile and textile products
        Leather and leather products
        Wood and wood products
        Pulp, paper, publishing and printing
        Coke, refined petroleum products and nuclear fuel
        Chemicals and manmade fibers
        Rubber and plastic products
        Other nonmetallic mineral products
        Basic metals and fabricated metal products
        Machinery and equipment (not elsewhere classified)
        Electrical and optical equipment
        Transport equipment
        Manufacturing (not elsewhere classified) and recycling

---

Source: Eurostat.

days after the end of the reference period. Member States are required to transmit working day adjusted series. They are encouraged to transmit seasonally adjusted data and trend-cycle indexes as well. Data are revised when additional information from national statistical authorities becomes available. Working day adjusted data are used to calculate a weighted mean in order to compile working day adjusted EMU and EU series. The weight for aggregating this index among Member States is generally value added, and comes from information from structural business statistics or from other statistics. Weights are revised every five years, and the current base year is 2000.

MERCHANDISE TRADE AND BALANCE OF PAYMENTS

External trade statistics are an important data source for many public- and private-sector decision makers. EU data are unique in that they cover both extra- and intra-European trade. External trade is the exchange of goods and services with non-EU countries. Intra-European trade describes the trade of goods and services within the members of the EU. While no one discounts the importance of intra-EU trade, analysts tend to focus on trade with the rest of the world. This is also true for the individual countries. For example, German trade with the rest of the world is monitored closely as a measure of economic growth prospects given the country's dependency on trade to grow. The same can be said for Italy.

At the EU level, external trade data are extensively used for multilateral and bilateral negotiations within the common EU commercial policy, to define and implement antidumping policy for example. It is also used to evaluate the progress of the EMU as an entity and many other policies. These data are an essential source for the balance of payments and national accounts statistics. Figure 9.6 shows the trade balance of the EMU with the rest of the world.

Merchandise Trade

External trade statistics cover both extra- and intra-EU trade. Extra-EU statistics cover trade of goods between a member and a nonmember country, while intra-EU trade statistics cover trade of goods between members. Goods include all movable property, including electric current. External trade data are published for the EMU as a whole, the EU-25 (all members) and the EU-15 (original members), as well as for each Member State separately. Data usually are provided by the traders on a customs basis for extra-EU trade and intrastat basis for intra-EU declarations. They are compiled by the appropriate national entities according to a harmonized methodology

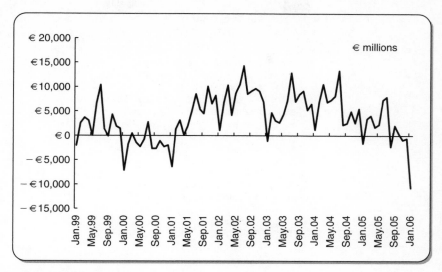

FIGURE 9.6 Unadjusted merchandise goods trade balance was negative at the end of 2005 and creates questions about the strength of demand outside the EU for European goods.
Source: Eurostat and Haver Analytics.

established by EU regulations before transmission to Eurostat. Products are classified by the Standard International Trade Classification (SITC Revision 3) and the Broad Economic Categories (BEC). Table 9.4 is a typical industry breakdown from the merchandise trade report.

Unadjusted data are preferred but seasonally and workday-adjusted data are available also. Merchandise trade data are available about 50 days after the reference month. For example, January 2006 data were available on March 22. Although the press release is brief (about six pages) when compared with the U.S. report of about 48 pages, the report contains data by reporting country, trading partners, and product. Data are revised frequently according to national needs and practices. They become final from six months up to possibly three years after the reference period (depending on the Member State).

Balance of Payments

Balance of Payments (BOP) data summarize harmonized information on all international transactions between residents and nonresidents of a country or of a geographical region during a given period. These transactions are part of the current account (goods, services, income, current transfers) and

TABLE 9.4 Merchandise Trade

Total
Manufactured products
Machinery and transport equipment
Chemicals and related products
Other manufactured goods
Manufactured goods classified by material
Miscellaneous manufactured articles
Raw materials
Crude materials (inedible fuels)
Animal & vegetable oils, fats and waxes
Mineral fuels, lubricants
Food, drinks and tobacco
Food and live animals
Beverages and tobacco
Goods n.e.s
Intra Euro-zone dispatches (exports)

Source: Eurostat.

also include transactions that fall in the capital and the financial accounts. Even though the BOP is an important macroeconomic indicator that can be used to assess the position of an economy with the rest of the world, analysts pay more attention to the merchandise trade reports than to the BOP. The ECB prepares monthly reports on extra-euro area transactions for the EMU only. These data are available about two months after the reference period. The first estimate of quarterly data is prepared by the ECB and released by Eurostat and is available about 10 weeks after the reference period. The complete quarterly data are available four months after the reference period.

M3 MONEY SUPPLY

While other central banks have virtually ignored money supply data, the ECB has not. Thanks to the influence of the Bundesbank in organizing the ECB, M3 money supply has become one of the "two pillars" of monetary policy used by the ECB, the other being the HICP. While the target for HICP is under 2 percent, the target for M3 growth is 4.5 percent as measured by a three-month moving average, which is compared with the same three months a year earlier. See Figure 9.7 for a picture of M3 growth. Single-month data are also available. The data on a national level are broadly compatible with international accounting standards as compiled by national central banks.

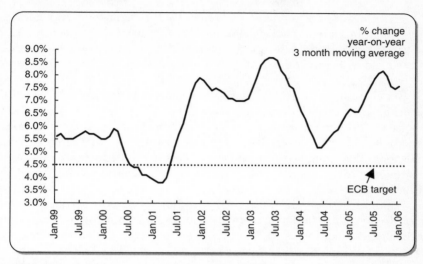

FIGURE 9.7   M3 is one of the two pillars of ECB monetary policy. A reason that the ECB was reluctant to lower interest rates below 2 percent was the abundant liquidity avaiable to the banking system as M3 expanded at a much faster pace than the Bank's 4.5 percent target rate of growth.
Source: ECB and Haver Analytics.

M3 measures overall money supply. It consists of M1, which is currency in circulation plus overnight deposits, and M2, which includes deposits with an agreed maturity up to two years plus deposits redeemable at up to three months notice. Not all M3 measures are alike. For example, ECB M3 is approximately equivalent to the Federal Reserve's M2 measure. Therefore, the brouhaha over the discontinuance of M3 data for the United States in the first quarter of 2006 missed the point—the two measures differ in scope.

The ECB compiles the money supply figures and they are available about a month after the reference month. For example, March 2006 data were available on May 2.

RETAIL SALES

Retail sales is an important indicator of domestic consumer demand and is monitored closely by analysts as an important input to GDP data. The data are available in both value and volume measures, although the press release deals only with volume. The base year is 2000. Unlike the United States and Canada, auto sales are not included in the retail sales data. Rather, auto vehicle sales are reported separately by the number of registrations rather than in monetary terms and are available from the Association des Constructeurs Européens d'Automobiles (ACEA), the European association of car makers. Figure 9.8 is a snapshot of the relative health of retail sales in the EMU.

Retail turnover is defined as goods and services market sales to third parties. Turnover includes all duties and taxes on the goods or services invoiced with the exception of the VAT and other similar deductible taxes directly linked to turnover. Turnover also includes all other charges (e.g., transport, packaging) passed on to the customer. Reductions in prices, rebates, and discounts, as well as the value of returned packing, must be deducted. Price reductions, rebates, and bonuses conceded later to clients, for example, at the end of the year, are not taken into account. Retail sales also include manufactured goods sales along with invoiced charges for packaging, installation, and transport but exclude items such as commission, leases, rentals, license fees, property sales, and so on. The data are available about five weeks after the reference month. For example, March 2006 data were available on May 4. Table 9.5 shows the various categories included in the report.

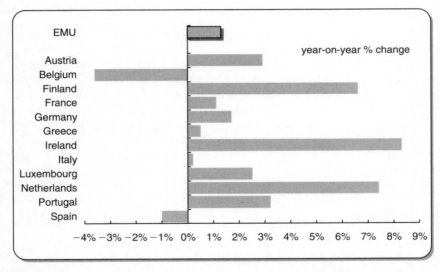

FIGURE 9.8 Continued weak domestic consumer demand especially in the big three countries of Germany, France, and Italy is a major reason why EMU growth has been anemic. The retail trade data are for January 2006.
Source: Eurostat and Haver Analytics.

TABLE 9.5 Retail Trade

Retail sales volume index (2000 = 100)
Food, drinks and tobacco
Sale in nonspecialized stores
Sale in specialized stores
Nonfood products
Textiles, clothing, footwear and leather goods
Household goods
Books, newspapers and other sales in specialized stores
Pharmaceutical and medical goods
Other sale in nonspecialized stores
Mail orders

Source: Eurostat.

In order to eliminate the price effect, data are deflated by a price index that is similar to the PPI and adapted to the particularities of retail trade but reflect price changes in the goods sold rather than the service provided. Goods are classified using the NACE Revision 1. Data are published for the EMU, the EU and for each country separately, if data are available. Member States are asked to transmit seasonally adjusted data and trend-cycle indexes. Data are revised when additional information from national statistical authorities becomes available.

EU BUSINESS AND CONSUMER SENTIMENT SURVEY

Unlike the other data described above, this survey is conducted by the EU. The official source is European Commission business and economic surveys, published in European Economy, Supplement B, by the Directorate-General for Economic & Financial Affairs. The index is a broad measure of both business and consumer sentiment in all EU Member States. Data are available for each country and are aggregated for EMU members only and for all EU members. Because of its coverage, it is highly regarded in the financial markets as a good indicator of the mood of consumers and industry in each country. Figure 9.9 is a sample of one month's sentiment for EMU members.

Confidence indicators are calculated for industry, services, construction, retail trade, and consumers. In turn, they are combined into an overall composite economic sentiment indicator (ESI). The data are seasonally adjusted and defined as the difference (in percentage points of total answers) between positive and negative answers. The overall index is a weighted average of these components. A mean index level is imposed by setting

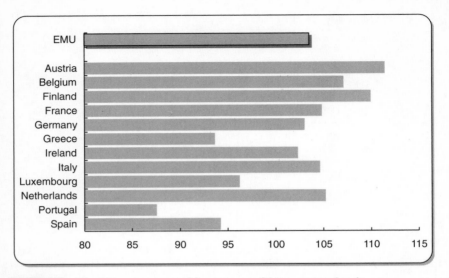

FIGURE 9.9   The EU consumer and business confidence survey has been more positive in the first quarter of 2006 even though growth continues to lag. *Source:* European Community and Haver Analytics.

the long-term average equal to 100. Values greater than 100 indicate an above-average economic sentiment whereas values below 100 indicate a below-average economic sentiment. It is published on the last working day of the reporting month.

Private Surveys

There are numerous private, nongovernmental surveys published in the EMU. Probably the most highly regarded are the purchasing managers' surveys. The surveys are available for both manufacturing and services industries and are prepared by NTC Research in the United Kingdom. They are published on the first and third business days of each month, respectively. Historical data are available on a subscriber basis only. Given the lag before government data are available, these are widely followed in the financial markets as an early harbinger of things to come.

The next sections of this chapter are devoted to the national statistics of Germany, France, and Italy. While they all comply with EMU criteria, some of these indicators are unique to these countries and are watched closely by investors. The French and German Web sites are bilingual for the most part. The German Federal Statistical Office has a good deal of descriptive material in English, but key reports with detail such as the GDP report are in German. The same holds true for France, but in French. In Italy, all reports are in Italian. A couple of years ago, the Italian statistical agency Istituto Nazionale di Statistica (ISTAT) modernized its web site. The old web site had a good deal of English material on it, but the new one has only the calendar in English. Therefore, it is a good idea to subscribe to a data service to escape the pain of trying to find the information if you cannot read Italian. A partial solution for the tables that are not in English is to have them translated once and then use them as a template for future releases. (for example, I did that with the Japanese GDP table.)

GERMANY

Germany had long been considered the engine of growth in Europe. However, it has been struggling for the past several years. The economy has been dependent on exports to grow because of anemic domestic consumption. Yet analysts still expect Germany to lead the EMU out of its malaise. Therefore, it is not surprising that analysts avidly study German data as reflective of the EMU as a whole. Data that draw particular attention are manufacturing orders, industrial production, and merchandise trade, along with the private surveys, including the ZEW and Ifo sentiment indexes, and the purchasing manager indexes.

German influence is evident in the evolution of EMU institutions. The Bundesbank, for example, served as a model for the design and formation of the ECB and its policies. While several of the EU member countries have outperformed the German economy, it remains as one of the most powerful. It was the largest of the organizing countries, and its economy still carries a heavy weight in EU calculations.

While the country's data conform for the most part to Eurostat standards, there are idiosyncrasies. National data are issued by both the Federal Statistical Office (Statistisches Bundesamt Deutschland) and the Deutsche Bundesbank (the German central bank). The Statistical Office is more user friendly for non-German-speaking data seekers. Recently, the Statistical Office has been upgrading its data. For example, little by little, it is doing away with the separate statistics for East and West, which had been a fixture of economic data since reunification back in the early 1990s. Surprise unannounced midmonth revisions are going away as well. Rather, revisions are being incorporated in the next month's release as they are in the United States. While a bilingual release calendar is now available, many of the dates are approximate, stating that the release will be available after a certain date. Every Friday, the Statistical Office releases a firm calendar for the following week, even though some indicators such as the consumer price index are not announced until immediately before release time. Most data are released at 2:00 A.M. ET.

However, it still pays to know German. Most statistical data such as GDP from the Bundesbank are in German.

Until recently, a unique feature of these data had been that two different agencies would release the same data and they would differ. The primary difference between the Statistical Office and Bundesbank was in their seasonal adjustment methodology. The Statistical Office still uses the so-called Berlin method but now also uses the U.S. Census Arima X12 method as well—the same as the Bundesbank. As a result, most data no longer differ. But market watchers still prefer Bundesbank data because they are used in GDP calculations. The release time for the Bundesbank version is generally sometime after that of the Statistical Office.

Gross Domestic Product (Bruttoinlandsprodukt)

In an effort to release data in a timelier manner, the flash report for GDP was created. The data are now available about six weeks after a quarter's end (first-quarter 2006 flash GDP was released on May 11). The flash release consists of one number—year-on-year percent change. The first of three subsequent releases for a given quarter is available about 10 days later. This release includes data on the composition of growth. Because of its size and position within the EMU, economic performance is watched closely. The economy has been struggling because of structural rigidities, especially in the labor market, that has put it at a competitive disadvantage. Germany changed to chain methodology to calculate GDP in 2005. Data are available only from 1991. With this revision, Germany moved from fixed 1995 prices to chained prices with a reference year of 2000. Figure 9.10 shows GDP back to 1992. Major revisions generally occur about every five to 10 years to introduce new concepts, definitions, classifications, and so on in the accounting system; and modernize the way of presentation and introduce new terms where necessary.

Price Measures

Consumer Price Index (Verbraucherpreisindex)   Germany, like other EMU countries, has both a national CPI and a harmonized index of consumer prices. The HICP is calculated to give a comparable inflation measure for the EMU. Components and weights within the national CPI vary and reflect national idiosyncrasies. The preliminary release is based on key state numbers, which are released prior to the national estimate. The states include North Rhine-Westphalia, Baden-Württemberg, Saxony,

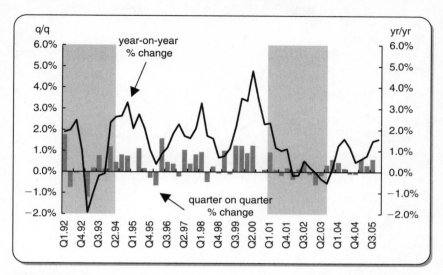

FIGURE 9.10   The German economy is a shadow of its vibrant past, when it was Europe's engine of growth. The graph shows a dramatic slowdown in GDP growth since 2001.
Source: Statistical Office (Statisches Bundesamt) and Haver Analytics.

Hesse, Bavaria, and Brandenburg. The release date is not announced in advance, but the preliminary estimate of the CPI follows the state releases by a day or two. The data are revised and considered final about two weeks after preliminary release.

While the CPI is a national inflation measure, the HICP is more of an international or intra-European measure of inflation. Its calculation relies on harmonized concepts, methods, and procedures, but reflects price developments in the individual states and based on national consumption patterns.

The CPI is based on the international Classification of Individual Consumption by Purpose. The same prices are used to calculate both price measures. An important difference between the national CPI and the HICP is that the national CPI includes owner-occupied residential property and motor vehicle tax while the HICP does not.

A provisional and a final result are released for both the CPI and HICP. While the first estimate is published around the 25th day of a calendar month, the final result is released between the 10th and the 15th day of the month following the reference month. The provisional data are released during the day, so no specific time is available. The final data are usually

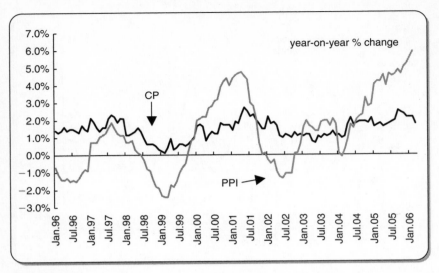

FIGURE 9.11 Producer prices have soared due to crude oil and commodity price increases while the consumer price index has remained cosistent within a narrow range
Source: Deutsche Bundesbank and Haver Analytics.

available at about 2 A.M. ET. Figure 9.11 shows year-on-year percent changes for the CPI and PPI.

Index of Producer Prices for Industrial Products (Index der Erzeugerpreise)

The index of producer prices measures price changes at an early stage in the economic process and therefore serves as an indicator of future inflation trends. The producer price index (PPI) and its subindexes are often used in business contracts for the adjustment of recurring payments. They also are used to deflate other economic statistics such as the production indexes. It should be noted that the PPI excludes construction.

The PPI for industrial products (domestic sales) measures prices for products that are produced in mining and manufacturing or in the energy and water industries and are sold within the country. The reference quantity for the overall index is the total domestic turnover of industrial products in the base year. In other words, these price statistics cover both the sales of industrial products to domestic buyers at different stages in the economic process and the sales between industrial enterprises.

The index is based on a total of about 13,000 individual price series which are indexed on the base year of 2000. The prices are transaction prices, not list prices, and exclude turnover tax. The PPI uses the same methodology as the CPI, is a Laspeyres price index. A characteristic feature of this index is that it reflects the price changes over time without quantity changes.

Monthly results are published in a press release around the 20th day of the following month. For example, data for March 2006 were available on April 19. The index is published for a large number of individual products at different aggregation levels. There are indexes for the major industrial groups including intermediate goods, investment goods, consumer goods and energy and core indexes that exclude energy.

Labor Markets (Erwerbstätige, Erwerbsoise, Erwerbslosenquoten/ILO-Arbeitsmarkstatistik)

Analysts in Germany and Europe tend to focus on the number of Germans out of work rather than the unemployment rate as we do in the United States. However, it is difficult to get a meaningful grasp of the numeric change and what it means. While the distinction between East and West German data is disappearing for other indicators, they are still a feature of the unemployment data. Therefore, data are available for East, West, and all of Germany.

A snag to understanding German unemployment data comes from the fact that there are several measures of unemployment bandied about when the data are released. Unemployment rates calculated by the Bundesbank are preferred, but some German analysts prefer the unadjusted rates, which are also published. And then there are still different rates for unemployment that are used by Eurostat to compute their unemployment rate. The spread between the Bundesbank rates and Eurostat can be quite significant. For example, the July 2005 unemployment rate from the Bundesbank was 11.7 percent, while that used by Eurostat to calculate EMU unemployment was 9.3 percent. The reason for the vast differential is found in the interpretation of the International Labour Organisation definition. Figure 9.12 shows the unemployment rates for the East, West, and all of Germany.

German national unemployment data are based on the number of unemployed persons who are registered with an official government employment office (registered unemployed) and have an official residence in Germany. They can work less than 15 hours a week, however, and still be counted as unemployed. Recent changes in the labor market have moved some people collecting long-term disability to the unemployment rolls, creating a jump in unemployment. As a result, the jobless register jumped by the addition of as many as 360,000 former welfare claimants in 2005. They were forced to register as unemployed under a new law aimed at increasing incentives for those without a job to find work. While German labor data are also

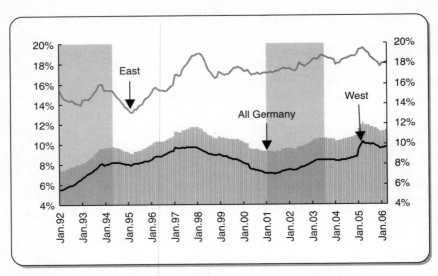

FIGURE 9.12 The labor force remains resistant to change, especially in the East, where the unemployment rate has hovered around 18 percent.
Source: Deutsche Bundesbank and Haver Analytics.

based on the ILO methodology—but with changes—Eurostat calculates harmonized unemployment strictly according to ILO methodology, which excludes people even if they work as little as one hour in the reference week. Unemployment data are available at the end of the reference month March 2006 unemployment data were available on March 30. Until recently, employment data lagged unemployment by two months, however that is no longer so. Employment data are also calculated using ILO methodology. However, there is no detail available that is comparable to that found in the U.S. employment situation report.

Output

Manufacturers' orders and industrial production data are keenly awaited by analysts each month. The data present a detailed breakdown by various sectors and a reading of the pulse of a major sector of the economy.

Manufacturing orders and industrial production data release schedules are known in advance. They are released at 6 A.M. ET within a day or two of each other. Unannounced revisions are no longer published; now they are available with the next release. Data for the reference month are available about five weeks later. For example, data for January 2006 manufacturers' orders were available on March 7, while industrial production data were available the next day. Like the PPI, industrial production data exclude construction, which is the preferred Eurostat measure.

Manufacturers' Orders (Aufragseingangs Umsatzatzindex/verarbeitendes Gewerbe)

The manufacturers' orders data rank high among indicators when monitoring and analyzing German economic well-being. Because these data are available for both foreign and domestic orders, they are a good indication of the relative strength of the domestic and export economies. The results are compiled each month in the form of value indexes to measure the nominal development of demand and in the form of volume indexes to illustrate the price-adjusted development of demand. Unlike in the United States, orders data are not collected for all manufacturing classifications—but only those parts in which the make-to-order production plays a prominent role. Not included are, for example, mining, quarrying, and the food industry. In Figure 9.13, as one would expect, orders and industrial production track each other closely.

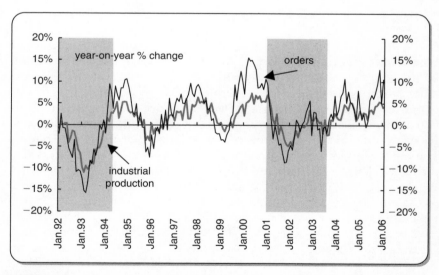

FIGURE 9.13   Industrial production and manufacturing orders are two of the most closely watched data series. Their weakness has translated into slow growth from 2001 through 2005.
Source: Federal Economics and Technology Ministry, Deutche Bundesbank, and Haver Analytics.

Industrial Production (Produktionsindex)

Like the orders data, the production index has the advantage of being available in a timely manner, giving a more current view of business activity. Those responding to the data collection survey account for about 80 percent of total industrial production. Like the PPI, construction is excluded from the data. The base year is 2000 and is classified using NACE, Revision 1.1. Unadjusted data along with working-day and seasonally adjusted data are published. The seasonally adjusted results are prepared in partnership by the Federal Statistical Office and the Bundesbank and delivered to the Federal Ministry of Economics and Technology, who then releases the data.

Merchandise Trade and Balance of Payments

Merchandise trade is vital to the economy because of its reliance on exports to grow. The country runs a large trade surplus, especially with other EU members. Trade with the rest of the world has fluctuated with the value of the euro. In 2003 and 2004 especially, trade was negatively affected by the euro's strength relative to other currencies, along with weak growth in most of the world economy (other than in the United States). A strong currency makes exports more expensive to purchasers and generally reduces demand for exporters' products.

Merchandise Trade (Außenhandel) Foreign trade data describe the cross-border goods transactions between the Federal Republic of Germany and other countries. General trade, as a rule, covers all goods that move into or out of Germany. Special trade, however, covers only goods that are imported into Germany for use, consumption, treatment, or processing, and goods exported that were produced, treated, or processed in the country. The difference consists mainly in not counting imports and exports that arrive or depart via customs and free-zone warehouses.

The relevant surveys are organized and conducted by the Federal Statistical Office using a centralized system. Since January 1, 1993, when internal borders were abolished between EU members, foreign trade data have been collected based on two different concepts. Intracommunity trade statistics cover the trade in goods with other EU Member States. Businesses engaged in foreign trade directly submit their declarations to the Federal Statistical Office. Extra-Community trade statistics or trade with the rest of the world are collected in the traditional way by customs authorities. The results of extra- and intra-Community trade statistics are published together as Germany's foreign trade data. The foreign trade statistics results are used in the Federal Statistical Office in the compilation of the national accounts

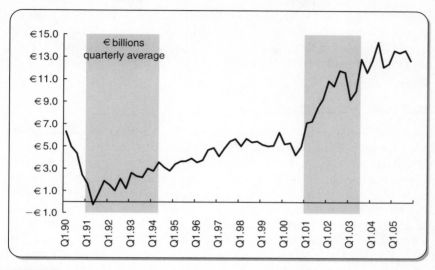

FIGURE 9.14   German exports translated into a healthy merchandise trade surplus. However, export did not carry over to the domestic economy. Slow overall growth was laid at the feet of the domestic economy.
Source: Deutsche Bundesbank and Haver Analytics.

and at the Bundesbank for preparing the balance of payments. Figure 9.14 shows Germany's hefty trade surplus.

Preliminary foreign trade data are released monthly about 40 days after the reference month. For example, February 2006 data were available on April 7. More detailed data in a breakdown by countries and commodity groups become available approximately two weeks later. A calendar is available on the Federal Statistical Office web site but like all other German data, the release date is confirmed on the previous Friday.

Balance of Payments (Zahlungsbilanz)

Germany follows the methodology set out by the IMF's *Balance of Payments Manual,* 5th edition. The data, available monthly in unadjusted and seasonally adjusted formats, include total goods exports and total imports; services exports and imports; net income flows; net current transfers; net capital account; portfolio investment; direct investment; other investment; and the change in official reserve assets. The data are published five to six weeks after the reference month. For example, data for February 2006 were available on April 11. An advance release calendar that gives the approximate or no later than release dates for the coming year, and for January of the following year, is available at the end of September each year on the Deutsche Bundesbank Web site. The precise release dates are announced on Friday of the week prior to the release. The press release is available only in German. Balance of Payments statistics are collected and published by the Deutsche Bundesbank.

Retail Sales (Umsatz/einzelhandel)

Retail sales are a measure of consumer well-being. Weak growth has been put at the feet of the consumer as they remained cautious in light of high unemployment. Lagging retail-sector reforms have not helped either, given the restrictions on shopping hours, for example. Both the Federal Statistical Office and the Bundesbank publish retail trade data. Until recently, there were vast differences between them, primarily because they each used a different seasonal adjustment program. This difference ended when the Statistical Office began using the U.S. Census Arima X12 methodology as well as their Berlin method. Another difference is that the Federal Statistical Office data are generally for total retail sales, while the Bundesbank data features sales excluding autos and petrol stations or excluding only autos. Obviously, everyone has their favorite!

Retail turnover measures retail trade sales in the form of nominal and real (price-adjusted) index numbers and their change rates, rather than

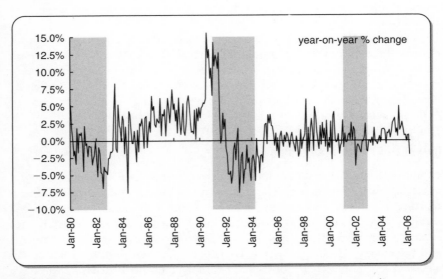

FIGURE 9.15 Germany's weak spot has been lackluster consumer spending.
Source: Deutsche Bundesbank and Haver Analytics.

absolute monetary turnover. The results, which are available both for total retail trade and for its components are based on the NACE classification system and are calendar and seasonally adjusted. The data are based on a sample of about 24,000 retail businesses. The base year, which is updated in five-year intervals, is currently 2000. The preliminary estimate is available about a month after the reference month. For example, March 2006 data were released on May 2. About two weeks later, detailed information is accessible on the Federal Statistical Office web site. Figure 9.15 shows Germany's lackluster retail sales.

Surveys from the Private Sector

As in other European countries, survey data gets analysts' attention primarily because it is available on a much timelier basis than the official data. There are four surveys of great import to those following the German economy—the Ifo Sentiment Survey, the ZEW Indicator of Economic Sentiment, and the manufacturing and services sectors purchasing managers' surveys.

Ifo   The Ifo Sentiment Survey is published by the Ifo Institute. The Institute surveys more than 7,000 enterprises on their appraisals of the business situation, current and future. This German business sentiment index is closely watched as an early harbinger of current conditions and business expectations. It is generally published during the last week of the month for the current month, with more detailed information available about a week later. For example, the April 2006 survey results were available on April 25. It is widely followed in the financial markets as a good indicator of business sentiment. Figure 9.16 tracks business sentiment since 1991.

ZEW   The ZEW Indicator of Economic Sentiment is calculated from the results of the ZEW Financial Market Survey (Finanzmarkttest). The ZEW is followed closely as a precursor and predictor of the Ifo. The data are available the second week of the month for the preceding month. For example, March 2006 data were available on April 11. The series shows the difference between the percentage of financial analysts that are optimistic and those that are pessimistic about the German economy in the next six months. For example, if 30 percent of participants expect the economy to improve within the next six months, 30 percent expect no change, and 40 percent expect it to deteriorate, the series would have a value of minus 10. Therefore, a positive number signifies that the share of optimists outweighs the share of pessimists and vice versa. Figure 9.17 portrays shows the ups and downs over time of sentiment by financial experts.

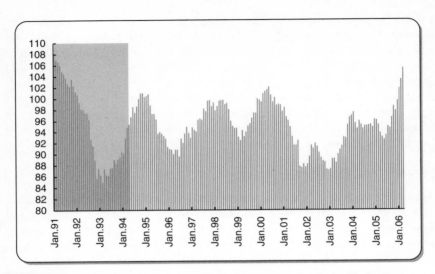

FIGURE 9.16 One of the financial market's favorite surveys is the Ifo business climate index. This business sentiment index is closely watched as an early indicator of current conditions and business expectations.
Source: Ifo and Haver Analytics.

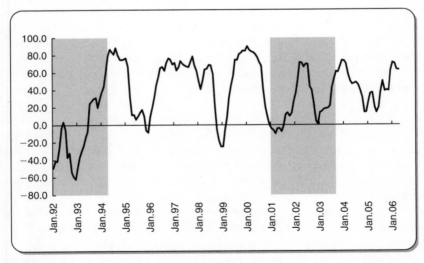

FIGURE 9.17 The ZEW is usually available about a week before the Ifo. Investors hone in on the index as a precursor to the Ifo. However, the ZEW surveys financial experts while the Ifo surveys businesses.
Source: ZEW and Haver Analytics.

PMI The purchasing managers' surveys for manufacturing and services are available on the first and third business days of each month. The index is produced by NTC Research of the United Kingdom and is co-sponsored by the German purchasing managers' organization, BME. The web site is bilingual and can be read in both English and German.

FRANCE

French economic data follow pretty much the same pattern as other EMU countries. There is only one statistics agency—Institut National de la Statistique et des Etudes Economique (INSEE). Much of the information available is in both English and French, but the major reports are available in French only. Release dates are available on INSEE's Web site for a rolling four-month period— in April, a calendar through July was available. Data are usually released about 8:45 A.M. local time or 2:45 A.M. ET.

Gross Domestic Product (Comptes Nationaux Trimestriels)

GDP data have been released in three versions since 2003. INSEE issues a flash GDP report about six weeks after the reference quarter's end in an effort to speed up data availability. The flash GDP report consists of one number—year-on-year percent change. In the past, they also have released a "flash" range (GDP grew 1.5 percent to 2 percent, for example), rather than a precise numerical estimate. Preliminary GDP results are released about 10 days later, with final figures available around 90 days after the end of each quarter. For example, fourth-quarter 2005 flash GDP estimate was released on February 10, with the preliminary data following on February 21. The final GDP report was not available until March 31. France was one of the last of the large EMU countries to change to a chain-weighted methodology for constructing its GDP accounts. It did so with the first-quarter 2006 data on May 19, 2006. Figure 9.18 below depicts GDP growth since 1990.

French Quarterly National Accounts are based on the European System of Accounts 1995 (ESA95) and are compiled using both production and expenditure methods. Data are published on GDP, private consumption, general government consumption, gross fixed-capital formation, and exports and imports of goods and services.

Prices

Prices are monitored closely in France just as in other EMU countries, especially given the ECB's focus on inflation. But while investors probably

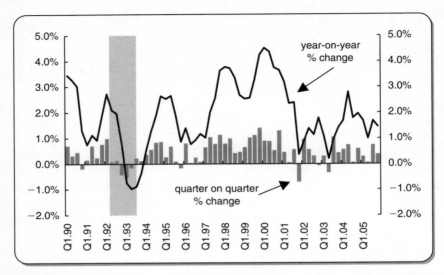

FIGURE 9.18   France was one of the last of the EMU countries to shift its GDP methodology to chain weighting. France has also been struggling economically, but has been better off than Germany mainly due to consumer spending.
Source: INSEE and Haver Analytics.

pay more attention to German data, French data are noted as well, especially given France's role as one of the big three along with Italy.

Consumer Price Index (Indice des Prix à la Consommation)   INSEE issues both a national rate of inflation and the harmonized version for Eurostat as do other members of the EU. The CPI also includes overseas areas, such as Guadeloupe, Martinique, Guyana, and Réunion, with a population greater than 2,000, as well as all mainland France cities. The index covers over 95 percent of final consumption. A seasonally adjusted global index has been published monthly since June 1996. (The HICP has been available since February 1997.) The CPI is constructed using an annually chained Laspeyres-type index with a base year of 1998. The CPI is available about 13 days after the reference month, with the exception of January, when it is not available until 22 days after the end of December. For example, March 2006 CPI data were released on April 13. The data are not revised except in unusual circumstances. Figure 9.19 shows price fluctuations in the CPI and PPI since 2000.

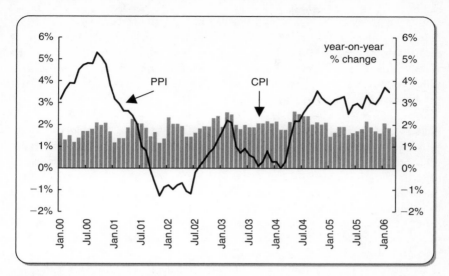

FIGURE 9.19 The PPI is reflecting higher energy and commodity prices while the CPI has managed to stay at or just below the 2 percent inflation ceiling mandated by the ECB.
Source: INSEE and Haver Analytics.

Producer Price Index (PPI) (Indice des Prix á la Production dans l'industrie)
The PPI or IPVI conforms to the general standards set out in Chapter 8. Like the CPI, it is a Laspeyres index but the base year is 2000. About 24,000 domestic ex-factory prices, exclusive of VAT, are collected and classified according to NACE, Revision 1. The nondomestic market has been followed since 2001 and import prices since 2004. The data are available about one month after the reference month. For example, April 2006 PPI was available on May 31.

Labour Force

INSEE measures employment and unemployment using ILO criteria. The unemployment data are available monthly, while employment data are available quarterly.

Employment (Emploi Salarié) Employment data are available quarterly and count the number of employed persons regardless of how long they worked.

Employment estimates include those working in all sectors, excluding agriculture, public services, education, and health services. The data cover all of metropolitan France and Corsica. The data are released about six to seven weeks after the reference quarter. For example, preliminary first-quarter 2006 data were available on May 16, while the revised data were not published until June 15.

Unemployment (Statistiques Mensuelles des Demandeurs d'emploi) Unemployment data cover metropolitan France and Corsica. The seasonally adjusted data are updated monthly, using ILO unemployment criteria to identify the unemployed. Data are based on the results of the annual Labor Force Survey (LFS), carried out in March of each year. They are defined as number of month-end job seekers registered at the Agence Nationale pour l'Emploi (national employment agency, ANPE) and the number of temporary workers. The data are revised once a year when the results of the latest labor force survey are available.

Periodically, the unemployment data are "leaked." Most typically, the data appear late in the afternoon of the day prior to the scheduled release and when the markets are closed. This dulls the market-moving ability,

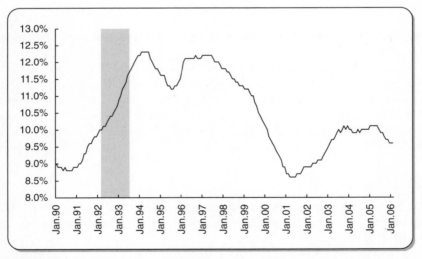

FIGURE 9.20 Unemployment has dropped from its 12.3 percent rate of 10 years ago, but is still hovering around 9.5 percent. While some labor market reforms have occurred, the population has resisted further changes that would introduce more flexibility into the marketplace.
Source: INSEE and Haver Analytics.

especially when the report is worse than expected. Figure 9.20 above tracks the unemployment rate since 1990.

Output

Industrial Production (Indice de la Production Industrielle)   As with most EU output data, the French data exclude construction, the preferred Eurostat number. The industrial production index (IPI) covers manufacturing, mining, construction, and energy, with a base year of 2000. Including subsectors, the index accounts for about 90 percent of the total industry value added. The IPI is available on an unadjusted basis as well as a seasonally and calendar-adjusted basis. The data are available about five weeks after the reference month. For example, April 2006 data were available on June 9. Figure 9.21 below illustrates French industrial weakness.

Merchandise Trade and Balance of Payments

Both the merchandise trade and balance of payment reports follow the standard procedures outlined above and utilize the intrastat forms for EU internal trade.

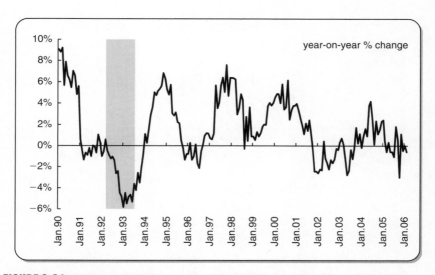

FIGURE 9.21   Industrial production less construction (Eurostat's preferred measure) growth has crumbled over the past five years as intensified competition from Asia has eroded the market for French manufactured goods.
Source: INSEE and Haver Analytics.

Merchandise Trade (Le Chiffre du Commerce Extérieur) Monthly merchandise trade data cover continental France and the overseas areas of Guadeloupe, Martinique, Guyana, and Réunion without any restriction on goods or countries. The data are available about six weeks after the reference period. For example, March 2006 merchandise trade data were available on May 12. Revisions are published monthly, along with the new monthly data. Figure 9.22 shows the deterioration in the French merchandise trade balance.

Balance of Payments (Balance des Paiements) BOP data are available quarterly on both an unadjusted and a seasonally adjusted basis. Included are data for imports and exports of goods; services trade including transportation, travel, insurance, construction, financial, leasing, and so on; receipts and payments for compensation of employees and receipts and payments for investment income; receipts and payments for transfers; capital account in net with capital transfers; financial accounts, including direct investment with components breakdown (including equity capital and reinvested earnings), portfolio investment with separate recording for assets and liabilities (showing financial derivatives and treasury securities), other investment with a sector-based breakdown for assets and liabilities; international reserves;

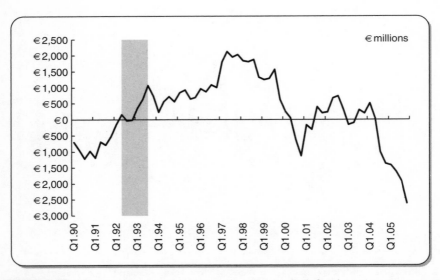

FIGURE 9.22 The burgeoning French merchandise trade deficit has put pressure on the overall EMU trade balance, despite Germany's large surplus.
Source: DGDDI and Haver Analytics.

and errors and omissions. The data are compiled in accordance with the methodology of the fifth edition of the IMF's *Balance of Payments Manual*. The data are available about eight or nine weeks after the end of the reference quarter. For example, first-quarter 2006 data were available on June 16.

Retail Sales

With the French economy reliant on consumer spending, these data, which account for about 25 percent of overall spending, are watched carefully by analysts.

Household Consumption Expenditure in Manufactured Goods (Dépenses de Consommation des Ménages in Pruduits Manufacturés) This indicator is a measure of retail sales and is unique to France. It measures consumer spending for household durable goods such as autos and furniture. The data are published monthly about three weeks after the reference month. For example, May 2006 data were published on June 21. There is no report in August because it is the traditional French vacation time. Instead, both the July and August reports are published in September. The data are seasonally and workday adjusted. These adjustments eliminate the fluctuations that

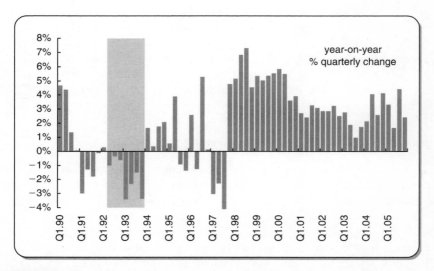

FIGURE 9.23 France's measure of consumer spending focuses on spending for manufactured goods such as household durables and autos.
Source: INSEE and Haver Analytics.

are solely due to changes in the number of working days. The data appear to be particularly sensitive to the number of worked Saturdays. The data are in constant 2000 prices and are published in volume terms and do not reflect price changes. The data are subject to revision as new information becomes available and the seasonal pattern is updated. Figure 9.23 shows the relative strength of retail sales when compared with pre-1998 years.

Private and Government Surveys

The purchasing manager's surveys for manufacturing and services follow the same pattern as in Germany. They are available on the first and third business days of the month and are prepared by NTC Research in the United Kingdom.

In addition to the private surveys, INSEE conducts both a monthly and a quarterly survey on business as well as a consumer confidence survey. It also conducts a monthly business investment survey.

ITALY

Little information is available about Italian indicators in any language. The data follow the same pattern as other EMU countries. There is one statistics agency—L'Istituto Nazionale di Statistica (ISTAT). Release dates for the following year are available on ISTAT's Web site in December. Data are usually released at 11 A.M. or noon local time or 3 or 4 A.M. ET. The reports are in Italian. A table is available in English. I have excluded retail trade data here because the report is ignored by virtually everyone and is not linked in any way to the consumption data that appears in the GDP accounts.

Gross Domestic Product (Conti Economici Trimestrali)

GDP data follow the general pattern of other EU countries and basically comply with the rules and procedures established by Eurostat. The data are estimated in accordance with the ESA95. ISTAT releases a flash estimate of GDP data about 45 days after the end of the reference quarter. The flash includes an estimate of total GDP in euros along with the percent change. (France and Germany do not publish a currency amount in their flash releases.) Figure 9.24 shows GDP growth since 1990.

The first full set of GDP data are available about 70 days after the reference quarter's end. These data are seasonally and workday adjusted and are available in current and constant prices. ISTAT converted to chain

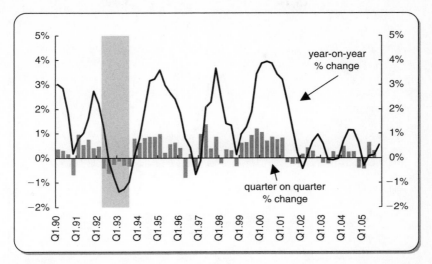

FIGURE 9.24 Italy's GDP growth has been virtually stagnant since 2001 with little or no growth. Their manufacturing industries have been particularly hard hit by Asian imports, while domestic consumption has lagged.
Source: ISTAT and Haver Analytics.

methodology with the release of fourth-quarter 2005 data with history back to 1981. The major categories for expenditure data include compensation of employees (by productive sector); gross fixed-capital formation (by productive sector); final domestic consumption (by purpose and by type of good); and labor input (in full-time equivalents). The data are preliminary when first released and are subsequently revised every 80 days, both in the current year and during the following two years. The data become final four or five years after their first release.

Prices

Price data are similar to other EU countries. ISTAT produces a national index of consumer prices as well as the HICP.

Consumer Price Index (Prezzi al Consumo, Provvisori and Definitivi) The CPI
is an annually chained Laspeyres-type index with a base year of 1995 and covers all of Italy. ISTAT changed to the chain Laspeyres index in January 1999. Prices are collected monthly with the exception of durables, semidurables, and rents. These are collected quarterly, while prices for seasonal goods are collected twice a month. Price changes are also measured

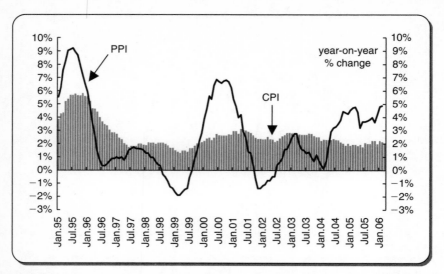

FIGURE 9.25 Italy's price patterns for both the PPI and CPI parallel Germany and France. While PPI prices press upward, the CPI increases remain contained and near the 2 percent on year rate.
Source: ISTAT and Haver Analytics.

monthly by the CPI for white- and blue-collars workers. The calculations for the HICP use the same methodology. Core CPI excludes tobacco and is widely used for indexing purposes in Italian laws and regulations. A preliminary estimate is available at the end of the reference month or a few days later. For example, the CPI for February 2006 was available on February 28. The final CPI was available two weeks later on March 15. Figure 9.25 shows price movements in the CPI and PPI.

Producer Price Index (Prezzi Alla Produzione) The PPI is a Laspeyres index with a base of 2000 that measures the change in the prices of goods sold by industrial producers within the domestic market. Prices are ex-factory, net of VAT and any other type of charges borne by the purchaser, and defined in accordance with contractual language commonly in use. The data are available one month after the reference month. For example, May 2006 data were available on June 28. The data are subject to revision.

Labour Force (Forza di Lavoro)

Both employment and unemployment data are available on a quarterly basis and follow the ILO criteria. Both series are published about 11 weeks after the reference quarter. For example, first-quarter 2006 data were available on June 20. The data are seasonally adjusted and not subject to revision. The report includes data on the participation rate; employment; unemployment and inactivity broken down by gender, age, and education; and employment by economic activity, profession, employee/self-employed position, part-time/full-time working time, permanent/temporary employment, and so on. The data are also available by geographic areas.

Employment (Occupazione) The data are obtained from the Labour Force Survey, a sample survey of resident population living in private households throughout Italy. People living in collective households are excluded. The definition corresponds to those recommended by the ILO and adopted by Eurostat. Those that are employed include persons 15 years of age or older who, in the reference week worked at least one hour for payment in money or kind or for a profit to the enterprise. Persons temporarily absent from work due to sickness, holidays, leave, and so on are also considered as employed.

Unemployment (Disoccupazione) Unemployment data are published both by the number of persons out of work and by the unemployment rate. The unemployment rate is obtained from the ratio between persons seeking employment and the total labor force as measured by the LFS. Unemployment includes persons aged 15 to 74 not employed in the reference week who were actively seeking employment in the four weeks preceding interview and were immediately available (within two weeks) to accept a position should one be forthcoming. The data are seasonally adjusted and not subject to revision. Figure 9.26 below shows the relative improvement in Italian unemployment.

Output

Industrial Production (Produzione Industriale) Industrial production is an important indicator for Italy as the country relies on merchandise trade for growth. The index is calculated as a Laspeyres index with a base year of 2000. The index, which is survey based, covers the mining, manufacturing, and energy sectors, and excludes construction. The data are classified according to ATECO 2002, Italian version, which is the same as NACE Revision 1.1 and ISIC Revision 3. The data are published in an unadjusted format as well as one adjusted for working days and seasonality. The data are published about six weeks after the reference month's end. For example, April 2006 data were published on June 12. The data are preliminary and are revised the following month and at least once a year thereafter. Figure 9.27 shows Italy's struggles in production.

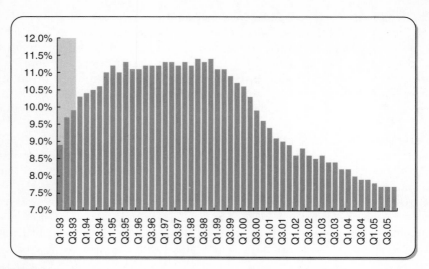

FIGURE 9.26   Italy's unemployment data are available on a quarterly basis. The unemployment rate declined rapidly in the late 1990s and continued to drop at a slower pace in later years. In 2005, it hovered around the 7.7 percent rate. *Source:* ISTAT and Haver Analytics.

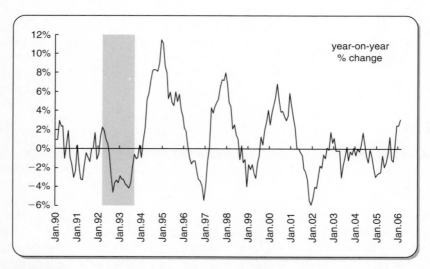

FIGURE 9.27   Industrial production less construction (Eurostat's preferred measure) has always fluctuated wildly. Italian industry has been moribund for the past several years and one the whole has suffered more than lackluster Germany and France. *Source:* ISTAT and Haver Analytics.

Merchandise Trade and Balance of Payments

Merchandise trade (Commercio Estero UE e Mondo and Commercio Estero Extra UE)   Merchandise trade data generally follow Eurostat's methodology. Separate reports are published for external and internal EU trade. The extra-EU trade data are compiled on the basis of customs declarations with non-EU countries. The intra-EU trade data (Intrastat) are derived from surveys and provide statistics on trade between Italy and other EU Member States. The data are available monthly. World trade data are available within one month after the reference month while intra-EU trade data are available within seven weeks after the reference month. For example, the March 2006 merchandise trade data with the rest of the world were available on April 21, while the February data for intra-EU trade were available on April 13. The data are subject to revision until they become final within one year after the end of the reference year. Figure 9.28 shows how the merchandise trade balance has deteriorated.

Balance of Payments   BOP data are available from Ufficio Italiano dei Cambi rather than ISTAT. The data, available monthly according to EU rules, are

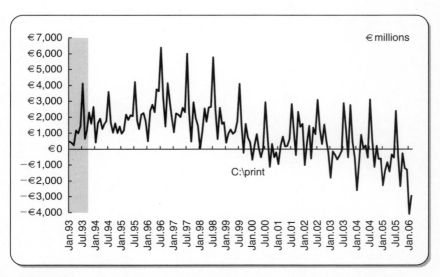

FIGURE 9.28   Italy's merchandise trade balance reflects the lack of markets for expensive Italian manufactures. Constrained by the euro's exchange rate, the country has been unable to devalue the currency to make its products more competitive as it did in the pre-EMU days.
Source: ISTAT and Haver Analytics.

published in millions of euro. Since 1999, the data have been compiled and presented in accordance with the fifth edition of the IMF's *Balance of Payments Manual*. Data include the current account, including imports and exports of goods and services, net income receipts, and net current transfers; the capital account; and the financial account showing data for: net flows of assets and liabilities for direct investment, portfolio investment, other investment, and financial derivatives; and reserve assets. Data are available about 30 working days after the reference month. For example, February 2006 data were available on April 14. The data are subject to revisions. The report is available in English.

Private Surveys   The purchasing managers' surveys for manufacturing and services are available on the first and third business days of each month. The index is produced by NTC Research of the United Kingdom.

In addition to the PMIs, ISAE or Istituto Di Studi E Analisi Economica conducts numerous surveys including one on consumer confidence and another on business confidence that are followed by market watchers.

CHAPTER 10

UK Indicators

Finding information on United Kingdom indicators is easy. There is only one source for government statistics—the Office for National Statistics (ONS). Complete releases for each indicator including data and analysis are available on their web site. Data are generally released at 8:30 Greenwich Mean Time (GMT), which translates to 4:30 A.M. ET in the United States. A release calendar is available for a rolling year in advance, but the schedule gets a bit sketchy toward the end of the year. Although ONS provides a vast quantity of data, this chapter focuses on major economic indicators that are important to market players. Since the United Kingdom is a member of the European Union, they are required to submit data to Eurostat that conform to its rules of the road.

In addition to the indicators available from the ONS, there are privately generated indicators available from sources that include the Chartered Institute of Purchasing (CIPS), which publishes the purchasing managers' surveys in conjunction with NTC Research, Confederation of British Industry (CBI) surveys, and house price surveys conducted by Nationwide Building Society and The Halifax, to name a few.

GROSS DOMESTIC PRODUCT

Gross domestic product (GDP) is an integral part of UK national accounts and is a primary indicator of economic activity. It generally provides the basis for most central bank, government, and private forecasting models. It is a vast source of data on just about anything you might want to know about the British economy.

GDP is measured on a quarterly basis and represents the total value of the country's production. It consists of domestically produced goods and services purchases by individuals, businesses, foreigners, and government entities. Data are available in nominal and real (inflation-adjusted) pounds sterling. Gross national product (GNP), which includes those overseas activities that generate income for UK nationals but excludes activities in the country that generate income for foreign nationals, is also available.

Economists and market players monitor real growth rates. The customary measures for analyzing GDP are quarter-on-quarter and year-on-year percent comparisons rather than the annualized growth rates used in the United States. Quarterly percent changes tend to be volatile, so it is wise to focus on the annual percent change when tracking GDP. The data are published in both seasonally adjusted and unadjusted formats and have been compiled in accordance with the European System of Accounts (ESA95) methodology (which was discussed in the previous chapter) since September 1998. The ONS computes GDP using chained volume index measures. In 2005, the base year was revised to 2002. Figure 10.1 tracks UK growth since 1975.

GDP data are released quarterly. The UK is usually the first of the major countries to release an estimate, just three and a half weeks after the reference quarter's end. For example, the initial release of first quarter 2006 data was on April 26. ONS uses three different theoretical approaches in estimating GDP. Each provides a more detailed layer of information.

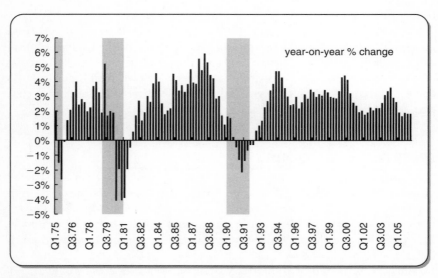

FIGURE 10.1 Thanks to the consumer, there has been solid growth since 1991. This has made it unnecessary for the UK to join the EMU.
Source: Office for National Statistics and Haver Analytics.

- GDP from the output or production approach or GDP (O) measures the value added that is created through the production of goods and services. This first estimate can be used to show how different industries contribute to the economy. It includes data on four major industrial categories:
  - Agriculture, hunting, forestry, and fishing
  - Production industries such as mining and quarrying including oil and gas extraction, manufacturing, and utilities
  - Construction
  - Service industries including distribution, hotels, catering and repairs, transport, storage and communication, business services and finance, and government and other services.
- GDP from the income approach or GDP (I) measures the total income generated by the production of goods and services. These data are available about seven weeks after the end of a quarter. Data for first quarter 2006 were available on May 25. As one would expect, the information available expands and includes output analysis in both current and constant 2002 prices in millions of pounds sterling. The data are classified, for example, as income earned by companies (corporations), employees, and the self-employed. Detailed data are published showing breakdowns by productive activity, by expenditure category, and by income.
- GDP from the expenditure approach or GDP (E) measures the total expenditures in current and constant prices on all finished goods and services produced within the economy. These data are available 12 weeks after the end of the quarter. First-quarter 2006 data were available on June 22. Expenditure analyses show consumer expenditures, government expenditures, capital formation (fixed investment), and stock building or inventory accumulation; and imports and exports along with the factor cost adjustment, which deducts expenditures on taxes after having allowed for subsidies. Transfer payments such as taxes and benefits are not related to production and therefore do not contribute to GDP. Payments related to production are called factor payments.

While overall GDP can tell you whether the economy is growing, the components can help you find which sectors are growing more than others and provide a clue as to where to find investment possibilities. GDP is the consummate measure of economic activity. Investors need to closely track the economy because it usually dictates how investments will perform. The stock market likes to see healthy economic growth because it translates to higher corporate profits. The bond market does not mind growth but

FYI

World economies are not isolated from one another. For example, in September 2005, the U.S. Gulf of Mexico coastline of Louisiana (including New Orleans) and Mississippi suffered from a catastrophic hurricane—Katrina. This U.S. storm became a footnote to the third-quarter 2005 UK GDP data because of the large role UK property insurers play in the international market. In the note, ONS said, "The volume measure of insurance output within this estimate of real GDP for the third quarter of 2005 is not affected by Hurricane Katrina. Under national accounting conventions the increase in insurance claims has an impact on the current price estimate (nominal GDP) and on prices, but it does not affect the volume measure of insurance."

is extremely sensitive to whether the economy is growing too quickly and paving the road to inflation. By tracking economic data like GDP, investors will know what the economic backdrop is for these markets and their portfolios.

The quarterly national accounts report contains a treasure trove of information similar to what is found in U.S. National Income and Product Accounts (NIPA). The data not only paint an image of the overall economy, but provide investors with information about important trends within the big picture. GDP components like consumer spending, business and residential investment, and price indexes illuminate the economy's undercurrents, which can translate to investment opportunities and guidance in managing a portfolio. Unlike in the U.S. NIPA accounts, government purchases of goods and services are distributed among the other categories. For example, in each investment category, there are data available for central and local governments.

While the amount of data available in this report is vast, it is presented in an entirely different format than that of the U.S. GDP accounts. The U.S. data tables have the descriptors on the left side vertically, with the dates horizontal. It is just the reverse in British data. Descriptors are horizontal, while dates are vertical on the left. Each sector in the UK data is on a separate page.

The UK economy is driven by consumer spending just as it is in the United States. To find what the consumer has been doing, check out Table A7 entitled "Household final consumption expenditures" in the ONS release. The breakdown here is much broader than in the retail sales release. For example, no data on transport (a category that includes autos and other transport equipment) are available in the monthly retail sales report but are included here.

If you are interested in investing in consumer products, expenditures are available for major consumer industries such as clothing and footware, home furnishings, communication, transport, health, food, and alcoholic beverages and tobacco. In addition, expenditures are parsed by durable, semidurable, and nondurable goods and services.

To see which sectors are investing to expand, check out gross fixed capital formation. Within each category, investment is divided among public, private, and households. Data are available for construction investment as well as transport equipment, other machinery and equipment, and intangible fixed assets. It is useful to distinguish between private demand versus growth in government expenditures. Growth in the government sector is discounted by market players because it depends on fiscal policy rather than economic conditions. Increased investment expenditures are viewed favorably by market participants because they expand productive capacity without inciting inflationary pressures.

THE BLUE BOOK

Published annually in July, the *Blue Book* is a compendium of national account data and is an essential data source for anyone concerned with macroeconomics. It provides detailed estimates of national product, income, and expenditures. All tables contain at least nine years of data, with some containing data for 18 years. For investors, it covers value added by industry, full accounts by sector including financial and nonfinancial corporations, central and local government, and households and capital formation.

PRICE MEASURES

While all central banks monitor inflation, those with inflation targets need to choose an appropriate measure to reflect their policies. In the United Kingdom there are two monthly indexes to measure consumer prices: the consumer price index (CPI, formerly called the harmonised index of consumer prices) and the retail price index (RPI). In brief, the CPI is used to set and monitor the Bank of England's inflation target, while the RPI is used for just about everything else. Although there is a quarterly price deflator in the GDP accounts, the CPI and RPI garner most of the attention by investors.

Until January 2004, the major measure of inflation for monetary policy purposes was the retail price index excluding mortgage interest payments (RPIX). At that time, the major inflation measure shifted to the harmonised index of consumer prices as defined by Eurostat. This index, which had been previously published as the HICP, was renamed the consumer price index or CPI. The change was in response to conditions set for the United Kingdom's possible entry into the European Monetary Union. While both the CPI and RPI rely on the same price information and are calculated from the same base price surveys, there are key differences between the two. A major difference is the exclusion of council taxes and owner-occupied housing costs from the CPI.

Historically, there has been a substantial spread between the two measures of inflation, which in part can be traced to the way they are calculated. Arithmetic means are used to combine individual prices to construct the RPI, while geometric means that allow for substitution are used in calculation of the CPI. This formula differential accounts for nearly half of the difference in the two indexes. As with most consumer price indexes, there is an overall measure and a core reading that excludes food and energy.

Consumer Price Indexes

Both the RPI and the CPI are described as fixed quantity or Laspeyres price indexes. As prices change over time, they assume that the relative quantities of each product purchased remain constant. This deliberate design choice is critical in ensuring that within year movements reflect only changes in prices. For this reason, they are sometimes referred to as "pure" price indexes.

The CPI is a chain-linked Laspeyres index (2005 = 100), which measures the average change in the prices of consumer goods and services. The expenditures include all private households, foreign visitors, and residents of institutional households. The index is compiled using a sample of more than 650 goods and services for which price movements are regularly measured. Domestic prices are collected by the private-sector company Research International on the second or third Tuesday of each month, although some prices are collected a day on either side of that Tuesday. In addition, data are collected by ONS staff from some major suppliers. Prices include taxes such as the value added tax (VAT) and insurance tax, as well as duties. The item weights used to calculate the index are derived largely from the annual UK Expenditure and Food Survey. Weights for higher-level CPI aggregates are derived from Household Final Consumption Expenditure data from the national accounts. All weights are updated each year, as is goods and services. The CPI and RPI are

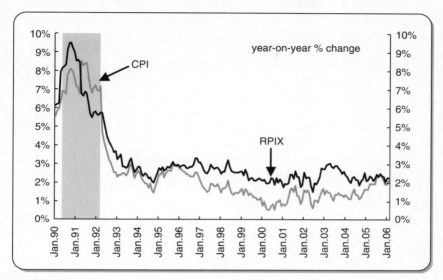

FIGURE 10.2   The exclusion of housing and council taxes contributes to the differential between the two indexes. The large difference in the late 1990s and early 2000s reflects the house price boom in the United Kingdom.
Source: Office for National Statistics and Haver Analytics.

released about two weeks after the reference month. For example, May 2006 data were published on June 13. Figure 10.2 shows inflation since 1990.

Retail Price Indexes

Another inflation measure is the retail price index. It is an average measure of change in the prices of goods and services bought for the purpose of consumption in the United Kingdom. It is compiled and published monthly. Once published, it is never revised. Although no longer officially used for monetary policy, the RPI continues to be used for the indexation of pensions, state benefits, and index-linked gilts. Wage agreements, leases, maintenance, and child support payments are often linked directly to this index. Also, utility regulators impose restrictions on price movements based on the RPI.

There are three versions of the retail price index: the overall index, the RPIX, and the RPIY. The RPI is the overall measure of inflation, while the RPIX is the old inflation measure used by the Bank of England as its inflation target. Mortgage interest payments were excluded because they are directly affected by Bank policy. The RPIY excludes mortgage interest rates and indirect taxes (VAT) council tax, duties vehicle excise duty, insurance tax, and air passenger duty).

What Is the Difference between the CPI and RPI?   The CPI excludes a number of items that are included in RPI, mainly related to home ownership, which is a more important component in the United Kingdom than on the European continent. These include council tax and a range of owner-occupier housing costs such as mortgage interest payments, house depreciation, building insurance, and estate agents' and conveyancing fees. The CPI covers all private households, while the RPI excludes the top 4 percent by income and pensioner households who derive at least 75 percent of their income from state benefits. The CPI also includes the residents of institutional households such as student hostels, and also foreign visitors to the United Kingdom. This means that it covers some items that are not in the RPI, such as unit trust and stockbrokers' fees, university accommodation fees, and foreign students' university tuition fees.

Although the same underlying price data are used in most cases to calculate the two indexes, there are some specific differences in price measurement. For example, different methods are used in the CPI and RPI to compile the index for new cars. Individual prices are combined in the two indexes within each detailed expenditure category according to different formulas. The CPI uses the geometric mean whereas the RPI uses arithmetic means. This lowers the CPI inflation rate relative to the RPI.

Another reason that the CPI is generally lower is mainly due to the index's exclusion of most housing costs that are included in the RPI, such as council tax and house depreciation. Housing prices soared for about three years (2002 through 2004) until the Bank of England's higher interest rates deflated them. Analysts think that the CPI benefits from greater coherence with macroeconomic data because the index's coverage of spending and households is based on the National Accounts. It also has the advantage of cross-country compatibility, at least with other EU members.

The retail price indexes benefit from their familiarity and credibility based on their longer history. Inevitably, it will be some time before the CPI becomes as widely recognized. The CPI's exclusion of most elements of owner-occupied housing costs lessens its relevance for some users, but this must be weighed against the significant difficulties encountered in measuring such costs appropriately, as reflected in the absence of any international consensus in this area.

Producer Price Indexes

The producer price index (PPI) is a monthly survey that measures the price changes of goods bought and sold by UK manufacturers. There are separate indexes for input prices and output prices. The indexes are calculated as a base-weighted Laspeyres index, which covers the UK manufacturing industry. Investors watch these indexes for upward price pressures that could feed through to consumer prices in the future and, in turn, impact central bank decisions. Investors are paying more attention to these indexes as they try to track the impact of soaring commodity prices through the economy.

The PPI provides a key measure of inflation, alongside the CPI, RPI and GDP deflators. The output price indexes measure the change in manufacturers goods prices. They are often referred to as factory gate prices. Input prices are not limited to just those materials used in the final product, but also include what is required by the company in its normal day-to-day operations. The index is rebased and the weights are revised every five years. An overall summary of both input and output prices are released monthly around midmonth for the previous month. Figure 10.3 show input and output price changes from 1990.

The price movements for a selected basket of goods are weighted to reflect the relative importance of the products in the base year, which is currently 2000. These are aggregated for various sectors of industry. For example, import price indexes measure price changes of goods and

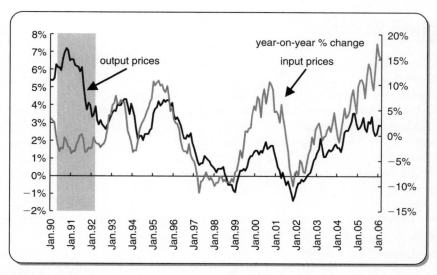

FIGURE 10.3 Soaring energy prices account for the run up in input prices, while a weak manufacturing sector unable to pass on those additional costs, is illustrated by the mild trend for output prices.
Source: Office for National Statistics and Haver Analytics.

raw materials brought into the United Kingdom and are a key component of input prices. (Export price indexes measure price changes of goods manufactured in the UK but destined for export markets.) The core measures exclude food, beverages, tobacco, and petroleum.

Prices are collected monthly from about 3,000 manufacturers covering a wide range of products. Approximately 9,000 price quotes are obtained, covering 980 products. The index is rebased and the weights are revised every five years. The prices include excise duties but exclude VAT. The weights are derived from data on sales in the base year as provided by the Prodcom inquiry, the manufacturing products inquiry required by Eurostat. Producer input and output prices are available about seven to 10 working days after the reference month. Data for May 2006 were available on June 12.

Although not followed closely, the ONS also measures services prices quarterly in the corporate services price index. This index is aimed at adding to and improving statistics for service industries, the fastest-growing sector of the economy. Briefly, the index includes prices for freight transport, telecommunications, property rentals, hotels, and banking. Indexes for computer services, legal services, and accounting are currently under development.

LABOUR MARKETS

Labour market data give investors a head start on understanding an economy's strengths and weaknesses. The United Kingdom's labour market reports are comprehensive and include data most important to analysts including employment, unemployment (two ways), and average earnings. The latter is a key inflation benchmark for the Bank of England's monetary policy as they look for potential inflationary pressures from wage increases.

The data are eagerly awaited by investors who look to the labour force data to provide more recent data on industry performance as well as the possible direction of central bank policy. The data are available about six weeks after the end of the reference period. May 2006 data were available on June 14. UK labor force data are available before most other major European countries with the exception of Germany, but later than the United States and Canada.

The Labour Force Survey (LFS) is a random survey of approximately 57,000 households every three months and is conducted by the ONS. It is the basis for both employment and unemployment data. The survey includes people living in student residence halls and National Health Service accommodations.

Employment

The ONS makes a distinction between the number of jobs and the number employed, given that a person can have more than one job. Employment is defined by the International Labour Organisation (ILO) criteria, which include anyone who did work during the survey period. Specifically, the number of those with jobs includes people aged 16 or over who did paid work either as an employee or was self-employed, had a job but was on temporary leave, in government-supported training and employment programs, and doing unpaid family work. The number of jobs is the sum of employee jobs, the self-employed, and those in HM forces and government-supported training programs. Unfilled jobs are not included. The data are seasonally adjusted and available monthly as a three-month moving average.

People aged 16 or over are classified as employed if they have done at least one hour of work in the reference week or are temporarily away from a job, that is, on a vacation. The ONS stresses that the number employed differs from the number of jobs simply because of the number of people holding multiple jobs. The data are classified in numerous ways. For investors, occupation and industry classifications are probably more

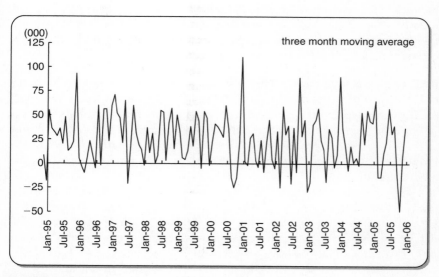

FIGURE 10.4 Even using a three-month moving average, employment change data are volatile. Labor force data reinforce the view that the United Kingdom has a vigorous economy.
Source: Office for National Statistics and Haver Analytics.

important. Aside from the broad breakdown in the monthly report, more extensive data are published quarterly in the LFS Quarterly Supplement and Labour Market Trends. Figure 10.4 shows the changes in employment since 1995.

Unemployment Two Ways

There are two separate ways to measure unemployment. The first or official estimate is based on the ILO definition. A second series—the claimant count—measures the unemployed who are claiming unemployment-related benefits. There is a large difference between the two series, and although they move broadly in line, one measure can increase while the other declines. The reason for this is simply that they measure different things.

Unemployment data are useful for a variety of reasons. For investors, a falling unemployment rate could be good news for those interested in consumer-oriented companies, for example. Consumers are employed and would have more money to spend. And hiring could mean a growing demand for a company's products. Obviously, the reverse would be true as well. A rising unemployment rate would tell you where demand could be weakening. Besides investors, governments use unemployment data along with other labor market indicators for macroeconomic and labor market management. In addition, the data are supplied to a range of international organizations including the European Central Bank. The ILO measure is the government's main unemployment measure, although many prefer the claimant measure because it is more current.

ILO Unemployment Measure   The "official" unemployment number is a count of jobless people who want to work, are available to work, and are actively seeking employment. It is calculated using data gathered by the Labour Force Survey and using the ILO definition. The advantage to the ILO definition is that it is used internationally (although there are national variations). However, comparisons can be made both among countries and over time, albeit carefully.

This measure like that of employment is based on the ILO definition that excludes job seekers who did any work during the month and covers those people who are looking for work and are available for work. The definition specifies that people aged 16 and over are unemployed if they are out of work, want a job, have actively sought work in the past four weeks, and are available to start work in the next two weeks; or are out of work, have found a job, and are waiting to start it in the next two weeks.

The unemployment rate is the number of people who are unemployed as a proportion of the resident economically active population of the area concerned. (Economically active is defined as people who are either employed

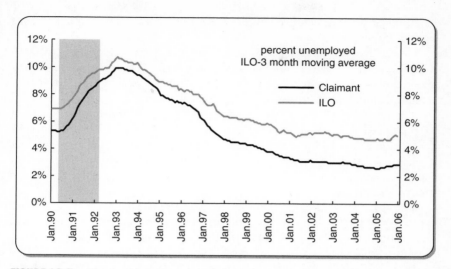

FIGURE 10.5 Along with robust growth has come record low unemployment rates by any measure.
Source: Office for National Statistics and Haver Analytics.

or unemployed.) The rate is published as a three-month moving average. Analysts tend to look at the numeric change rather than the unemployment rate, although some market watchers do look at both. All sectors of the economy are covered. The unemployment data are derived from the LFS. Figure 10.5 shows unemployment measured two ways since 1990.

Claimant Count The claimant count measures only those people who are claiming unemployment-related benefits or job-seeker's allowance. It is always lower than the ILO measure simply because not all unemployed people are entitled to claim benefits or they choose not to do so. The claimant count data comes from the administrative records of Jobcentre Plus (formerly Employment Service), and are available earlier than the LFS-based unemployment data. The claimant count rate is the number of people claiming unemployment-related benefits as a proportion of claimants and jobs in each area.

When employment is high, the gap between unemployment and the claimant count tends to widen, as some jobless people reenter the labor force. By actively looking for work, they may become classified as unemployed under the ILO definition. However, they are not in the claimant count unless they also claim benefits. The difference between the two measures is wider for women than for men. According to the ONS, fewer than 50 percent of unemployed women claim unemployment-related benefits, compared with around 75 percent of men.

Unemployment data are available in their current format back to 1984 (nonseasonally adjusted and seasonally adjusted). The present seasonally adjusted claimant count series goes back to 1971 and is adjusted to allow for significant changes to benefit rules.

The reference period is the second Thursday of every month. The data are published in both unadjusted and seasonally adjusted form five weeks after the date to which the figures refer. The claimant count is a by-product of the administrative system used to pay benefits and can therefore reflect changes in that system. The nonseasonally adjusted claimant count data are final when first released.

The seasonally adjusted claimant data for the latest month are identified as provisional in the first release and are revised in the subsequent month. Each year the seasonal adjustment for the claimant count is reviewed, taking account of the additional information about seasonal patterns provided by the previous year's data. The seasonal factors are recalculated and the previous seasonally adjusted estimates are amended accordingly.

Average Earnings

The average earnings index (AEI) dates back to 1963 and is a key indicator of how fast earnings are growing in Great Britain. The index measures how earnings in the latest month compare with those in the base year, which is currently 2000. A moving average of the latest three months compared with those in the prior year is the measure of choice, although month-on-month and year-on-year comparisons are also available. The data are seasonally adjusted. The three-month average rate of increase, introduced in April 1998, replaces the previously published underlying rate.

The data are closely watched by the Bank of England for signs of wage inflation. The Bank has a target of 4.5 percent increase in the three-month moving average measure. Indexes are published for the whole economy and the public and private sectors along with indexes for manufacturing and services, including private-sector services. The index is based on information obtained from the Monthly Wages and Salary Survey and is available at the same time as the LFS. Average earnings are obtained by dividing the total amount paid by the total number of employees paid, including those employees on strike and temporarily absent. Figure 10.6 tracks average earnings increases since 1990.

The average earnings index does not measure earnings levels—these are estimated by the New Earnings Survey and the Labour Force Survey. The AEI covers earnings only in Great Britain, as earnings information is not collected for Northern Ireland and regional data are not available.

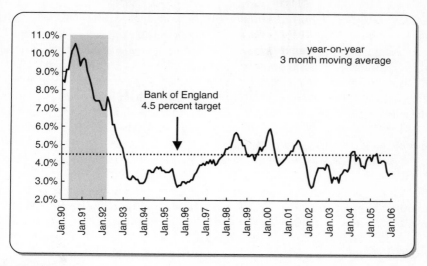

FIGURE 10.6 Average earnings have not posed an inflationary problem for the Bank of England. Increases have stayed close to or below the Bank's target of 4.5 percent.
Source: Office for National Statistics and Haver Analytics.

No adjustments are made for changes in hours worked, notably overtime, although increases in average pay as a consequence of increased overtime is reflected in the index.

Information on bonuses is provided by all respondents who pay them during the reference period. Bonus payments are recorded for the month in which they are paid, rather than for the period to which they relate. For example, an annual performance bonus paid at the end of a financial year might be recorded in March or April. Bonus data have been available since May 1996, and therefore it is possible to calculate growth in pay excluding bonuses only since May 1997. In addition, the bonus data are subject to a discontinuity in the series. This is a result of a change in the survey questions on bonuses in February 1999. Prior data are not comparable with those that follow it.

MERCHANDISE TRADE AND BALANCE OF PAYMENTS

Merchandise Trade

Ever since statistics on exports and imports of goods were first collected in 1697, trade has been one of the country's key economic indicators. The

United Kingdom has traditionally run a large merchandise trade deficit, which is offset in part by services. Its main trading partners are other EU members and the United States. The relatively high value of the pound sterling to the U.S. dollar and the European Monetary Union euro has made British exports expensive and has been blamed in part for the trade deficit. The data are available on a monthly basis within 40 calendar days after the end of the reference month for both non-EU and EU trade. Data for April 2006 were available on June 9. A single news release is published each month with data for all world trade.

Goods trade statistics are compiled by the ONS and are derived principally from data provided by HM Customs and Excise on the physical movement of goods in and out of the country. However, in order to conform to the International Monetary Fund definitions for balance of payments statistics, the ONS makes various adjustments to the customs data. These adjustments include transactions that are not reported to customs and exclude certain transactions that are reported to customs but where there is no change of ownership.

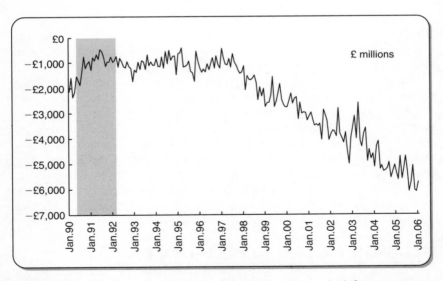

FIGURE 10.7 Like the United States, the UK merchandise trade deficits continue to set new records. Traditionally, the United Kingdom has run a surplus in services that offsets part of the goods deficit.
Source: Office for National Statistics and Haver Analytics.

Statistics on services trade such as international transport, travel, and financial and business services are derived principally from surveys conducted by the ONS. Additional data for both goods and services comes from a variety of other sources, including other government departments. All information included in the monthly Trade First Release is on a balance of payments basis, is seasonally adjusted and is used as a direct input into the quarterly Balance of Payments and National Accounts.

The release includes tables that show the total value of trade in goods together with index numbers of volume and price. The data are analyzed by broad commodity groups and according to geographical area as well. The release also includes early monthly estimates of the value of services trade. Trade in gold (i.e., gold bullion, gold coin, unwrought or semimanufactured gold and scrap) is excluded from the statistics of total exports and imports. However, trade in ores and concentrates as well as finished manufactures of gold (e.g., jewelry) are included. Revisions are made periodically during the year to ensure that fully consistent trade data are used in the BOP and the National Accounts calculations. Data are subject to revision for two years after the first publication. Figure 10.7 above graphically shows the burgeoning trade deficit.

Balance of Payments

The quarterly balance of payments is one of the United Kingdom's key economic statistics. It measures the overall net flow of transactions between UK residents and the rest of the world and reports how those flows are funded. Data cover the following components: imports and exports of goods and services; current transfer credits and debits; income credits and debits that include investment income and employee compensation; capital account credits and debits that include capital transfers and nonproduced, nonfinancial assets; and the financial account broken down into direct and portfolio investment, other investment, assets and liabilities of general government, and assets and liabilities of other UK residents. The data are available quarterly, with a one-quarter lag. First quarter 2006 balance of payments data were available on June 30.

Trade in gold (i.e., gold bullion, gold coin, unwrought or semimanufactured gold and scrap) is excluded from goods trade. However, it is included in the financial account. But trade in ores and concentrates and finished manufactures of gold such as jewelry are included in goods trade.

The data are predominantly derived from surveys conducted by the ONS and the Bank of England, as well as directly reported data from other government departments such as HM Treasury and Inland Revenue, along with other suppliers including the Bank of International Settlements and the European Investment Bank.

Monthly Balance of Payments The ONS has been developing an experimental monthly balance of payments (MBOP) as part of its statistical preparations for possible future membership in the eurozone. Monthly BOP statistics are required by the European Central Bank for the purposes of monetary policy and foreign exchange operations within the euro area. Even though not a member, the United Kingdom has accepted the need to provide monthly BOP estimates to the Bank, and the ONS manages a joint program with the Bank of England to meet ECB requirements. The data have been available to the public on request since December 1999 and are now available on the ONS Web site.

OUTPUT

Industrial and Manufacturing Output

Industrial and manufacturing output are watched carefully by market participants despite the decline in the importance of manufacturing in the economy. Manufacturing output is the preferred number rather than industrial production, which can be unduly influenced by electrical generation and weather. The manufacturing index is widely used as a short-term economic indicator in its own right by both the Bank of England and the UK government. Market analysts also focus on manufacturing and its subsectors to get insight on industry performance. Analysts' preferred measure is the monthly change in the index, even though the ONS gives prominence to a three-month moving average. Figure 10.8 on page 197 shows ailing UK output.

Manufacturing has been struggling, even though the UK economy has managed to stay recession free since 1992. The indexes are monitored by both the Bank of England and the government as an important early indicator of the industrial economy. The data are a major contributor to the National Accounts.

The index of production measures the volume of production of the manufacturing, mining and quarrying, and energy supply industries. Although it accounted for about 18.6 percent of the economy in 2003, it continues to slip. It is now estimated to account for about 16 percent. The index of manufacturing includes 13 subsectors and is considered by many to be an indicator in its own right. The First Release disaggregates manufacturing into seven industrial sectors. It also shows main industrial groupings as well as the oil and gas extraction industry.

The monthly index is published about 26 working days and no later than six weeks after the reference month (May 2006 data were published on July 6). About 8,300 businesses are surveyed or sampled through the Monthly Production Inquiry, which covers around 90 percent of total

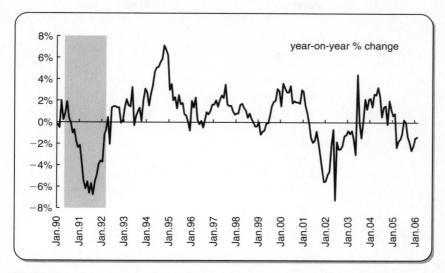

FIGURE 10.8 Manufacturing output has been a drag on the UK economy for some time now. Every now and then, there are flickers of light, but it has been a tough struggle. Part of the problem has been the relatively high value of the pound sterling against both the the euro and U.S. dollar, the currencies of their two largest trading partners.
Source: Office for National Statistics and Haver Analytics.

manufacturing or 75 percent of the industrial sector including energy. Other data sources include the Iron and Steel Statistics Bureau for iron and steel output and the Department for the Environment, Food and Rural Affairs for food. The data for the energy sector are based on surveys conducted by the Department of Trade and Industry.

The index is chain linked with a base year of 2002 = 100 and uses weights based on value added at factor cost in that year. The index covers the mining and quarrying, manufacturing and electricity, and gas and water supply sectors of the Standard Industrial Classification 2003. The data are deflated by using a combined domestic and export price deflator. Because month to month changes can be volatile, the ONS prefers a three month moving average which is compared with the previous three months as their primary measure.

RETAIL SALES AND RETAIL SALES VOLUMES

With consumer spending a large part of the economy, market players continually monitor spending patterns. There are three major sources—the retail sales monthly release, the quarterly household final consumption data found in the national accounts and the Confederation of British Industry (CBI) monthly survey on retail and wholesale distributive industry trades.

The monthly retail sales report contains sales data in both pounds sterling and volume. Because of month-to-month volatility, the ONS tracks data using a three-month moving average.

The retail sales report data are based on sample survey of 5,000 Great Britain businesses including both large retailers and a representative panel of smaller businesses. The data are indirectly used to calculate quarterly consumer spending on goods which, in turn, feeds into the compilation of the National Accounts. The retail sales index reference year is 2000 = 100. The data are available about two to three weeks after the reference month. Data for May 2006 were available on June 15. Figure 10.9 illustrates the strength of retail sales within the economy.

UK retail sales data exclude auto sales. To find these data, check the quarterly national accounts and household final consumption expenditures category. Household final consumption expenditure is roughly equivalent to quarterly personal consumption expenditures in U.S. GDP accounts. It represents traditional consumer spending but also includes imputed rent for

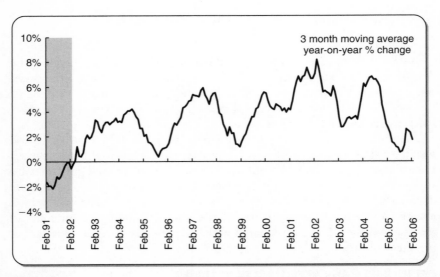

FIGURE 10.9   Like the U.S., the UK economy is consumer oriented. Higher interest rates and a slowdown in house price inflation dampened consumer exuberance in 2005.
Source: Office for National Statistics and Haver Analytics

the provision of owner-occupied housing services and consumption of own production.

Household consumption expenditures cover all goods and services purchases. However, it excludes housing purchases and expenditures on valuables such as antiques and some jewelry. These items are part of capital formation. Household consumption does include households' income paid in lieu of cash including company cars for private purposes and free or subsidized accommodation or meals.

Distributive Trades' Survey

The CBI monthly distributive trades report provides a vital update on volume of sales, orders, and stocks. The data are available on a timelier basis than either the retail sales report or the consumption expenditures from the quarterly GDP data. The distributive trades survey covers 20,000 outlets of firms responsible for 40 percent of employment in retailing. It includes measures of sales activity across the distributive trades. It was first introduced in 1983 and the retail results form the UK component of the EC survey of retail trades.

OTHER INDICATORS

Government indicators are not the only data keenly watched in the financial markets. Those below give a preview of what can be expected in the official statistics.

Chartered Institute of Purchasing Purchasing Managers' Survey

CIP publishes the monthly purchasing managers' surveys for both manufacturing and services that are watched closely for early signals of expansion and contraction. With the 50 level the breakeven point, anything above that level is considered expansion—and the higher the number the faster the expansion. Conversely, the lower the number under 50, the faster the contraction. The data are calculated by NTC Research.

Confederation of British Industry

Another source of industry performance originates with the CBI. It publishes a series of monthly surveys on such topics as industrial trends, retail and wholesale distributive industry trades, and the business and economic outlook. Surveys are followed because they focus on specific areas of the economy and are an excellent way to keep your finger on the pulse of a wide range of economic issues. The data are especially helpful if investment is being considered in a specific sector.

Nationwide and Halifax House Price Indexes

Two indexes that were followed closely during the housing boom were the Halifax house price index and the Nationwide house price index. They continue to be monitored as analysts look for a renewal of house price increases. One of the reasons that the Bank of England began to increase interest rates in 2004 was to rein in the housing market. They succeeded.

CHAPTER 11

Japanese Indicators

J apanese indicators present a challenge to data watchers. Many government agencies are responsible for issuing key economic data here, unlike other countries covered in this book. And while the releases are, for the most part, chock full of data, they lack the analysis found in British, Canadian, and U.S. reports. Another impediment to Japanese data analysis is the inconsistent availability of English translations. For example, there are more data available in Japanese only, including retail sales data revisions. To circumvent some of these problems, a subscription to a data service such as Haver Analytics gives you the data without the hassle of dealing with multiple government Web sites or, for that matter, understanding Japanese. There is no comprehensive calendar listing data releases for all agencies, nor are there annual calendars for several of the individual indicators. When a calendar is available, it generally coincides with the Japanese fiscal year, which begins April 1.

There are many issuers of government data, including:

- Ministry of Finance (MoF): merchandise trade
- Ministry of Economy, Trade and Industry (METI): industrial production, tertiary and all-industry indexes, retail sales
- Bank of Japan (BoJ): Tankan Survey, corporate goods price index (CGPI),
- Ministry of Health, Labour and Welfare: unemployment, worker household expenditures,
- Cabinet Office: gross domestic product (GDP)
- Ministry of Internal Affairs and Communications (MIC): consumer price index (CPI)

Figuring out when data are to be released can be difficult for the clock challenged. Essentially, if the calendar says that an indicator will be released on Friday morning Japan time, early birds will be checking for the data Thursday night in the United States. And Japan does not go on daylight savings time. Therefore, release times in the United States and Europe fluctuate by an hour when daylight savings time begins (data are an hour later) and ends (data are an hour earlier). Most data are released at either 30 minutes past the hour or 50 minutes past the hour. For example, first-quarter gross domestic product (GDP) data were available at 7:50 P.M. EDT. It is important to be aware of these differentials in release time if you are following Japanese events from the United States and Europe!

Another issue is analyst skepticism about the quality of Japanese data. Even when there are no changes in base year or methodology, indicators tend to have more volatility than in other industrial countries, making it harder for analysts to get their bearings. Three recent changes in the methodology used to calculate GDP data, and in particular deflation, have resulted in continued wariness of the calculations, and in turn, has led to the use of other data to measure growth. According to the Organisation for Economic Co-operation and Development (OECD), Japanese revisions swing far more wildly than those of other countries, even though the reasons for the revisions are not unusual. Under pressure to publish a more timely release simply means that the inputs are merely estimates that will be subject to larger revisions later on. For example, third-quarter 2005 GDP growth was revised downward to an annual growth rate of 1 percent from the 1.7 percent originally reported. And the country had not been in a recession in 2004 after all.

So what data do the data watchers watch? On a monthly basis, industrial production, unadjusted merchandise trade data, and the CPI. On a quarterly basis, the Bank of Japan's Tankan Survey wins.

One of the analysts' favorites is industrial production, which is volatile but gives a detailed look at manufacturers. For example, in the United States, data are collected from a sampling of companies. However, in Japan much more detail is required, so the data cover a majority of manufacturers. Economists also prefer Japan's unadjusted merchandise trade data rather than the seasonally adjusted estimates, since exports are an important driver of Japanese business cycles. And, as with production figures, the data provided are extremely detailed. The CPI is monitored zealously by analysts and politicians on the deflation watch.

Key data releases tend to clump during the last week of the month with retail sales, industrial production, unemployment rate, CPI, and workers' household spending occurring on the same day or within a day or two of each other.

GROSS DOMESTIC PRODUCT

Despite analysts' wariness, they still follow GDP data closely. The results can move markets—especially when the outcome varies from the consensus forecast. A sign that analysts have been looking for finally emerged at the end of 2005 and into the first quarter of 2006. The domestic economy (and the consumer) finally began to show signs of life after a long period of economic malaise. However, during that time, when the economy did expand sporatically, it did so on exports.

GDP follows the basic description of the indicator. But the methodology used to calculate GDP has changed several times over the past few years, contributing to analysts' doubts about data accuracy. The System of National Accounts (SNA) for Japan shifted from SNA68 to SNA93 on October 27, 2000. That, in turn, was followed by a change in the estimation method for preliminary quarterly GDP less than two years later. The most recent change has been to chain-linking methodology (December 8, 2004). Japan's methodology now is aligned with most of the industrial world, including the United States. However, as a result of these changes, GDP history now begins in 1994. (History from 1955 to 2001 is available from Haver Analytics and is based on SNA68, the precursor to SNA93.) The calculation of the GDP price deflator in a country plagued by deflation was an important element in the switch to chain linking. Now the GDP deflator will be rebased annually rather than once every five years. Even though deflation has eased as measured by the CPI, the GDP deflator shows that prices continued to fall at a healthy clip on a year-on-year basis in 2005 and into 2006. Figure 11.1 shows GDP and the persistent decline in the deflator.

The GDP accounts are the responsibility of the Cabinet Office. They are compiled using GDP by expenditure for flow accounts and private capital assets for stock accounts, both of which cover the entire economy. The data are organized by major expenditure categories such as private consumption, which is further broken down to household consumption and household consumption excluding imputed rents; private residential investment; nonresidential private investment; private inventory change; government consumption; public investment; public inventory change; and exports and imports of goods and services. For stock accounts, constant price data are broken down by major private industry. Data are also available for national income, the savings rate, and other figures related to national wealth.

The Quarterly Estimates of GDP report is prepared twice each quarter—the first about six weeks after the end of the reference quarter. Revised data are available about two months and 10 days after the end of the reference

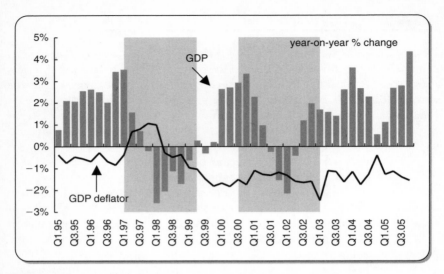

FIGURE 11.1 Despite an economic recovery as measured by GDP, deflation remains a nagging problem according to the GDP deflator measure of prices. *Source:* Cabinet office and Haver Analytics.

quarter. For example, first-quarter 2006 data were released on May 19, 2006. The second release for the same quarter was published on June 12. Data are disseminated in thousand millions of yen (¥) in nominal and real terms, together with the implicit deflators. Data are published in both original and seasonally adjusted formats and are preliminary when first released. They are revised continuously as new data becomes available and become final at the end of the following year.

TANKAN SURVEY

The Tankan is the most widely followed measure of business sentiment in Japan. It is unique to Japan and probably moves the markets more than any other indicator except possibly prices. Developed by the Bank of Japan, its purpose is to help the Bank gauge business conditions and trends for the purpose of setting and administering appropriate monetary policy. Literally thousands of subcategories are available to look at, and everyone has their favorite. It is prepared by the Research and Statistics Department of the Bank. The Tankan underwent major design changes in the way the data are categorized and collected in 2003. Due to the changes in the selection and grouping criteria for companies in the sample, the new

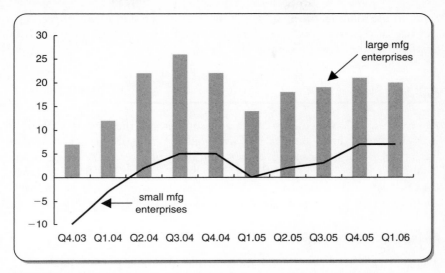

FIGURE 11.2 The Tankan is truly a market-moving indicator. Consisting of thousands of measures, the graph above shows the well-being of two major categories—those of large and small manufacturers. Large manufacturers include the multinational exporters while the small manufacturers generally include smaller domestic producers.
Source: Bank of Japan and Haver Analytics.

data are not comparable with the old. *This means that we no longer have history for comparison!* Figure 11.2 shows the limited data available for historic comparisons.

Data are categorized by size and type of business. For example, there are large enterprises, large manufacturing enterprises, and large nonmanufacturing enterprises, as well as small enterprises in each category. The surveys are published quarterly in April, July, October, and December. For example, first-quarter 2006 data were published on April 3. Respondents are asked about business conditions, supply-and-demand conditions for products, inventory levels, production capacity, financial position, and changes in prices. They are also asked about sales, current profits, fixed investments (semiannual and annual actual results and forecasts), and loans from financial institutions, number of employees, and other operational questions (actual results at the end of each quarter).

The data are presented as a diffusion index (positive responses less negative responses) on a level basis as well as year-to-year percent changes. Data are included for such things as revision rate in comparison with the previous survey and estimates of population by the type of industry (16 types in the manufacturing and 14 types in the nonmanufacturing) and by the size of the enterprise (i.e., large, medium-sized, and small enterprises classified by the size of capital.)

PRICES

Analysts as well as members of the government and the central bank have been holding a long vigil as they awaited the end of the deflation that has crippled the economy. Even into the third quarter of 2006, there are disagreements on whether deflation has finally ended. The Bank of Japan thinks it has, while members of the government are not so sure. And they disagree on the appropriate price measure to use to make the call.

Consumer Price Index

The CPI is one of the more important monthly releases for Japan. It is the primary inflation measure for the BoJ, even though it does not have an inflation target. Analysts have waited for the index to turn positive for many years. It would signal that the deflationary spiral that has gripped the country is finally at an end. Like other CPIs, the index is not designed to measure living-expense changes that arise from changes in the types, qualities, or volumes of the goods and services purchased. Rather, it measures a fixed basket of goods and services. The primary core measure excludes only fresh food.

Every five years, the base year of the CPI shifts to reflect changes in the mix of goods and services the public buys. Since consumers usually shift more of their purchases to items whose prices have risen more slowly, the updates generally have lowered reported inflation. In the summer of 2006, the base year shifted to 2005. At the same time, new core measures, one of which excludes both fresh food and energy, were formally added. (A provisional core CPI excluding food and energy had been available since December 2005.) Now there are three new core inflation measures: the first excludes fresh food and energy, the second excludes energy and all types of food, and the third excludes energy, food, and telecommunications charges. In addition to the shift in base year, the basket of items included in the index was updated to reflect more recent consumer purchase patterns. For example, gone from the index are sewing machines; but now doughnuts and flat screen TVs are included.

The general index increased continuously in terms of year-on-year comparisons from 1950 to 1995, when it declined for the first time. After that, the index was up for three years because of a consumption tax rate increase and the soaring prices of fresh vegetables due to bad weather. However, in 1999, the index declined for a second time, and continued to drop for five consecutive years, mainly because of the decline of industrial product prices for durable consumer goods.

The CPI is usually released at 8:30 A.M. on Friday (local time) of the week that includes the 26th of the month. The CPI for May 2006 was released on June 30. The release includes the national index for the previous month and the midmonth preliminary report for the current month for the Ku area of Tokyo. A release schedule for the new fiscal year is published at the end of March. The data are produced by Price Statistics Office of the Ministry of Public Management, Home Affairs, Posts and Telecommunications.

The CPI is calculated as the weighted arithmetic mean with a fixed base (Laspeyres formula, 2005 = 100). It covers all of Japan but excludes one-person households. (The CPI that covers the all households, including one-person households, is also calculated as a supplementary index.) The index covers about 584 items including four items of imputed rent for owner-occupied housing. The prices of index items are collected in the monthly Retail Price Survey. The weights are based on the 2005 Family Income and Expenditure Survey and are revised once every five years. The base year is also changed every five years. The data for the whole country are final when released and as a rule are not subject to revision. Only the seasonally adjusted monthly data are revised at the time December data are released. Figure 11.3 on page 208 shows two measures of price change: the CPI and the CGPI.

Corporate Goods Price Index

The CGPI focuses on goods prices as transacted between companies. It is Japan's version of the producer price index. The index reflects the price level for the supply and demand of individual industrial goods. Unlike the CPI, this index is calculated by the BoJ Research and Statistics Department. The indexes of less aggregated products such as commodities are the deflators that translate nominal output values into real quantities. The basic grouping index classifies selected commodities by their attributes. In reality, three indexes—the domestic corporate goods price index, the export price index, and the import price index—are released simultaneously. It is the domestic index that market players follow.

The domestic CGPI uses a chain-weighted Laspeyres formula, which is the weighted arithmetic mean based on the chained value-based weights. The data are not seasonally adjusted. The CGPI is revised at five-year

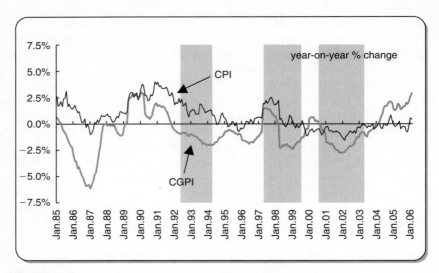

FIGURE 11.3   The graph above pictures consumer and corporate goods prices. The CGPI emerged from deflation and has been climbing for a year while consumer prices have barely shown any positive price changes. Once again, it is the typical picture of producers unable to pass along price increases.
Source: Bank of Japan, MIC, and Haver Analytics.

intervals. At that time, there is a review of the commodities covered, their classifications, and a change in the base year and the calculation of the weights. The 2000 revision changed the name of the index from wholesale price index to corporate goods price index.

There is a distinct difference between the way prices are collated for the CPGI and the CPI or GDP deflator. For the CPGI, the commodities representing each stage of production, that is, the raw material, semifinished goods, and finished goods stages, are counted at each stage of production. For example, when crude oil prices go up and are passed on to the next stage(s) downstream, the increase is counted repeatedly at each stage. As a result, simple comparisons cannot be made between the commodities of the domestic CGPI and other price indicators such as the CPI and GDP deflator that count commodities only once.

Preliminary figures are released on the eighth working day of the following month after the reference month. For example, the February 2006 data were published on March 9. The final figures are released two months after the reference month. The precise release date is generally announced in the BoJ Statistical Releases scheduled for the next six months, which is published at the end of every quarter.

MEASURES OF PRODUCTION

Production measures are watched closely by the financial markets. Japan's production has long been its source of growth and this is especially true for output that is destined for export. Analysts have been watching industries that are more oriented toward the domestic economy as well. During the recent recovery, they have lagged firms that are export oriented. Analysts feel that a full Japanese economic recovery will not occur until this sector turns around as well.

Industrial Production

Industrial production provides key industry data for this export-dependent economy. Japan does not highlight total industrial production, and you would have a problem finding the number in their press release. Rather, the Ministry of Economy, Trade and Industry (METI), the producing agency, highlights mining and manufacturing activity. The data are issued twice a month—a preliminary estimate at the end of the month for the preceding month and a revised estimate about two weeks later. For example, February 2006 data were available on March 30. The revised data were available on April 17. According to METI, the report's intent is multi-faceted—it gives readings of production while at the same time, it provides an indication of product and equipment demand as well as operating rates. Currently, the base year is 2000 = 100. The Economic Analysis Office, Research and Statistics Department, and Economic and Industrial Policy Bureau of the METI prepare the report. A calendar for the full year is available on the METI Web site. Figure 11.4 gives a long-term view of industrial production.

Other indexes are calculated and reported in this release as well. In addition to production, indexes for shipments and inventories are also included. The shipments index is a measure of factory shipments for mining and manufacturing component products such as electronics and transport equipment. The inventory index aligns inventories at the same producers with those in the production and shipments indexes. The producer's product inventory rate index provides a direct view of supply-and-demand trends for mining and industrial products. This index is sensitive to inventory increases as demand drops and shipments decline. Therefore, it is an important leading economic indicator.

Revisions for the previous year are usually published in February or March of the following year. At the same time, the seasonal indexes are updated. The METI notes that although the term industry classification is used to describe the subcategories, it is more accurate to say that the classification is by product groups. Most of the line items covered by the

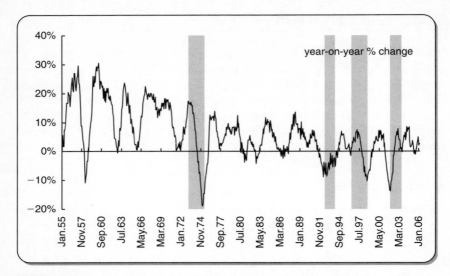

FIGURE 11.4   Swings in the industrial production index have calmed somewhat but still show volatility.
Source: METI and Haver Analytics.

indexes are taken from the METI Current Survey of Production, while the remaining are from other government ministries and agencies and industry organizations.

TERTIARY AND ALL-INDUSTRY INDEXES

The tertiary and all-industry indexes are unique to Japan. The tertiary index is a monthly measure of the service sector of the economy, while the all-industry index combines the tertiary index with most other industries. Analysts sometimes favor the all-industry index since it encompasses the entire economy. The indexes are published around midmonth, with about a six-week delay. For example, January 2006 data were published on March 23. METI's Economic Analysis Office prepares both the tertiary and all-industry indexes. Both indexes use the year 2000 as the base year. The data are seasonally adjusted.

Tertiary Indexes

A tertiary industry is defined by what it is not. A tertiary industry, therefore, is any industry specified in Japanese Standard Industry Classification

(JSIC) that is not in the agricultural, forestry, or fisheries (primary) industry or mining, manufacturing, or construction (secondary) industry. The tertiary index reflects activity in utilities, transport and telecommunications, wholesale and retail trade, finance and insurance, real estate, and services. The index excludes public-service and nonprofit organizations such as labor unions from coverage. The index is very volatile on a month-to-month basis. Service activity is notoriously difficult to measure so METI measures the activities within industry segments rather than by volume of output activity. Figure 11.5 tracks service industry behavior over since 1991.

The objective of the indexes is to give a comprehensive reading of service-sector production activity. The overall index is a compilation of several subseries that indicate productive activity in services as provided by individual industries using a measure of relative importance or value added of each industry as a weight.

The tertiary indexes were first published as estimates in 1976. In 1978, the estimates were verified, and adjustments were made to both the data and estimation method. The index was published with the base year of 1975 and is revised every five years. The 1995 revision changed the publication cycle from quarterly to monthly and also revised the scope of coverage to clarify the indexes' functions as economic indicators. The base year currently is 2000.

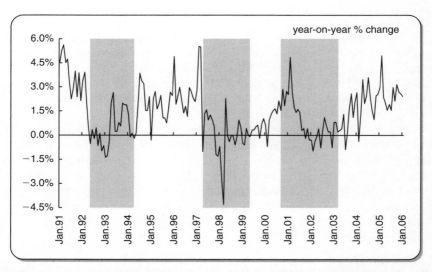

FIGURE 11.5 The tertiary index is a market favorite because it measures output in the service sector. While volatile, it generally moves with the business cycle.
Source: METI and Haver Analytics.

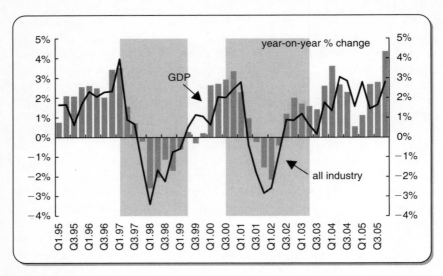

FIGURE 11.6   A companion index to the tertiary, the all-industry index adds all other major industries to the tertiary. The outcome is considered a good approximation of GDP.
Source: METI and Haver Analytics.

All-Industry Index

The all-industry index, the tertiary index's companion, combines the six industries that comprise the tertiary index with the construction, agricultural, and fisheries industries; the public sector; and industrial output. This index is considered a close proxy for GDP. Like the tertiary index, it is very volatile on a month-to-month basis. Figure 11.6 shows the close relationship between the all-industry index and GDP.

The all-industry index gauges production activity for all industries from the viewpoint of supply. As such, they are a proxy for GDP from the supply side. Specifically, weights are assigned, based on relative proportion of added value, using the 1995 input-output tables. Until the summer of 2006, the tertiary and all-industry indexes were released simultaneously. Since that time, the all-industry index lags the tertiary index release by about a week.

LABOR MARKETS

As in most countries, the employment data are sought as an early warning signal to economic performance. But analysts were puzzled by the relatively low unemployment rate given the dire economic conditions in the late 1990s and early 2000s. Although traditionally a lagging indicator, these carefully monitored data did not reflect the severity of the economic malaise. Rather one had to look below the unemployment rate for the reason. In part, it had to do with the tradition in Japan of having one job for life and the general cultural reluctance to fire employees. Although companies did cut employment, the cuts tended to be in facilities not located in Japan. Offered severance packages, many workers left the labor force entirely, reducing the numbers of workers looking for a job.

Labour Force Survey

The Labour Force Survey has been conducted every month in the post–World War II years since July 1947 after a trial period that began in September 1946. The survey provides information on the country's employment and unemployment. The data are compiled by the Labour Force Statistics Office of the Population Census Division of the Statistical Survey Department of the Statistics Bureau of the Ministry of Public Management, Home Affairs, Posts and Telecommunications.

Like most industrial economies, the data are compiled in accordance with the international guidelines set out by the International Labour Organisation (ILO). The survey is conducted on the last day of each month with the exception of December, when it is conducted between the 20th and 26th of the month. The report is published a month after the reference month. For example, February 2006 data were available on March 30. An annual calendar is available for the new fiscal year beginning April first at the end of March.

The survey targets about 100,000 household members who are 15 years old and older and are selected at random nationwide. The survey asks them about their employment and unemployment status. The ILO defines the employed as all persons above a certain a certain age who are paid employees, who worked one hour or more during the survey period with the goal of earning wages/salary, or who are self-employed and worked one hour or more for profit or family profit.

Unemployment

The unemployment rate is defined as the percentage of the unemployed to the total labor force (sum of the employed and unemployed). The number of unemployed is defined as persons 15 years old and over who did not work at all during the survey week, but were currently available for work and were actively seeking a job or were waiting for the results of past job-seeking activity. This differs slightly from the ILO standard that includes all persons who, during the reference period, were either without work, currently available for work, and seeking work. A Special Labor Force Survey is conducted to find out why people left the labor force. This survey captures those who left the labor force because of their severe economic situation, including those who wanted to work but gave up looking because they thought that no suitable work is likely to be available. Figure 11.7 shows that the unemployment rate is high by Japanese standards.

Both the United States and Japan broadly follow the ILO international standards. But their unemployment rates differ because each defines its employment situation differently. For example, Japan's definition of the criterion for seeking work is broader and includes persons who made arrangements to begin paid employment or have undertaken a self-employment activity within the past week as well as those who are waiting for the results of the past job-seeking activities. In the United States, however, the definition is narrower and includes only those who were seeking jobs within the past four weeks.

Unemployment data are derived from the Labour Force Survey. The survey covers all persons 15 years old and over; usually resident in Japan,

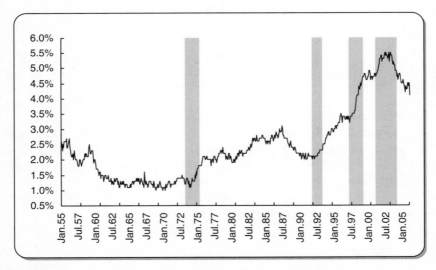

FIGURE 11.7 Although recovering, the unemployment rate still has a long way to go to reach its all-time lows. It should be noted that at its peak, the unemployment rate was 5.5 percent. This is lower than the unemployment rate lows in most of Europe.
Source: MIC and Haver Analytics.

except the foreign diplomatic corps, their staff, and dependents; and foreign military personnel and their dependents. The data are available on a seasonally adjusted and unadjusted basis. The unadjusted data are final and not subject to revision. The seasonally adjusted monthly data for the previous years are revised at the time of the January release at the end of February. More detail is available in Japanese only.

Employment

The number of employed persons covers both those 15 years old and over who are defined as employed and at work and those who are defined as employed but not at work. Employed and at work includes those persons who worked for pay or profit for at least one hour during the reference period. Family workers are also included in this category, even if they were not paid. Employed but not at work includes those employees who did not work during the reference period, but who received or expected to receive wages or salaries. The category also covers self-employed workers who did not work during the reference period and whose absence from work has not exceeded 30 days.

The data are reported on both a seasonally and nonseasonally adjusted basis. The nonseasonally adjusted data are final and are not subject to revision. The seasonally adjusted monthly data for the previous years are revised with the January release.

MERCHANDISE TRADE AND BALANCE OF PAYMENTS

International trade has been Japan's engine of growth. Trade statistics are published by the Ministry of Finance (MoF) and Customs under the provision of the Customs Law and the relevant international conventions. These data, and especially the bilateral trade balances, are followed closely by investors of exporters' stocks. China has replaced the United States as Japan's largest trading partner, but the importance of the United States remains huge. The Bank of Japan, at the request of the MoF, has tinkered with the value of the yen at times so that exports would be favorably priced in the United States and repatriated profits would be higher.

Merchandise Trade

Even though the Tokugawa Shogunate proclaimed Japanese isolation in 1633, trade and the country's external relations were confined to China and

Holland until the middle of the nineteenth century, and the only port open for these purposes was Nagasaki. Isolation ended when Western countries, including the United States, started to seek markets in the East. In June 1853, the U.S. East India Fleet, commanded by Commodore Matthew C. Perry, entered Uraga Harbor near Yokohama. In March 1854, acceding to Commodore Perry's demands backed by armed threats, the Japanese government signed a Treaty of Peace and Amity between the emperor of Japan and the United States of America. This was the very first step taken by Japan toward joining the international community. Eventually, the door to Japan was opened wider. In 1858, the first Treaty of Amity and Commerce was signed with the United States. It was followed by similar treaties with Holland, Russia, the United Kingdom, and France. Customs houses were opened in accordance with the treaties of commerce, and the ports of Hakodate, Nagasaki, Yokohama, Hyogo, Osaka, and Niigata were opened to international trade.

From around 1931, international trade was increasingly subjected to protectionist policies such as tariff barriers, and the world was divided into economic blocs. In Asia, the Manchurian Incident of 1931 was followed by the North China Incident in 1937. In Europe, hostilities led to the outbreak of war in 1939, and the whole world soon followed.

Japan's external trade declined with the intensification of the wartime regime. After the outbreak of war in the Pacific in December 1941, external trade was limited mainly to southern Asia and Manchuria. Shipping was brought under state control to reinforce military transport capacity.

External trade remained under the strict control of the occupation forces in the post–World War II years. However, this control was gradually relaxed, and was withdrawn completely in January 1950. The Japanese economy resumed its growth and Japan rejoined the international economic community. Additional impetus to external trade was given by Japan's accession to the General Agreement on Tariffs and Trade (GATT) in 1955. At that time, Japan embarked on a modernization of its customs laws and tariffs.

Preliminary data are issued on a monthly basis with a lag of a month. For example, data for February 2006 were available on March 22. But the data are not final until they are revised in March of the following year. The data are prepared by the MoF. Although an advance calendar does exist, the release dates are listed as not yet confirmed (NYC) until a week before the actual release. The data are based on customs declarations. The export and import statistics do not include goods of small value (less than ¥200,000), samples, goods smuggled, gifts, ships' and aircrafts' stores, personal effects of travelers, traveling entertainers' props, U.S. and UN Forces goods, and

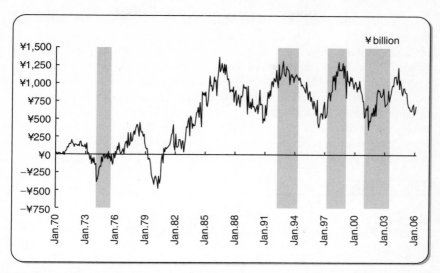

FIGURE 11.8 Merchandise trade kept at least part of the economy afloat when the domestic economy plummeted. Japan has always been a trade-driven economy. *Source:* Ministry of Finance, JTA, and Haver Analytics.

shipping containers that are repeatedly used. Figure 11.8 shows Japan's hefty trade surplus.

Balance of Payments

Data are compiled by the central bank and the MoF in accordance with the fifth edition of the International Monetary Fund's (IMF's) *Balance of Payments Manual*, and record all external economic transactions in Japan in a fixed period. Unlike the United States and the United Kingdom, where the data are available on a quarterly basis, data here are published monthly about six to seven weeks after the reference month (April 2006 data were available on June 12). They cover exports and imports of goods and services; net income flows; net current transfers; and capital and financial account items with separately identifiable data for direct investment, portfolio investment, financial derivatives, other investment, financial account items excluding securities lending, and changes in reserve assets. The data are provisional when first released. The final data are published on a quarterly schedule about four months after the end of the reference quarter.

The BoP compiles the transactions between residents and nonresidents, which consist of those involving goods, services, and income; those involving financial claims and liabilities; and transfers. A transaction is defined as an economic flow that reflects the creation, transformation, exchange, transfer, or extinction of economic value and involves changes in ownership of goods and/or financial assets, the provision of services, or the provision of labor and capital. To facilitate comparison with domestic statistics, foreign currency–denominated transactions are converted into yen at the prevailing rate in the foreign exchange market.

RETAIL SALES

The consumer was missing in action as the Japanese economy struggled to recover from its deflationary malaise. With prices falling and employment faltering, the consumer had little impetus to buy. Two of the more important indicators of consumer spending are workers' household spending and retail sales. The former details the expenditures by wage earners, a most important component of the economy, while the latter breaks down sales by establishment.

Workers' Household Spending

The Family Income and Expenditure Survey was developed to track income and consumption trends monthly, particularly in workers' households. This segment of the population is viewed as a critical component of consumer spending. Since the collapse of the bubble economy, analysts looked to worker spending as a guide toward the revival of consumer spending as a whole, which accounts for about 60 percent of the economy. The data for the reference month are available at the end of the following month. For example, April 2006 data were available on May 30. The data are in yen. Most observers track the year-on-year percent change.

Retail Sales

Retail sales data are published by the METI in the Current Survey of Commerce and give the yen value of sales in the reference month. Data are available about a month after the reference month. For example, February 2006 data were available on March 29. Retail sales are available in total and for large-scale retailers. There are also commercial sales and wholesale sales in the report. Retail sales are revised about two weeks later, but these data are available only in Japanese. Figure 11.9 graphically illustrates the weakness in consumer demand.

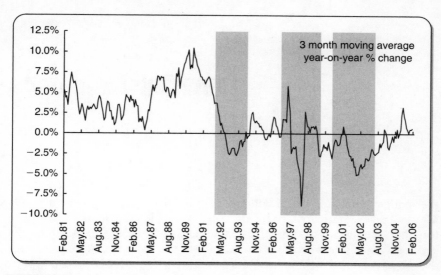

FIGURE 11.9   The weakness of the domestic sector over the years has been evident in consumer spending as illustrated by retail sales.
Source: METI and Haver Analytics.

CHAPTER 12

Canadian Indicators

Canadian indicators are straightforward. There is one governmental statistics agency, Statistics Canada or StatCan—which is a definite advantage for data watchers. An annual calendar is available in December of the previous year. Release dates seldom change. A notable exception was after the August 2003 blackout in Ontario and parts of the U.S. East Coast, which forced delays—but mainly because businesses were closed and could not get data to StatCan. Data are released at 8:30 A.M. ET with the exception of the Labour Report and the consumer price index (CPI) releases. They are released at 7:00 A.M. ET. Each indicator report provides complete description of the indicator. The report also contains analysis in easy-to-read language and graphs.

Proximity to the United States invites comparisons with U.S. performance and data. However, it should be emphasized that Canadian indicators are unique to Canada and not the mirror image of the United States. The one exception is bilateral merchandise trade data. Here, the U.S. Commerce Department and StatCan exchange data for purposes of accuracy and both the Canadian and U.S. reports are released at the same time and on the same day of each month.

STATISTICS CANADA

Statistics Canada is responsible for all government data collection and reporting, including a census that is conducted every five years. Its mission is to provide objective information and analyses about all aspects of Canadian society and its economy. The agency is mandated by law to collect, compile, analyze, and publish information on the economy, institutions, and population. The data are used by the government and the Bank of Canada to analyze and develop fiscal and monetary policies. In the private sector, the data are used to evaluate economic performance and investment opportunities that are available in Canada. The information in this chapter is based on readily available information about each indicator on Statistics Canada's bilingual web site, www.statcan.ca.

GROSS DOMESTIC PRODUCT

StatCan issues two distinct gross domestic product (GDP) reports: the standard quarterly report, similar to those of other countries, and a monthly GDP report. Their methodology follows most of the international guidelines set out in the System of National Accounts 1993 (see Chapter 8).

Quarterly GDP

The National Income and Expenditure Accounts give the basic data by which one can assess Canadian economic performance. While gross national product (GNP) measures the earnings of all factors of production regardless of where they are located, GDP measures the unduplicated value of production that originates only within the country's geographic boundaries, regardless of ownership. The more important measure is GDP. Figure 12.1 shows GDP along with the investment and consumption components.

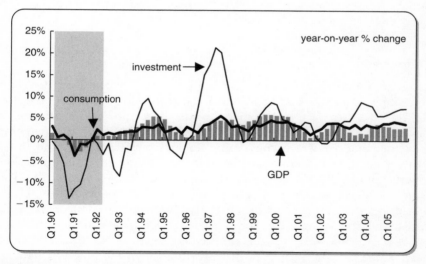

FIGURE 12.1   Like other English-speaking countries, the backbone of the Canadian economy is the consumer. And like the United Kingdom and Australia, the Canadian economy has been growing since 1992.
Source: Statistics Canada and Haver Analytics.

GDP data are issued two months after the quarter's end and trail most other industrial countries with the exception of Australia. For example, first-quarter 2006 data were released on May 31, 2006. But, unlike the United States and many other countries, the data are issued once a quarter and do not go through a monthly revision cycle even though changes are made on a rolling basis. (In the United States, advance, preliminary, and final estimates are published in three consecutive monthly releases after the quarter ends.) The Canadian quarterly estimates are revised when those for subsequent quarters of the same year are published. When the first quarter of a new year is released, annual revisions extend back for four years. Usually, the data are not revised again except when historical revisions are carried out, about once every 10 years.

GDP is measured three ways: by incomes arising from production, by final expenditures on production, and by value added for a particular time period. The statistical discrepancy measures the difference between the income and expenditure estimates. The data are derived from the Canadian System of National Accounts (CSNA), which provides the integrated framework for measuring the economy. The accounts are centered on the measurement of activities associated with production of goods and services and the sales of goods and services in final markets. GDP estimates are broken down to show how the various sectors of the economy (businesses, persons, governments, and nonresidents) interact with one another to produce output.

Monthly GDP

Unique to Canada is a monthly GDP report prepared by StatCan. (A private consulting firm, Macroeconomic Advisers, calculates a monthly GDP for the United States.) These data give investors a comprehensive estimate of the economy's performance on a monthly basis and could help pinpoint industries that are worth considering for investment purposes and those that are not. These data are published in lieu of the industrial production reports found in the United States and elsewhere. The data are calculated at basic prices and provide information from an industry point of view. These data also serve as a check on the quarterly GDP data. The data are released with about a two-month lag. For example, March 2006 data were released on May 31, 2006—at the same time as first-quarter 2006 quarterly GDP data. These data are subject to more revisions than the quarterly data as more information becomes available. Figure 12.2 shows monthly GDP and its components—manufacturing and services.

GDP by industry at basic prices is a measure of the economic production that takes place within Canadian borders. According to the Organisation

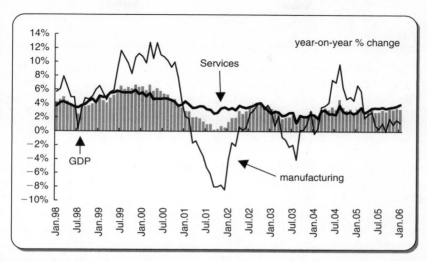

FIGURE 12.2 Monthly GDP faltered in 2001. Manufacturing sank after the 1990s dot-com boom. However, services remained on an even keel and kept overall growth positive.
Source: Statistics Canada and Haver Analytics.

for Economic Co-operation and Development glossary, basic prices are the amounts that are receivable from the purchaser by the producer for a unit of good or service output. They exclude any taxes that might be payable or any transportation charges that might be invoiced separately by the producer. Basic prices include any subsidy that might be receivable because of its production or sale. Capital consumption costs are associated with depreciation on buildings, machinery, and equipment and are included. The production estimates are prepared for 215 individual industries using the North American Industrial Classification System (NAICS). Estimates are included for such industries as fishing, logging, mining, manufacturing, construction, utilities, wholesale, retail, communications, transportation, finance and insurance, real estate, business services, government, education, accommodation, food, and health services. The data are seasonally and trading-day adjusted. Trading-day adjustments are based on the number of days in the month as well as on the relative importance of each day of the week.

PRICE INDEXES

Price data are important in any economy, but the measures take on heightened significance when the central bank uses an inflation target as a guide for

> ## FYI
>
> The Bank of Canada Web site has an interactive inflation calculator that uses monthly CPI figures from 1914 to the present to show users the impact of inflation on purchasing power.

setting its monetary policy. Financial markets monitor price index changes for clues to possible changes in interest rates. Although the Bank of Canada still pays attention to policy changes south of the border, they have managed in the past several years to unshackle themselves from their previous reactive posture. And although the Bank carefully weighs many other indicators, inflation targeting forces them to hone in on the consumer price index.

Consumer Price Index

Overall inflation is measured by the CPI. The monthly survey tracks about 600 goods and services, including food, housing, transportation, furniture, clothing, and recreation, that reflect an average family's typical spending patterns. The basket is updated periodically to reflect changes in consumer spending patterns. Data are available by region and nationally for many of the major expenditure categories. The base year is 1992.

While most data watchers in the United States prefer seasonally adjusted values, it is not so in Canada. Rather, the unadjusted percent rate of change is typically reported compared with the previous month and over the past 12 months. But a seasonally adjusted CPI is also calculated to provide an alternative picture of the short-term inflationary trend.

The central bank watches the CPI closely, given its focus on controlling inflation. The Bank aims to keep inflation within the range of its current target of 1 to 3 percent (see Chapter 5). Not content with the more common core CPI measure that excludes food and energy, the Bank developed its own operational core measure, which excludes the eight most volatile components—fruit, vegetables, gasoline, fuel oil, natural gas, mortgage interest, intercity transportation, and tobacco products—as well as the effect of changes in indirect taxes on the remaining components. Figure 12.3 shows the CPI and core.

Between 1913 and 1926, both the Department of Labour and the Dominion Bureau of Statistics (now Statistics Canada) produced separate CPIs, each using a different target population. But in the early 1920s, the

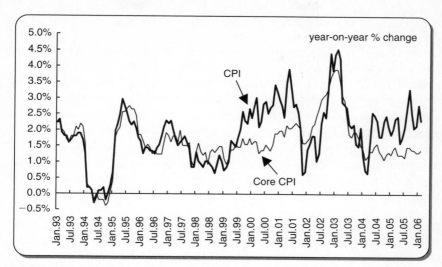

FIGURE 12.3 The CPI less food and energy kept its cool while the overall CPI was pushed upward by climbing energy prices, especially gasoline.
Source: Statistics Canada and Haver Analytics.

Dominion Bureau of Statistics started using Labour Department data to construct a monthly series beginning in January 1914. The present CPI has its roots in that set of indexes.

The CPI is used for a myriad of purposes in addition to serving as the central bank's inflation target. Contract payments such as wages, rents, leases, and child or spousal support allowances are adjusted for price increases based on the CPI. Adjustments to private and public pension programs and personal income tax deductions, along with some government social payments, rely on it as well. The index is used as input to government analysis as they evaluate and initiate new economic policies. It is also used as a deflator when converting current-dollar estimates to constant-dollar estimates, to eliminate price change effects. As discussed, the Bank of Canada uses the CPI along with special aggregates of the index in determining its monetary policies and to measure the success of its inflation-fighting policies. Finally, business analysts and economists use the CPI for economic analysis and research into inflation's causes and effects.

Producer Price Indexes

There are two sides to producer prices: input and output. In Canada, the raw materials price index (RMPI) reflects input prices or the cost of raw materials used to create a product, while the industrial product price index (IPPI) reflects output prices or those prices charged after manufacturing input. Data watchers carefully note whether manufacturers have pricing power—that is, whether they have the ability to pass increased costs on to their output prices. Investors watch the relationship between the two so that they can judge whether increased costs will influence profit margins.

Industrial Product Price Index   In the 1920s, the Dominion Bureau of Statistics began to cover the change in wholesale prices and manufacturing industries output. Some of their output had been included in the general wholesale index (GWI), but in a very incomplete manner. After World War II, the need to create national accounts led to the development of the industry selling price index (ISPI). The first ISPI series tracked a limited number of industries. But over the next 20 years, the remaining industries were included. In the early 1980s, the IPPI replaced the ISPI, covering commodities as well as manufacturing industry output. The index measures the price movements for domestically manufactured goods that are targeted for either domestic or export consumption. The IPPI series is used in monthly GDP calculations as well.

The IPPI reflects the prices that Canadian producers receive when goods leave the factory gate, that is, what producers receive for their output. This index is similar to the United Kingdom's producer output index. The index includes prices for major commodities sold by manufacturers, but it excludes indirect taxes and items such as transportation and wholesale and retail costs. The base year is 1997 and is subject to revision for six months.

The index is affected by the foreign exchange rate of the Canadian dollar versus the U.S. dollar, and each month StatCan notes its impact. For example, in November 2003, when the U.S. dollar was weakening, I noted in my weekly article, "International Perspective" (January 12, 2004), that during the month of November, the value of the U.S. dollar weakened against the Canadian dollar and pushed down prices of products that are quoted in U.S. dollars, notably motor vehicles and lumber products. As a result, the total IPPI excluding the effect of the exchange rate would have gone up 0.1 percent instead of declining 0.4 percent. However, when compared with November of the previous year, the influence of the exchange rate was much stronger. As a result, the IPPI excluding the effect of the exchange rate would have increased 1.0 percent rather than declining 4.0 percent between November 2002 and November 2003.

The IPPI series is used in a variety of analytical studies on price formation and is also used as an input to other price series as well as in calculating contract escalation clauses. The index was used, for example, in the long-running softwood lumber trade dispute with the United States.

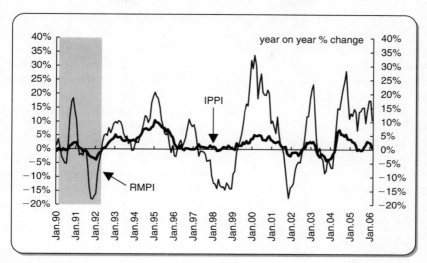

FIGURE 12.4 Commodity prices are notorously volatile and that volatility is obvious in the raw materials or input price index. The industrial product price index or output price index was less affected by the swings in crude oil and other commodity prices.
Source: Statistics Canada and Haver Analytics.

Some provinces tie their stumpage fees (those fees that forestry companies pay for logs taken from Crown or government land) to the relevant IPPI series. Manufacturing establishments are identified through the Annual Survey of Manufactures for data collection purposes. Industries are classified by NAICS.

Briefly, there are three sets of price indexes. The first is grouped by commodities; the second covers the total commodity output for individual industries; and the third, by stage of processing. Goods are divided into those used mainly as inputs or intermediate goods and those that enter directly into final demand or finished goods. Figure 12.4 shows the IPPI and RMPI.

Raw Materials Price Index (RMPI) The RMPI reflects the prices paid by Canadian manufacturers for key raw materials, either domestically or in world markets. It is published simultaneously with the IPPI and, like that index, has a base year of 1997 and is subject to revisions for six months. This index is analogous to the producer input price index published in the United Kingdom.

Unlike the IPPI, it includes all charges purchasers incur and includes transportation charges, net taxes paid, and custom duties, as well as the effects of subsidies, if any are paid to the purchaser. There are seven major product groups into which about 80 individual raw material price indexes are aggregated. The unique feature of the RMPI is that many of the prices are set in world markets and it includes non-Canadian goods.

In 1978, this index replaced the obsolete GWI, which had been produced since 1926. While the IPPI covered manufactured goods prices, there were no indexes covering unprocessed materials (other than agricultural products). In addition, there was a growing interest in energy prices, which had not been included at all in the GWI. The RMPI was introduced in January 1981 to ensure continuity with those in the earlier index.

The RMPI, like the IPPI, is used in the calculation of real GDP by industry. The RMPI basket weights are generally updated every five years. As in the IPPI, the RMPI uses NAICS and includes all industrial goods manufactured in Canada.

LABOUR FORCE

Labour force data provide investors with the earliest signs of industry performance. While other data are produced with a month or two delay, these data are available only a week to 10 days after the end of the latest month and 13 days after data collection. For example, February 2006 employment data were available on March 10. The data are compared with GDP to see if labor market trends are in line with general economic performance. The labor market is a lagging indicator and generally lags overall economic growth. For example, employers are usually reluctant to hire at the beginning of an economic recovery until they are assured that growth will continue. And they will continue to hire after the economy slows because employers want to be sure that they keep their trained personnel on hand to meet demand. But knowing the relationship between employment and GDP growth can help give the investor a more accurate reading of the economic tea leaves. As with all labor data, these have widespread use in government and in the private sector. Government uses the data to evaluate the effectiveness of many employment-related programs and initiatives including unemployment benefit criteria and policies. In the private sector, employment data provide fodder for academic research, while in the business sector, they provide important information in the nonstop search to learn how the economy is functioning. Figure 12.5 shows the improvement in the unemployment rate.

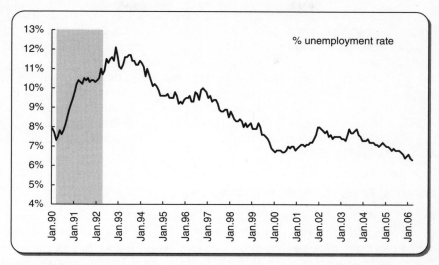

FIGURE 12.5   Since its peak in 1993, the unemployment rate has continued to edge downward.
Source: Statistics Canada and Haver Analytics.

Labour Force Survey

The Labour Force Survey (LFS) provides employment and unemployment data, which are among the most timely and important measures of the economy's performance. LFS estimates are the first of the major monthly economic data series to be released. The report is the resource for basic employment, unemployment, and participation rate data. The survey was initially developed in the aftermath of World War II to provide reliable and timely data on labor market conditions as the economy reverted to a peacetime footing.

Employment data, along with the rate of unemployment and the participation rate, are the survey's main components. Estimates for full-time and part-time employment are included along with employment estimates classified by industry, occupation, public and private sector. Data on hours worked, and much more, all cross-classified demographically are also included. Geographically, estimates are produced for all of Canada, the individual provinces, and a large number of subprovincial regions. Data about wage rates, union status, job permanency, and workplace size are also produced.

The LFS covers the civilian, noninstitutionalized population 15 years of age and over. Residents of the Yukon, Northwest Territories, and Nunavut;

those living on Indian reserves; full-time members of the Canadian armed forces; and inmates of institutions are not included in the count. Significant changes were made to the questionnaire in 1997 to upgrade and fill in data gaps and to make more use of computer-assisted interviewing.

The data adjustments are made every five years after new population estimates from the most recent census become available. At that time, all LFS data back to the previous census are reweighted using the new population estimates. For example, at the beginning of 2005, all estimates were adjusted to reflect 2001 census population counts, and LFS estimates were revised back to January 1976.

Survey of Employment, Payrolls and Hours

Payroll and hours data are released midmonth in a second report, about two weeks after the LFS. This is in contrast to the United States, where the employment situation report contains all relevant labor force data. The Survey of Employment, Payrolls and Hours is the only source of detailed information on the total number of paid employees, payrolls, and hours at detailed industrial, provincial, and territorial levels. The target population is composed of all employers except those primarily involved in agriculture, fishing and trapping, private household services, religious organizations, and military personnel of defense services. This report does not garner the attention in the financial markets that the LFS gets.

MERCHANDISE TRADE AND THE BALANCE OF PAYMENTS

Merchandise trade data are an important indicator of the Canadian economy's well-being and are keenly watched by market analysts. In particular, the Canadian dollar's value against the U.S. dollar will fluctuate on the news. The economy is dependent on exports, particularly of commodities and manufactured goods. Exports account for more than 41 percent of GDP, while imports account for over 37 percent. Over 87 percent of Canada's commodity exports go south of the border to the United States. As such, analysts watch the trade balance between the two countries carefully. Canada runs a deficit with virtually all countries with the exception of the United States and sometimes Japan. However, its positive balance with the United States more than offsets the deficit with other countries. The data are integral to the government's formulation of trade and budgetary policies. In the private sector, investors use the data to monitor import penetration and export performance as they look for investment opportunities. The data also serve as a vehicle for monitoring commodities prices, which in turn have affected virtually everything from stock prices of commodities firms to the value of the country's currency in 2005 and 2006.

Merchandise Trade

A unique feature in the collection of bilateral trade data is the cooperation between the Canadian Customs and Revenue Agency and United States Customs Service in preparing the report. Merchandise trade data are released at the same time each month by StatCan and the U.S. Bureau of Economic Analysis in conjunction with the Census Department. This ensures that the balances reported by the two countries are the same. Both classify data using the NAICS.

The merchandise trade data are derived from customs data and go through several iterations as they are converted first to a Balance of Payments (BOP) basis and then included as inputs in the Canadian System of National Accounts and GDP. The customs basis measures the change in the stock of material resources into or out of Canada as a result of the physical movement of merchandise. BOP information is adjusted to conform to the national account concepts and definitions so that all economic transactions that involve merchandise trade between residents and nonresidents are covered.

On a BOP basis, transactions are defined in terms of ownership change, while on a customs basis, a transaction occurs when a good crosses the border. Other major differences involve the country of attribution for imports (BOP is country of shipment, while customs is country of origin) and valuation. For example, freight is excluded from merchandise trade and added into transportation services for BOP purposes. An obvious example here is the classification differences for goods originating in Europe. The classification of goods made in Germany highlights the differences that can occur. For the purpose of customs classification, Germany is the country of origin. But since the goods were shipped from Rotterdam, for BOP purposes they are classified as goods from the Netherlands.

The International Trade Division of StatCan is similar to most other countries in its use of administrative data derived from customs sources to produce merchandise trade data.

Merchandise trade data are released midmonth, about six weeks after the end of the reference month. For example, January 2006 data were released on March 9. All data for the current year are subject to revision on a monthly basis. In February of each year, the revisions for customs-based data for the previous three years, along with the current year's customs-based data, are released. Figure 12.6 shows imports and exports along with the trade balance.

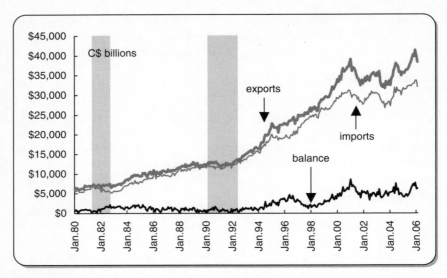

FIGURE 12.6   Merchandise trade has benefited from Canada's vast crude oil supplies as demand soared in the 2000s, especially from Canada's neighbor in the South.
Source: Statistics Canada and Haver Analytics.

Balance of Payments

The BOP covers all economic transactions between Canadian residents and nonresidents. It includes the current account and the capital and financial accounts. The current account covers transactions on goods, services, investment income, and current transfers. Transactions in exports and interest income are examples of receipts, while imports and interest expense are examples of payments. The balance from these transactions determines whether Canada's current account is in surplus or deficit. The data are compiled in accordance with international standards as put forth in the fifth edition of the International Monetary Fund's *Balance of Payments Manual.*

The capital and financial account is mainly composed of transactions in financial instruments and are classified into direct investment, portfolio investment, and other investment. These investments belong to either Canadian residents (Canadian assets) or foreign residents (Canadian liabilities). Transactions resulting in a capital inflow are presented as positive values, while capital outflows from Canada are shown as negative values.

A current account surplus or deficit should correspond to an equivalent outflow or inflow in the capital and financial account. In other words, the two accounts should add to zero. In fact, because the data are compiled from multiple sources, the two rarely match. As a result, the statistical discrepancy is needed to balance the accounts. (A statistical discrepancy occurs when balancing the income and expenditure accounts in GDP as well.)

RETAIL SALES

Retail sales are a key indicator of consumer health and a key monthly indicator of consumer purchasing patterns. Furthermore, retail sales are an important component of GDP and are input to many economic models used in both the public and private sectors to project economic performance. For example, the Bank of Canada uses the data in its interest rate decision-making process. Businesses use retail sales estimates to track their own performance against industry averages and to prepare expansion plans along with investment strategies. They are keenly watched by analysts looking to invest in Canada. Unlike European data, auto sales are an important component of the overall series. And it is not uncommon for analysts to look at retail sales excluding the automotive sector, which in Canada includes new and used auto dealers, including parts and gasoline station sales. This differs from the U.S. automotive component of retail sales, which does not include gasoline sales. Similarly, the various segments that would indicate the strength or weakness of the housing market are also monitored carefully. Figure 12.7 on page 234 illustrates the pattern of retail sales in the Canadian economy.

The Monthly Retail Trade Survey collects data on sales and the number of retail locations by province and territory using a sample of about 12,000 establishment groups. Retail sales estimates do not include any form of direct selling that bypasses the retail store such as direct door-to-door selling, automatic vending machine sales, newspapers or magazines sold directly by printers or publishers, and book and record club sales. Internet retailing activities are included in the survey only when conducted through the same legal structure as the retail establishment. The data are generally available about seven weeks after the reference month. For example, January 2006 data were available on March 21. Raw data are revised each month for the month immediately prior to the current reference month being published. In addition, revisions are made once a year, with the initial release of the February data, for all months in the previous year.

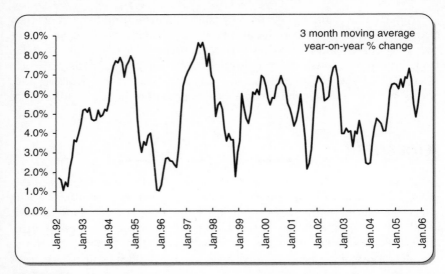

FIGURE 12.7   Retail sales provide a gauge of consumer spending. As such, they are monitored carefully by investors. Retail sales have been trending upward over the last several years.
Source: Statistics Canada and Haver Analytics.

MONTHLY SURVEY OF MANUFACTURING

Canada focuses on the shipments data of this report, which also contains information on inventories and new and unfilled orders. In the United States, the focus is on new orders. Shipments, which represent the monetary level of factory shipments for manufacturing durable and nondurable goods, are more relevant for this export-oriented economy. The data are used by analysts to evaluate the economic health of manufacturing industries. They are also used as inputs to GDP as well as for economic research. And, needless to say, retail sales data are used by the central bank in its decision-making process. Data for January 2006 were released on March 15, about six weeks after the end of the reference month. Figure 12.8 illustrates the large swings in shipments.

Since 1999, StatCan's Business Register has provided the sampling frame for the Monthly Survey of Manufacturing. The target population for the survey consists of all manufacturing-sector establishments that are on the business register. About 35,000 of the roughly 104,000 manufacturing establishments have a possibility of being selected to participate in the survey. An initial sample was drawn in 1998, when the survey was

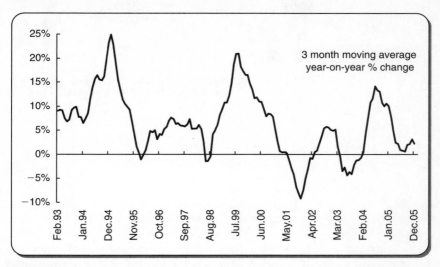

FIGURE 12.8   Canada monitors factory shipments, unlike the United States where orders are followed closely. The series reflects the downturn after the technology bust in the late 1990s.
Source: Statistics Canada and Haver Analytics.

converted to the NAICS and is refreshed each month. Every three years, all establishments in the sample are restratified to take into account changes in their value of shipments, while business units no longer in existence are removed. At the same time, some small units are replaced with others in the sample.

Monthly, preliminary estimates are provided for the reference month with revised estimates, based on late responses, for the previous three months.

CHAPTER 13

Australian Indicators

A ustralian data differ from other countries discussed here in many aspects. Traditional monthly data such as the consumer and producer price indexes, for example, are available only on a quarterly basis. Like Japan, release times are a challenge for data watchers in the Northern Hemisphere. Daylight savings time (DST) in Australia is the reverse of that in the United States and Europe. When the United States begins to observe DST, Australia ends its observance so that there is a two-hour swing when data become available in the United States. The Australian Bureau of Statistics (ABS) releases data at 11:30 A.M. local time. This translates to 7:30 P.M. ET the night before when Australia is observing DST and 9:30 P.M. ET when it is not. A release calendar is available six months in advance. (In March, a calendar was available through August.) There is a wealth of information on the ABS Web site on each indicator.

Data releases usually include nominal, seasonally adjusted, and trend estimates for the series in question. The ABS uses Henderson moving averages to produce trend estimates from the seasonally adjusted data. The month-to-month movements of the seasonally adjusted estimates might not be reliable indicators of trend behavior because they can include irregular or nonseasonal movements. Henderson moving averages were derived by Robert Henderson in 1916 and were originally developed for use in actuarial applications. They are trend filters, commonly used in time series analysis to smooth seasonally adjusted estimates in order to generate a trend estimate. They are used in preference to simpler moving averages because they are capable of capturing trend turning points.

AUSTRALIAN BUREAU OF STATISTICS

The ABS is one of the oldest government statistical agencies. Its roots go back over 100 years ago to 1901, when statistics were collected by each Australian state for its individual use. While attempts were made to coordinate collections through an annual Conference of Statisticians, it was quickly realized that the fledgling nation would require a unified statistical office to develop nationally comparable statistics. The Commonwealth Bureau of Census and Statistics (CBCS) was established under the Census and Statistics Act in 1905.

The states continued to maintain their own statistical offices and worked together with the CBCS to produce national data. However, some states found it difficult to finance a state statistical office at the proper competence level needed to provide an adequate statistical service. In 1924, the Tasmanian Statistical Office transferred to the Commonwealth. Unification of the state statistical offices with the CBCS occurred only in the late 1950s. In 1974, the CBCS was abolished and the ABS was established in its place. The Australian Bureau of Statistics Act in 1975 established the ABS as a statutory authority headed by the Australian Statistician and responsible to the treasurer.

AUSTRALIAN SYSTEM OF NATIONAL ACCOUNTS

The estimates of national income, expenditure, and product provide the framework for monitoring the Australian economy's health and are closely followed and analyzed by government and private-sector economists alike. The information is utilized in short-term economic forecasting and in the underlying analyses for forecasts and economic policy. The data provide input to economic activity models that simulate the effects of economic policy and behavior and in international comparisons of economic performance.

Market analysts tend to focus on trend and seasonally adjusted chain volume measures of key indicators, including gross domestic product (GDP) as an indicator of growth; measures of income such as compensation of employees and gross operating surplus of corporations; final consumption expenditure components of government and households; gross fixed capital formation; the ratio of net household saving to net household disposable income; and production classified by individual industry groupings.

The Australian System of National Accounts (ASNA) provides the source data that is used to develop GDP. The accounts provide information about economic assets and activities for sectors, industries, and commodities, and about different types of assets, liabilities, transactions, and other economic events. In terms of economic information, the scope of the statistics is therefore very wide, and the only economic activities omitted are those that fall outside the defined boundaries of production, consumption, accumulation, and economic assets.

The principal economic events recorded in the accounts are production, consumption, and wealth accumulation. However, they also record income generated by production, the distribution of that income among the factors of production, and the use of the income. The data also contain the value of the economy's stock of assets and liabilities, and record events unrelated to production and consumption that bring about changes in the value of wealth. The ABS uses a single business register as the source of survey populations for most ABS economic statistics and applies national accounting concepts in the design of the register and the surveys.

The ASNA is based on the standards set out in SNA93. It does not include all of its elements, although Australia's implementation is more extensive than most other countries. The concepts and definitions generally conform to SNA93 standards, but with some minor variations that have been adopted to allow for particular Australian data supply conditions or user requirements.

GROSS DOMESTIC PRODUCT

GDP data are awaited eagerly by analysts, but the wait is long. Australia is usually the last of the major industrial countries to report GDP. For example, first-quarter 2006 data were not released until June 6. But these data which are released over two months after the end of the reference quarter have an advantage—they are more complete and revisions are not as prevalent—nor as large.

Data are disseminated in millions of Australian dollars (A$) for both current price data and chained volume measures of GDP. The current price estimates are compiled using both the income and the expenditure approaches, while the chain volume estimates use both the production and the expenditure approaches. The chain volume measures are obtained by applying an annually reweighted chain Laspeyres volume changes to the current price values of the reference year, which is always the last but one full financial year ending June 30 for which the data are available. The so-called headline chain volume measure is referred to simply as GDP. GDP at current prices is obtained by reflating the chain volume measure of GDP using the expenditure implicit price deflator.

GDP data are available by expenditure categories including household consumption, government consumption, gross fixed capital formation by government and by enterprises, changes in inventories, and exports and imports of goods and services. The data are available also by productive sectors. Using the Australian and New Zealand Standard Industrial Classification (ANZSIC), information is provided by components for all industries. Additional breakdowns are provided for the agriculture, forestry, and fishing; mining; manufacturing; electricity, gas and water; and transport and storage industries. Data are also available by income components, including

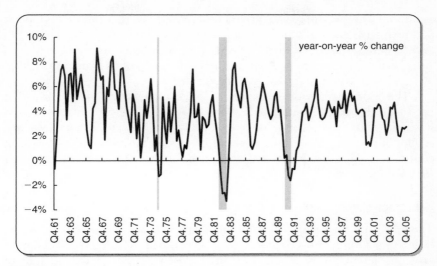

FIGURE 13.1 The economy has been averaging about 3.5 percent growth for the past 25 years. Like the United States, Canada, and the United Kingdom, the consumer is the primary engine of growth.
Source: Australian Bureau of Statistics and Haver Analytics.

compensation of employees, gross operating surplus, gross mixed income, and taxes less subsidies on production and imports. Figure 13.1 shows GDP growth since 1961.

Standard ABS seasonal adjustment methods are used except for various farm crops for which a special method is used. Seasonally adjusted estimates are provided for current price GDP and its income and expenditure components, the national income account, national capital account, external account, general government income account, household income account estimates and for chain volume measures for GDP and its expenditure and industry components as well.

Revisions to previously published data are made when the next quarter's data are released although most revisions are made in the September quarter release. In addition, long-term revisions to the chain volume measures are made in the June quarter release when all chain volume series are re-referenced to a new financial year. However, this change does not affect estimates of the movements in the volume series.

PRICE INDEXES

Unlike most other industrialized nations, Australia issues its consumer (CPI) and producer (PPI) price indexes on a quarterly basis. Price information is paramount to investors and analysts especially given that the Reserve Bank of Australia (RBA) uses an inflation target to set monetary policy. The PPI and CPI are released within a day or two of each other about three to four weeks after the quarter's end. For example, data for the first quarter of 2006 were released on April 23 and 25, respectively.

The indexes provide measures of price movements for a variety of product categories. Although they are followed closely by analysts, ABS has said that they are published primarily for use in the government's economic analysis. Price indexes are often used in business and government contracts to adjust payments and/or charges to take account of price changes (indexation clauses).

Consumer Price Index

The CPI is an important economic indicator and its movements have had direct and indirect effects on all Australians. The RBA's official inflation target is set in terms of the CPI and is used as its official measure of inflation for evaluating monetary policy success. Besides being an indicator of consumer price movements, the CPI has been used for pension and superannuation payments indexation and for determination of the size and nature of wage adjustments. Many business contracts are regularly adjusted to take account of changes in the CPI or in some of its components. Figure 13.2 shows how muted the CPI has become.

The CPI is regarded as Australia's key measure of inflation. It is designed to provide a general measure of price inflation for the household sector as a whole. The CPI measures changes over time in the prices of a wide range of consumer goods and services acquired by metropolitan households. It is revised only in exceptional circumstances, such as to correct a significant error. As is the case with all price indexes, the reference base year is changed periodically. Australia is unique in that its base period is not a calendar year but currently is the third quarter of 1989 to the second quarter of 1990 equals 100.

Producer Price Indexes

PPIs are published by stage of production (preliminary, intermediate, and final stage commodities) and by industry (selected manufacturing, construction, mining and services). The output indexes measure changes in the prices of goods and/or services sold by a defined sector of the economy while input indexes measure changes in the prices of goods and/or services purchased by a particular sector. The reference base year is 1998 to1999 equals 100.

The stage of production PPI includes indexes for the supply of commodities (goods and services) to the economy and covers those that are

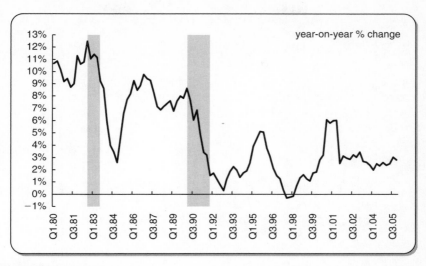

FIGURE 13.2   Inflation targeting has been credited with bringing a pesky problem under control. With an inflation target range of 2 to 3 percent, consumer prices have been under control for the past 10 years, with a brief break in 2000.
Source: Australian Bureau of Statistics and Haver Analytics.

domestically produced and as well as those that have been imported. Because they include imports, they are an alternative way to look at the largely existing PPI indexes that conventionally relate to the output of domestic industries at basic prices. These indexes may or may not include exports. Because the main focus is on domestic inflation, exports are excluded from the "headline" series. Figure 13.3 on page 242 shows changes in the PPI since the third quarter of 1999.

Other Price Indexes

There are other price indexes as well, although none are considered leading indicators of economic activity. They are the International Trade Price Indexes, which are intended to broadly measure changes in the prices of goods imported into Australia and goods exported from Australia; the Labour Price Index, which measures annual changes in the price of labor in the Australian labor market; and the Wage Price Index, which measures changes in the wages paid by businesses to employees.

Two types of price indexes covering a wide range of economic transactions are calculated as part of the National Accounts. The first is chain price indexes, which are calculated for all expenditure components and subcomponents of GDP. The second is the implicit price deflators, which

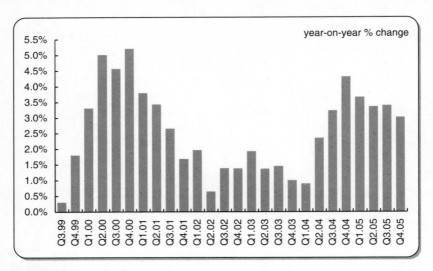

FIGURE 13.3 The PPI for finished goods has remained within a relatively narrow range after jumping in the second quarter of 2004 thanks to energy prices.
Source: Australian Bureau of Statistics and Haver Analytics.

are compiled at the same levels as for the chain price indexes but use the volumes of expenditure in the current period for their weights. Seasonally adjusted implicit deflators are preferred. Both chain price indexes and the implicit deflators are compiled quarterly and published along with the quarterly GDP report. Unlike the CPI and PPI, the National Accounts price indexes are often revised, sometimes to a significant extent.

LABOUR FORCE SURVEY

Given the long wait for GDP data, the monthly Labour Force Survey (LFS) takes on added importance for its insight into the economy. The economy, like those in the United States, Canada and the United Kingdom, are consumer driven. This makes employment data crucial to the analysts' arsenal when evaluating the economy's performance. The statistics of most interest are the estimates of the change in the number of employed and unemployed people, the unemployment rate, and the labor force participation rate.

The ABS has conducted the household survey since 1960. In February 1978, the survey shifted to a monthly basis from a quarterly one. The design of the survey has remained broadly the same since its inception but is regularly updated to ensure that it is the most appropriate for the provision of accurate labor force statistics. Unemployment has declined as pictured in Figure 13.4.

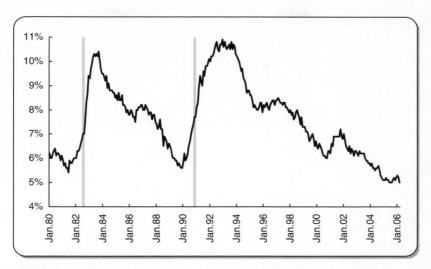

FIGURE 13.4 Unemployment has been declining for over 14 years—since the last recession ended in December 1991.
Source: Australian Bureau of Statistics and Haver Analytics.

The survey provides timely information on the labor market activity of the resident civilian population aged 15 and over. The unemployment rate is the main measure of unutilized labor, and the participation rate reflects changes in total labor availability. The data are seasonally adjusted and trend adjusted for selected series such as labor force status, employment by industry, and long-term unemployment. The survey contains detailed socio-demographic information along with the data on the size of the labor force and worker status, unemployment rate, participation rate, and gross changes in labor force status. It also includes employment data on a person's main employment and whether it is a full-time or part-time job, the hours worked in all jobs, job tenure, under employment, usual hours, hours in main job, preference for working more hours, reason for working less than 35 hours in the reference week, and occupation and industry in main job. Although most information is collected monthly, data on occupation, industry, status in employment, and under employment are collected quarterly in February, May, August, and November.

OUTPUT

There is no separately produced industrial production report. Rather, the data are included as part of the quarterly GDP report. (Canada includes industrial production data as part of its monthly GDP release.)

Industrial Production

The indexes are components of the production measure of GDP and are expressed as index numbers, rather than as chain volume estimates. Quarterly output indicators are weighted together using current price value-added estimates from the previous year. The resulting data are benchmarked to annual estimates compiled in supply-use tables. Indexes are available for aggregate industrial production along with the following industrial breakdown:

- Mining
- Manufacturing
- Food, beverage, and tobacco
- Textile, clothing, footwear
- Petroleum, coal, chemical, and so on
- Nonmetallic mineral products
- Machinery and equipment
- Metal products
- Wood and paper products
- Printing, publishing, recorded media
- Other manufacturing
- Electricity, gas, and water supply

Manufacturing output data are obtained from a quarterly ABS business survey covering around 16,000 management units. The data are deflated by the PPI to obtain chain volume estimates. Quantity output data are used for the other industries in the index. Mining data are obtained from the Australian Bureau of Agricultural and Resource Economics, as well as the state mining departments.

The data are provisional when first released and are subject to revision to reflect the more comprehensive data obtained from the annual data source. The data become final approximately three years after the end of the reference quarter.

MERCHANDISE TRADE AND BALANCE OF PAYMENTS

As in the United States, the United Kingdom, and Canada, the consumer generally supplies the stimulus to growth in Australia. However, Australia (along with Canada) is a key commodity exporter as well and its currency, the Australian dollar, is subject to market fluctuations depending on the supply and demand for major commodities (as is the Canadian dollar and for that matter the New Zealand dollar as well). Most investor reaction to new trade data takes place in the currency markets. Despite the heavy demand for its commodities, Australia has been running sizable trade and current account deficits thanks to heavy consumer demand for imports and fickle investment flows.

As with trade statistics everywhere, the data are used by analysts and the government alike to monitor overall demand for the country's products; to analyze the composition of commodity exports; to examine regional trading patterns; and to evaluate the impact on the domestic market of export activity, including opportunities for expanded production for export markets. The government uses the data to formulate and review trade policy as well as to support trade negotiation positions with the goal of developing or expanding overseas markets for its goods.

Merchandise Trade

Merchandise trade statistics are compiled from information submitted by exporters and importers or their agents to the Australian Customs Service. Adjustments for coverage, timing and valuation are then made to convert them to a balance of payments basis. The main source for services data is the quarterly Survey of International Trade in Services. To bring merchandise trade statistics on a recorded trade basis to a balance of payments basis, timing adjustments are made to ensure that the transaction is recorded in the period in which ownership changed, rather than in the period in which the transaction was recorded. Seasonally adjusted data are preferred in Australia unlike Japan where unadjusted data are key to analysts. Figure 13.5 on page 246 shows the deterioration in the trade balance.

Merchandise trade data are available on a monthly basis, usually about five weeks following the reference month. For example, March 2006 data were released on May 5. The data are classified by the various international systems including the Harmonized Commodity Description and Coding System or Harmonized System; the Standard International Trade Classification Revision 3 the Classification by Broad Economic Categories; and finally by the Australian and New Zealand Standard Industrial Classification.

Exports   International merchandise export statistics measure the quantity, value, and origin of all goods that are sent out of Australia permanently. The data provide information about the country's trading role within the global economy. Merchandise export statistics are inputs to the balance of payments and the national accounts.

Merchandise exports data follow United Nations Statistical Division recommendations and are defined as goods that subtract from the stock of material resources in Australia as a result of their movement out of the country. These include goods that have been produced or manufactured

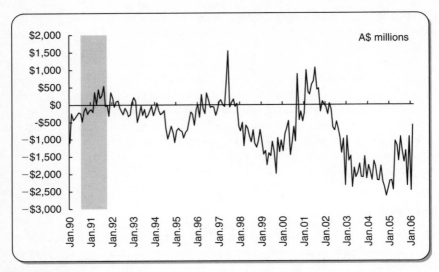

FIGURE 13.5 The merchandise trade balance has been mired in deficit despite the demand for Australian commodities.
Source: Australian Bureau of Statistics and Haver Analytics.

in Australia, and re-exports of imported goods (where the goods leave in essentially the same condition as when they entered the country). Merchandise exports exclude goods exported with the reasonable expectation of re-import within a limited time (goods exported for repair and return for example). Exports of goods which were imported with the reasonable expectation of reexport within a limited time (and were, therefore, excluded from merchandise imports) are also excluded.

Imports Like exports, imports are also inputs to the balance of payments and the national accounts. But they are also used to measure the country's dependency on foreign goods. And like exports, imports are evaluated for domestic market implications. They are also part of the government's formulation and review of trade policy and negotiations. Merchandise imports data follow United Nations Statistical Division recommendations and are defined as goods that add to the stock of material resources in Australia as a result of their movement into the country. These include goods brought into Australia directly for home consumption, plus goods imported into customs (bonded) warehouses. Goods are cleared from a bonded warehouse once the duty applicable has been paid. Merchandise imports exclude goods imported with the reasonable expectation of reexport within a limited time (e.g., goods for temporary exhibition in Australia).

Balance of Payments

The balance of payments provides a systematic record of economic transactions between Australia and the rest of the world. The data are compiled from a range of Australian Bureau of Statistics and other agency surveys, administrative data and special data sets. The data are a resource for a wide variety of users that range from economic analysts to policy advisers. The data help them monitor, evaluate, and forecast developments in the external sector accounts for domestic and international macroeconomic analysis and policy determination. The data are also used by government agencies, businesses, industry associations, research institutions, and others looking to study transactions and financial claims between residents and nonresidents. The uses vary from trade promotion and negotiations to market and industry performance studies. The framework used is based on the International Monetary Fund's *Balance of Payments Manual,* 5th edition.

There are four types of transactions recorded in the balance of payments accounts. The first involves transactions in goods, services, and income. The second involves the provision of financial resources such as foreign financial assets and liabilities. The third covers one-sided transactions or current transfers that are offsets to transactions in current real or financial resources that are undertaken without an exchange. An example would be foreign aid either in cash or kind. The fourth type is capital transfers that offset transactions that are undertaken, without exchange, in fixed assets or in their financing (such as development aid). The first and third make up the current account and the second, the financial account. The fourth type (capital transfers), together with a minor item for the acquisition and disposal of nonproduced, nonfinancial assets (such as patents), make up the capital account.

Unlike merchandise trade data, the balance of payments is available on a quarterly basis and is generally released about two months after the end of the reference quarter. For example, first-quarter 2006 data were available on June 6.

RETAIL SALES

Australia is a consumer-oriented country, so the monthly retail sales data are studied carefully by market participants. The two major series are total retail sales and retail sales less hospitality and services. Like retail sales reports in the United Kingdom, there are no auto sales data included in Australian report. The report does include monthly estimates of the value of turnover of retail businesses classified by industry and by state and territory.

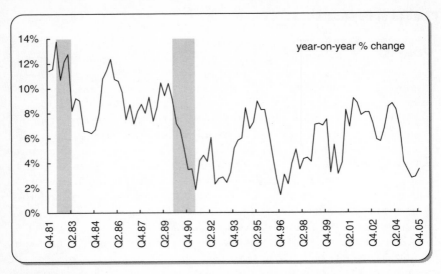

FIGURE 13.6   Investors watch retail sales closely, given the consumer orientation of
the economy.
Source: Australian Bureau of Statistics and Haver Analytics.

The principal objective of the series is to show month-to-month movement
of turnover as a percent change. The data are released about a month after
the reference month. For example, data for April 2006 were released on
May 30. Figure 13.6 shows retail sales since 1981.

The industry breakdown in the report follows the Australian and New
Zealand Standard Industrial Code (ANZSIC). Data are available for food
retailers, department stores, clothing and soft goods, household goods,
recreational goods, other retailing and hospitality and services. Retail trade
turnover includes net proceeds from licensed gambling activities undertaken
in the hotels and licensed clubs industry.

The data are seasonally adjusted by estimating and removing systematic
calendar-related effects from the original series. In addition, the data are
adjusted for increased Christmas spending in December and trading-day
influences that arise from the varying length of each month and the varying
number of Sundays, Mondays, Tuesdays, and so on in each month. The
data are also adjusted for Easter, when the holiday falls in March or April.
The monthly trend estimates are derived by applying the Henderson moving
average to the seasonally adjusted estimates. Trend estimates are used to
analyze the underlying behavior of the series over time.

MANUFACTURING SALES

Manufacturing sales are found in a report entitled Quarterly Business Indicators Survey. Only private-sector business units are included. Public-sector businesses such as all departments, authorities, and other organizations owned and controlled by Commonwealth, State and local government are excluded. Businesses with no employees are also excluded. Inventory data are not collected from businesses with fewer than 20 employees, because smaller businesses generally have more difficulty in providing accurate inventory data. Estimates for these businesses are derived by applying sales information to an estimated inventories-to-sales ratio. Profits data also are not collected from businesses with fewer than 20 employees. Estimates for these businesses are derived by applying sales information to an estimated profits-to-sales ratio. The data are classified according to the ANZSIC system.

The survey is conducted quarterly by mail and is based on a random sample of approximately 16,000 units which, in turn, is stratified by industry, state/territory and number of employees. All private-sector units with more than 250 employees, and other statistically significant units, such as joint venture partners, are included in the sample.

The data are seasonally and workday adjusted as they are for retail sales. The trend estimates are derived by applying a Henderson moving average to the seasonally adjusted estimates. The data are subject to revision.

CHAPTER 14

Chinese Indicators

THE WILD WILD WEST OF ECONOMIC INDICATORS

The Chinese economy is described widely as a developing one. And so too are their economic statistics. Analysts have long complained of their quality and although the government has tried to improve them, there is a long way to go. Even data that can be checked internationally such as international trade data are disputed by many. In China, it verges on black magic.

For example, the sum of gross domestic product (GDP) reported by the provinces regularly exceeds the national total. And different results emerge, depending on which measure is used. Measured by expenditure, growth accelerated in 2005 but measured by production, it is unchanged. So it is not surprising that private economists' efforts to make the numbers add up have produced a bewildering array of forecasts ranging from a crash on one extreme to a soft landing on the other. Early in 2006, China revised their GDP data to reflect the 2005 nationwide economic census, the first in six years. As a result, GDP was revised higher than originally reported in December 2005. The previous census was taken when private businesses and services generated far less activity than now.

Quite different from other developing economies, China suffers from too many statistics rather than too few. But China is also unique because of the size of its economy and the speed with which change is taking place. Now a mistake could be very costly, not just for China, but worldwide. China's economy has opened up dramatically. But its government has not. Information is viewed as a resource to be hoarded and as a means to exercise power. Free and accessible information is viewed as a modern economy's lifeblood. Without information, markets do not work properly, nor can rational investment decisions be made. Investors hate uncertainty. To feel more secure, investors need to trust the information at hand. This can be achieved by making economic information more transparent and more accurate.

Political and institutional problems bedevil statistics gathering. Different ministries collect their own data, each using its own methods. And so do the central bank and state planners, often measuring different things. The National Bureau of Statistics struggles to make sense of it all. But the bureau is weak, with only about 3 percent of its 90,000 statisticians having university degrees. It lacks both financial resources and political clout. Its local offices are often beholden to provincial governments, whose officials have a strong incentive to massage the numbers to suit their political masters. The bureau has to sell its data to cover its costs and, it is said, to pay ministries to part with information. And its methodology is obtuse.

The data for Hong Kong and Macao Special Administrative Regions and Taiwan Province of China are estimated and published separately and are not included in the national accounts of China.

Data are primarily the responsibility of the National Bureau of Statistics (NBS) of China. While international conventions such as the Standard National Accounts (SNAs) are followed, other international conventions are not. In short, there is no way to compare China with rest of the industrialized world.

GROSS DOMESTIC PRODUCT

China has been producing an annual national accounts since 1985. Between 1985 and 1992 the accounts were compiled according to both the Material Product System and the international convention of the System of National Accounts. The latter were essentially derived from the MPS accounts using a conversion system developed by the United Nations Statistical Office. In 1992, China adopted the SNA as its official accounting system, and since then national accounts data have been compiled in accordance with that methodology. Although quarterly national accounts have been estimated since the first quarter of 1992, unlike the usual international practice, the accounts are compiled on a cumulative basis—January to March, January to June, January to September, January to December, and not for discreet quarters.

Gross domestic product (GDP) at current market prices is classified by 16 industries and growth rates at constant prices are published. Agriculture and industry value added are estimated by the production approach (gross output minus intermediate consumption), while the value added for other activities is estimated by the income approach (sum of the components of value added). Although constant price estimates with a base year of 2000 are calculated, they are not published.

GDP by expenditure is compiled at current and constant prices, but constant price estimates are not published. These estimates are categorized by household consumption expenditure, government consumption expenditure, gross fixed capital formation, changes in inventories, and net exports of goods and services.

The data are compiled by the NBS and the People's Bank of China (PBOC). Estimates for nonfinancial corporations, financial corporations, general government, household, and the rest of the world sectors are available. The NBS also compiles production accounts, distribution and use of income accounts, and capital account data. They also develop the financial account by rearranging flow of funds financial transactions data that were originally compiled by the PBOC. There are no breakdowns of government consumption expenditures, gross fixed-capital formation, change in inventories, and net exports. Household consumption expenditures are divided into two components—urban and rural. The income components of GDP are published only in the input-output tables. The NBS uses the Chinese Industrial Classification of the National Economy. Figure 14.1 shows the annual change in GDP.

The preliminary estimates for a given year are published 20 days after the end of the year. Revised estimates, published nine months after the end of the year, are made independently from the quarterly estimates. The final estimates are published 17 months after the end of the year.

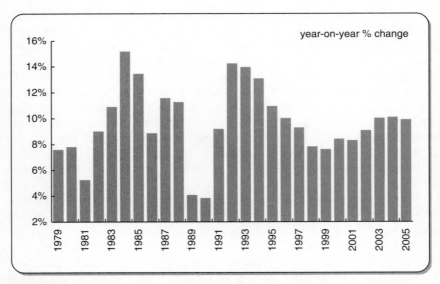

FIGURE 14.1   China's growth has averaged close to 10 percent, but substantiating the data is difficult.
Source: China National Bureau of Statisics and Haver Analytics.

LABOR MARKET

Unemployment

The data for the annual report on unemployment in urban and rural areas originate with the Ministry of Labor & Social Security, and the NBS uses the data as input for its report. There is some confusion here because the yearbook says that the data are collected and compiled by an NBS survey. The Department of Planning and Finance, Ministry of Labor and Social Security (MOLSS) compiles the data on number of registered unemployed persons in urban areas. The NBS data includes a breakdown by sex, age, and educational level, while the MOLSS data are published quarterly via a press release.

Those unemployed are defined according to International Labour Organisation (ILO) guidelines as those persons of the age 16 and above who are not working and are looking for work. The NBS compiles data on both employment and unemployment from the Labor Force Survey (LFS). From 1996 to 2001, the LFS was conducted three times a year. Since 2002, the survey is conducted twice a year—in May and November. The November survey covers all the country excluding Hong Kong and Macao Special Administrative Regions and Taiwan Province of China. The May survey covers urban areas only.

Employment

There are two main sources of data: the quarterly LFS and the quarterly establishment survey. Like unemployment, the LFS follows the ILO guidelines. The definition of employed includes persons who are 16 years of age and above, are engaged in economic activities, receive remuneration for their work, or earn income and have worked for one or more hours in the reference week. Those who have temporarily left their working place (for training, holiday, vacation, or other such reasons) are also considered as employed. Those who have left their working post while keeping their labor contract unchanged are excluded.

In the establishment survey, employed persons are defined as those who work in various urban units (excluding private and individual enterprises) and follow the ILO guidelines above. The LFS covers the whole country, excluding Hong Kong, Macao, and Taiwan. The establishment survey covers more than 2 million units in urban areas excluding private sector.

The employment data from the LFS are available on an annual basis, while the establishment survey data are published on a quarterly basis. The annual employment data are available two months after the end of the reference year and are made available through a press release. Eight months after the end of the reference year, detailed annual data are available in the *China Statistical Yearbook*. Quarterly data are available about 25 days after the end of the reference quarter in *China Monthly Economic Indicators*. The Department of Population, Social, Science and Technology Statistics in the NBS is responsible for compiling and disseminating employment statistics.

PRICES

Consumer Price Index

The CPI measures the change in the level of prices for a specified basket of goods and services normally purchased by urban and rural residents. Approximately 226 areas throughout the country are covered, including 80 counties and 146 cities. The current CPI is an annually chained Laspeyres price index and has been available since 2001. From 1978 to 2000, the index was compiled using current-year weights for most items.

The CPI is released around the 13th day following the reference month in an NBS news release. The monthly CPI is broken into eight categories. More detail is available on the day following the release and includes aggregate information by urban and rural areas and provinces. The data are posted on the NBS Web site. The first release of the annual CPI is in January and is published annually in the NBS publication *China Statistical Yearbook*, with detail including subcategories.

The CPI is a composite index that is derived from the urban and rural indexes. These are aggregated from city and county basic information. The index weights are updated every five years and are derived from the urban and rural household surveys that cover about 100,000 households (including 40,000 households in urban areas and the remaining in rural areas). The households also complete a diary of purchases for that year. The current weights are for the year 2000. Minor adjustments are made to the weights every January using the latest information from the household surveys. Figure 14.2 shows annual changes in prices as measured by the CPI.

In total, there are about 600 national items used in the calculation of the all-China CPI. Local authorities at the provincial and city level are allowed to add additional local area items that are important to the local area economy. The list of items is revised annually for representativeness based on purchases reported in the household surveys. The number of items can change from year to year, but rarely by more than 10 in any given year.

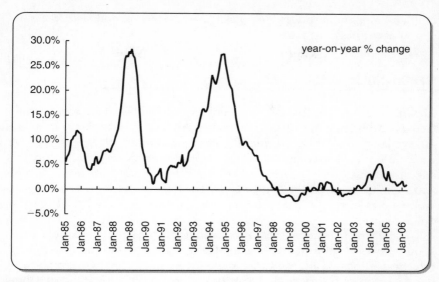

FIGURE 14.2 Inflation has been under control in China since the late 1990s, signifying that its rapid growth has not induced consumer price increases. *Source:* China National Bureau of Statisics and Haver Analytics.

Producer Price Index

The PPI measures the industrial products price changes for the domestic market. Unlike most other countries, China only produces a comparison with the same month in the previous year but not with the previous month. The PPI covers all manufacturing activities. The prices include excise taxes but exclude the value-added tax (VAT). The industry breakdown for the PPI follows China's Industrial Classification of the National Economy. The data include a 38-industry breakdown and are not seasonally adjusted. They are available by the 20th of the month following the reference month and are published in the daily NBS paper *China Information*.

The price data are collected from around 45,000 enterprises in 415 cities, in a special price survey and include about 2,700 items, which are then allocated into 186 subgroups. The current base year is 2000 and is updated every five years.

INDUSTRIAL PRODUCTION

The NBS does not publish an index of industrial production. Instead, it publishes estimates of value added in industry at current prices and growth rates in comparable prices, comparing the current period with the same period of the previous year.

MERCHANDISE TRADE

Merchandise trade statistics are compiled and published by the Customs General Administration (CGA) on a monthly basis. Preliminary estimates are available about 13 days after the reference month with details available within 25 days. The compilation of Customs statistics follows the concepts and definitions of the International Merchandise Trade Statistics: Concepts and Definitions, Revision 2 since 1980. Data are released for total imports and exports in the Chinese currency, the yuan or renminbi, and the U.S. dollar.

There are five main categories each for primary and manufactured goods. Detailed information is available by category, destination country, foreign enterprises, and domestic region, to name a few. Geographically, the data covers the customs territory of the People's Republic of China and excludes Hong Kong, Macao, and Taiwan. Figure 14.3 shows the U.S. merchandise trade deficit with China.

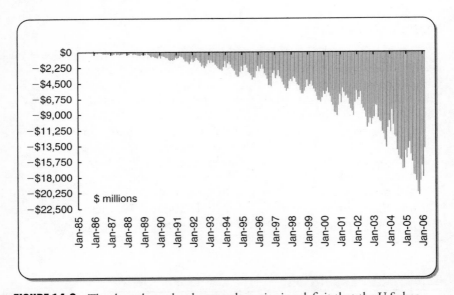

FIGURE 14.3 The data show the sharp and continuing deficit that the U.S. has incurred with China, especially in the past 10 years.
Source: U.S. Bureau of Economic Analysis, U.S. Census Bureau, and Haver Analytics.

Customs statistics cover all merchandise passing through the customs territory, excluding temporary imports or exports, goods on lease for less than one year, personal effects of travelers, goods consigned to diplomatic missions, confiscated contrabands, and goods in transit. Since 1995, goods entering bonded warehouses are recorded as imports when placed into the warehouses from abroad.

Since 1992, a classification based on the Harmonized System is used for collecting and compiling trade statistics. Imports are valued on a cost, insurance, and freight (CIF) basis and exports on a free on board (FOB) basis. Bilateral trade data are also available.

The Customs General Administration issues two publications of customs statistics, a monthly bulletin and a yearbook, both in Chinese and English. The monthly publication is available within 25 days after the reference month. The yearbook is available within six months after the reference year. Monthly preliminary trade data are released through China Central Television (CCTV) and the Xinhua News Agency, *China Daily*, *Economic Daily*, *International Business Daily*, *Economic Reference*, and *International Trade News*.

Key Indicators by Country and Issuing Agencies

European Monetary Union (Eurostat)

Gross Domestic Product
Unemployment
Harmonized Index of Consumer Prices
Producer Price Index
Industrial and Manufacturing Output
Merchandise Trade Balance
Retail Sales
M3 Money Supply

Germany

Gross Domestic Product (Federal Statistical Office, Deutsche Bundesbank)
Unemployment (Federal Statistical Office, Deutsche Bundesbank)
Employment (Federal Statistical Office, Deutsche Bundesbank)
Harmonized Index of Consumer Prices (Federal Statistical Office, Deutsche Bundesbank)
Consumer Price Index (Federal Statistical Office, Deutsche Bundesbank)
Producer Price Index (Federal Statistical Office, Deutsche Bundesbank)

Manufacturers' Orders (Federal Ministry of Economics and Technology, Deutsche Bundesbank)

Industrial and Manufacturing Output (Federal Ministry of Economics and Technology, Deutsche Bundesbank)

Retail Sales (Federal Statistical Office, Deutsche Bundesbank)

Merchandise Trade Balance (Federal Statistical Office, Deutsche Bundesbank)

ZEW Sentiment Index (ZEW)

Ifo Index (Ifo Research Institute)

France (INSEE)

Gross Domestic Product

Unemployment

Employment

Harmonized Index of Consumer Prices

Consumer Price Index

Producer Price Index

Industrial and Manufacturing Output

Merchandise Trade Balance

Consumer Spending on Manufactured Goods

Italy (ISTAT)

Gross Domestic Product

Unemployment

Employment

Harmonized Index of Consumer Prices

Consumer Price Index

Producer Price Index

Industrial and Manufacturing Output

Merchandise Trade Balance

Retail Sales

United Kingdom (Office for National Statistics)

Gross Domestic Product

Unemployment

Employment

Retail Price Indexes

Consumer Price Index

Producer Input and Output Price Indexes

Industrial and Manufacturing Output

Merchandise Trade Balance

Retail Sales

Japan

Gross Domestic Product (Cabinet Office)

Tankan Survey (Bank of Japan)

Unemployment (Ministry of Internal Affairs and Communication)

Employment (Ministry of Internal Affairs and Communication)

Consumer Price Index (Ministry of Internal Affairs and Communication)

Corporate Goods Price Index (Bank of Japan)

Industrial Output (METI)

Tertiary Index (METI)

All-Industry Index (METI)

Merchandise Trade Balance (Ministry of Finance)

Retail Sales (METI)

Canada (Statistics Canada)

Gross Domestic Product

Monthly Gross Domestic Product

Unemployment

Employment

Consumer Price Index

Industrial Product Price Index
Raw Materials Price Index
Industrial and Manufacturing Output
Merchandise Trade Balance
Retail Sales

Australia (Australian Bureau of Statistics)

Gross Domestic Product
Unemployment
Employment
Consumer Price Index
Producer Price Index
Merchandise Trade Balance
Retail Sales

China (National Bureau of Statistics of China)

Gross Domestic Product
Consumer Price Index
Merchandise Trade Balance

United States

Gross Domestic Product (Bureau of Economic Analysis)
Unemployment (Bureau of Labor Statistics)
Employment (Bureau of Labor Statistics)
Consumer Price Index (Bureau of Labor Statistics)
Producer Price Indexes (Bureau of Labor Statistics)
Industrial Production (Federal Reserve)
Merchandise Trade Balance (Bureau of Economic Analysis and the Census Bureau)
Retail Sales (Census Bureau)

National Income and Product Accounts vs. System of National Accounts

While most in the statistics community applaud the efforts to have comparable data, the United States is alone in using the National Income and Product Accounts (NIPA) rather than the standardized version. According to the U.S. Department of Commerce Bureau of Economic Analysis, the System of National Accounts (SNA) does not accurately reflect U.S. economic activity. But the Bureau of Economic Analysis (BEA) has been working with other members of the international statistical community to narrow those differences during the recently authorized review and update of the SNA. And BEA does restate gross domestic product (GDP) on an SNA basis on an annual basis for submission to the Organisation for Economic Co-operation and Development (OECD).

In an article in the December 2004 *Survey of Current Business* entitled "The NIPAs and the System of National Accounts" by Charles Ian Mead, Karin E. Moses, and Brent R. Moulton, the authors set out a detailed comparison between the SNA and NIPA accounts. The restated accounts are derived from published NIPA data that are then converted to the SNA basis in a series of reconciling adjustments that are based on underlying detail and related estimates. However, the adjustments do not deal with all the differences between the NIPAs and the SNA. For example, information is simply not available to cover illegal production, which, according to the SNAs, should be included as part of the production measured by GDP.

Both the NIPAs and the SNAs organize major economic institutions (households, businesses, governments, and nonprofit institutions) and their transactions so that the resulting estimates are meaningful for economic analysis, forecasting, and policy creation. The SNA is organized as a series of accounts that summarize the transactions of groups of institutions (or sectors), of groups of establishments engaged in production (or industries), and of the total economy. It includes a sequence of accounts that flow from one to another.

The SNA encompasses accounts that are organized as separate sets of accounts in the United States. The NIPAs are organized as seven summary accounts with nearly 300 underlying tables, and cover the transactions that are grouped in the SNA as the production account, the distribution and use of income accounts, and the capital accounts. In particular, in the NIPAs, the domestic income and product account provides estimates of GDP and corresponds to the SNA production account for the total economy. The domestic income and product account also provides information about the income from production that accrues to labor (compensation of employees), to capital (net operating surplus and consumption of fixed capital), and

TABLE B.1   Gross Domestic Product (SNA)

Gross domestic product
   Final (total) consumption
      Private consumption
         Households
         Nonprofit institutions
      Government consumption
         Individual consumption
         Collective consumption
   Gross investment
      Gross fixed investment
         Equipment
            Machinery & tools
            Motor vehicles
         Construction
            Residential construction
            Nonresidential construction
               Buildings
               Civil engineering
         Other fixed investment
   Total exports
      Exports of goods
      Exports of services
   Total imports
      Imports of goods
      Imports of services

Source: Eurostat.

TABLE B.2   Gross Domestic Product (NIPA)

Gross domestic product (GDP)
    Personal consumption expenditures
        Durable goods
        Nondurable goods
        Services
    Gross private domestic investment
        Fixed investment
            Nonresidential
                Structures
                Equipment and software
            Residential
        Change in private inventories
    Net exports of goods and services
        Exports
            Goods
            Services
        Imports
            Goods
            Services
    Government consumption expenditures
     and gross investment
        Federal
            National defense
            Nondefense
        State and local

Addenda:
    Final sales of domestic product
    Gross domestic purchases
    Final sales to domestic Purchasers
    Gross national product (GNP)
    Disposable personal income

    Current-dollar measures:
        GDP
        Final sales of domestic product
        Gross domestic purchases
        Final sales to domestic Purchasers
        GNP
        Disposable personal income

Source: Bureau of Economic Analysis

to government (taxes on production and imports) while in the SNA, these flows are included in the generation of income account.

Tables B.1 and B.2 show the difference between the NIPA and SNA categories for the GDP accounts.

According to the SNA, the accounts of the related estimates for each of the domestic institutional sectors can be added to obtain an account of the total economy. In the SNAs, a nation's economic institutions are grouped into five major sectors: nonfinancial corporations, financial corporations, general government, nonprofit institutions serving households, and households. Each institution is classified in one of these sectors, and all of the accounts for the institutions (production, distribution and use of income, capital, financial, and balance sheets) are included in the accounts for that sector. Each sector can be divided into subsectors; for example, in the general government sector, accounts can be compiled for central government, state government, local government, and social security funds.

In the NIPAs, economic institutions are also grouped into sectors, but the sector classification scheme is more complicated than in the SNA. Institutions are grouped in one way for measuring their contribution to production, and they are grouped in another way for measuring income, outlays, and saving. In contrast, the SNA sector definitions are the same for all of the accounts. For measuring the contribution, or value added, of various institutions to production, GDP, the nation's producers are grouped into three sectors: business, households and institutions, and general government.

Industrial Classification Systems

An important part of being able to compare data internationally is the manner in which the data are classified below the overall total. Standards have been developed to classify business establishments for the collection, analysis and publication of statistical data related to business economies. But clearly one size does not fit all. While national systems have been around for some time, only in recent years has there been an attempt to classify businesses across national borders. The United Nations Statistical Division has been working with the International Monetary Fund and the World Bank as well as statistical agencies worldwide to make national accounts data more compatible internationally via the International Standard Industrial Classification system (ISIC). This is one of several ambitious statistical efforts undertaken by international organizations. Under the aegis of Eurostat, the European Union has established a classification for its members (NACE) while in North America, the United States, Canada, and Mexico have established the North American Industry Classification System (NAICS). The purpose here is to familiarize the reader with the variety of industrial classifications that exist.

INDUSTRIAL CLASSIFICATIONS

North American Industry Classification System

North American Industry Classification System (NAICS) is the first-ever North American industry classification system. The system was developed under the auspices of the U.S. Office of Management and Budget in cooperation with Statistics Canada and Mexico's Instituto Nacional de Estadística, Geografía e Informática (INEGI) to provide comparable statistics across the three member countries of the North American Free Trade Agreement (NAFTA).

NAICS also provides better comparability with the International Standard Industrial Classification System (ISIC, Revision 3), which was developed and is maintained by the United Nations. In the United States, NAICS was adopted in 1997 to replace the old Standard Industrial Classification (SIC) system and is the first economic classification system to be constructed based on a single economic concept.

One of the goals for NAICS was to respond to increasing criticism about the Standard Industrial Classification (SIC) codes on the grounds that they did not reflect the economy's structure anymore. The new codes now reflect an updated structure of the U.S., Canadian, and Mexican economies including the emergence and growth of the service sector and new and advanced technologies. It is a flexible system that allows each country to recognize important industries below the level at which comparable data will be shown for all three countries.

Typically, the level at which comparable data will be available for the three countries is the detailed five-digit NAICS industry. However, this was not feasible for all subsectors or industries, so less detail is available. Canada and the United States agreed upon an industry structure and hierarchy to ensure comparability of statistics between them. They also established the same national detail (six-digit) industries where possible, adopting the same codes to describe comparable industries.

International Standard Industrial Classification system (ISIC)

The ISIC is a standard classification of economic activities arranged so that entities can be classified according to the activity they carry out. Now in its fourth revision, the ISIC is used worldwide in classifying economic data. The classification system provides a way to compare international data as well as providing guidance for national classification development that can help, in turn, develop sound national statistical systems. The categories at their most detailed level are delineated according to the customary combination of activities described in statistical units. While ISIC Revision 4 continues to use criteria such as input, output and use of the products produced, more emphasis has been given to the character of the production process in defining and describing ISIC classes.

Statistical Classification of Economic Activities in the European Community (NACE)

NACE Revision 1 provided the groundwork for a common classification system within the European Union and ensures comparability between

Member State and EU classifications for statistical purposes. Developed between 1961 and 1963, it was originally known by the acronym NICE. In 1965, the classification of trade and commerce in the European Communities was compiled to cover all commercial activities known as NCE. In 1967, a classification for services was compiled followed by one for agriculture. In 1970, the General Industrial Classification of Economic Activities within the European Communities was compiled and became known as NACE. And in 1970, NACE Revision 1 established a direct link between the European classification and the internationally recognized ISIC Revision 3 as developed under the auspices of the United Nations. These two classifications are directly compatible at the two-digit level. The French equivalent is called CITI.

The Australian and New Zealand Standard Industrial Classification (ANZSIC)

ANZSIC has been a combined effort of the Australian Bureau of Statistics and the New Zealand Department of Statistics for use in the collection and publication of statistics in the two countries. It replaced the Australian Standard Industrial Classification (ASIC) and the New Zealand Standard Industrial Classification (NZSIC). ANZSIC resulted from the need to improve comparability of industry statistics for the two countries. And international comparability has been enhanced by aligning ANZSIC with ISIC Revision 3, wherever possible. In preparing the classification considerable effort has gone into reaching a suitable balance between maintaining historic comparability and keeping pace with changes in technology and in the business environment. But while alignment with ISIC was considered to be desirable, ANZSAIC departed from the ISIC where it was inappropriate for local conditions and requirements. The basic design principle underlying the formation of categories in the ANZSIC is that the categories should reflect as realistically as possible the way in which activities are actually organized within business units.

All-industry index (Japan) The all industry index takes a reading of activity in the tertiary and index combines it with activity in the construction, agricultural, and fisheries industries; the public sector; and industrial output. This index is considered a close approximation for gross domestic product growth as measured by industrial and service sector output.

Average earnings (UK) The index measures how earnings in the latest month compare with those for the last base year when the index took the value of 100. The current base year is 1995.

Balance of Payments The Balance of Payments measures all monetary flows that enter a country from overseas less all that leave the country within a given time period. It is usually broken down into the current account and the capital account. The current account includes visible or merchandise trade and invisible trade, which is receipts and payments for services, such as banking or advertising, and other intangible goods as well as cross-border dividend and interest payments. The capital accounts include short- and long-term capital flows. They can include, for example, items such as repatriated profits that were made by selling investments (i.e., bringing profits home) and funds that are moved around the world by multinational companies in order to function.

Bank for International Settlements The Bank for International Settlements (BIS) is the central bankers' bank that fosters international monetary and financial cooperation.

Bank of Canada The Bank of Canada is responsible for monetary policy in Canada.

Bank of England The Bank of England, the oldest central bank, is responsible for monetary policy in the United Kingdom.

Bank of Japan The Bank of Japan (BoJ) is responsible for monetary policy in Japan.

Bank rate The interest rate charged by banks for loans.

Central bank policy announcements European Central Bank—announces its monetary policy with regard to interest rates usually during its first meeting of the month. The announcement is followed by a press conference where the president of the ECB briefs the press (and the markets) on their decision.

> Bank of Japan—issues a brief statement after its meetings, which are held every three to six weeks. The governor holds a press conference monthly after its meeting to discuss monetary policy.

> Bank of England—after its monthly monetary policy committee meeting, a statement is issued only if a policy change is made. Otherwise, no comment is made.

> Bank of Canada—issues a statement after each meeting, which occur about every six weeks to inform the financial markets of its policy decision.

Reserve Bank of Australia—issues a statement after each monthly meeting. They do not meet in January.

Federal Reserve—issues a statement at the conclusion of its meetings, which are held eight times a year to determine the near-term direction of monetary policy.

Consumer price index   The consumer price index (CPI) is a measure of the average price level of a fixed basket of goods and services that are purchased by consumers. Monthly changes represent the rate of inflation.

Core consumer price index   The consumer price index less volatile components is referred to as the core CPI. In Europe, a core measure excludes food, energy, and tobacco. In the United States and Canada, it is the CPI less food and energy. The Bank of Canada has an operational measure of the core CPI that excludes eight volatile items—fruit, vegetables, gasoline, fuel oil, natural gas, mortgage interest, intercity transportation, and tobacco products—as well as the effect of changes in indirect taxes on the remaining components.

Consumption of manufactured goods by consumers (France)   Consumption of manufactured goods by consumers is an indicator of consumer spending for household durable goods such as autos and furniture.

Corporate goods price index (Japan)   The corporate goods price index (CGPI), previously called the wholesale price index, is a measure of the average price level for a fixed basket of capital and consumer goods paid by producers.

Deflation   Deflation is a pervasive decline in the price level. Deflationary forces are often associated with extremely weak economic conditions.

Disinflation   Disinflation reflects a moderation in the rate of inflation. A period of disinflation can occur for any number of reasons, including healthy productivity growth, strong competitive pressures in global markets, and moderating economic growth.

Employment   Employment reports count the number of paid employees working part time or full time in a country's business and government establishments.

European Central Bank   The European Central Bank (ECB) is responsible for monetary policy in the European Monetary Union.

European Monetary Union   The European Monetary Union (EMU) consists of all EU Member States who have adopted the euro as their currency. There were 12 members until Slovenia joined on January 1, 2007. The EMU is also known as the eurozone.

European Union   The European Union (EU) is a federation of 27 European countries originally established as the European Economic Community in 1957 to enhance trade among members. It is expected that the number of members will continue to grow as other Eastern European countries join.

EU economic sentiment survey   Conducted by the European Union, the index is a broad measure of both business and consumer sentiment.

Factory shipments (Canada)   Factory shipments represent the dollar level of factory shipments for manufacturing durable and nondurable goods.

Federal Reserve Bank   The Federal Reserve (Fed) is responsible for United States monetary policy.

Federal funds rate This is the rate banks charge each other for the use of overnight funds in the U.S. federal funds rate target is the rate that the Federal Reserve controls by adding or removing reserves from the banking system.

Gross domestic product Gross domestic product (GDP) is the broadest measure of aggregate economic activity and encompasses every sector of the economy. In the EMU, it is an aggregate of all member countries.

Gross domestic product by industry (Canada) The gross domestic product by industry is the value added by labor and capital in transforming inputs purchased from other producers into that industry's output.

Gross domestic product—flash GDP flash is a preliminary estimate based on partial data from the GDP releases of Germany, Italy, and the Netherlands. The estimate also includes data from other indicators in France and Spain. The flash estimate, which is released about 45 days after the quarter's end, is an effort to speed up delivery of key economic data.

Harmonized index of consumer prices The harmonized index of consumer prices (HICP) is an internationally comparable measure of inflation calculated by each member of the European Union using a specific formula. Since January 1999, the European Central Bank has used the HICP as its target measure of inflation. The U.S. Bureau of Labor Statistics has recently created an HICP for the United States for international comparability purposes.

Harmonized index of consumer prices—flash The HICP flash is an early or flash estimate based on incomplete data is released about two weeks before the detailed release.

Household spending (Japan) Wage earner spending is an important gauge of personal consumption, which accounts for roughly 55 percent of Japan's gross domestic product.

Inflation targeting A monetary policy strategy aimed at maintaining price stability by focusing on deviations in published inflation forecasts from an announced inflation target.

Ifo survey Published by the Ifo Institute, this West German business sentiment index is closely watched as an early indicator of current conditions and business expectations. The Institute surveys more than 7,000 enterprises on their appraisals of the business situation and their short-term planning.

Industrial production or output The index of industrial production measures the physical output of manufacturing, mines, and utilities. In several European countries and in Japan, the preferred number is manufacturing output.

Industrial product price index (Canada) The industrial product price index (IPPI) reflects the prices that producers in Canada receive as the goods leave the plant gate. The IPPI excludes indirect taxes and all the costs that occur between the time a good leaves the plant and the time the final user takes possession of it, including the transportation, wholesale, and retail costs. In the United Kingdom, it is called the producer output price index.

Inflation Inflation is a steady increase in prices.

International Labour Organisation The International Labour Organisation (ILO) is the United Nations agency that seeks the promotion of social justice and internationally recognized human and labor rights. Most countries use the organization's employment and unemployment definitions as the basis of their labor force statistics.

International Monetary Fund The International Monetary Fund (IMF) is an international organization with 184 member countries. It was established to promote international monetary cooperation, exchange stability, and orderly exchange arrangements; to foster economic growth and high levels of employment; and to provide temporary financial assistance to countries to help ease Balance of Payments adjustment.

International System of Industrial Classification The International System of Industrial Classification (ISIC, Revision 3) is an industry classification system that was developed by the United Nations Statistics Division to provide a set of activity categories that can be used when analyzing statistics according to such activities. The detailed groups and classes of the ISIC are best suited for classifying the kind of economic activity of establishments.

Merchandise trade balance Merchandise trade balance measures the difference between imports and exports of both tangible goods and services. The level of the international trade balance, as well as changes in exports and imports, indicate trends in foreign trade.

Monetary Aggregates Monetary aggregates are alternative measures of the money supply by degree of liquidity. Changes in the aggregates can indicate the thrust of monetary policy as well as the outlook for economic activity and inflationary pressures. M3 money supply is the European Central Bank's broadest measure of money supply growth and measures overall money supply. It consists of M1, which is currency in circulation plus overnight deposits; and M2, which includes deposits with an agreed maturity up to two years plus deposits redeemable at up to three months' notice. Since January 1999, the ECB has used the three-month moving average compared with the same three months in the previous year as its target measure of money supply growth.

Monetary policy Central bank monetary policy is determined by targeting either interest rates and/or the money supply. A reduction in interest rates will spur growth while an increase may dampen growth. If a central bank were targeting money supply, increases would spur growth while decreases would curtail growth.

Manufacturers' orders (Germany) Manufacturers' orders measure new orders placed for manufactured goods, both domestic and foreign.

National accounts National accounts data provide the foundation for macroeconomic analysis. The information provides a multipurpose database that can be used to calculate gross domestic product, as well as to analyze a multitude of other areas of inquiry, including income and wealth distribution, financial and other markets, resource allocation, the incidence of taxes and welfare payments, environmental issues, productivity, industry performance, and so on.

National Income and Product Accounts National Income and Product Accounts (NIPA) is the format used exclusively by the United States to display its economic accounts. They include the value and composition of national output and the distribution of incomes generated in its production.

North American Industry Classification System   The North American Industry Classification System (NAICS) is an industry classification system that was developed as the result of the North American Free Trade Association (NAFTA), which joined Canada, Mexico, and the United States in a free trade zone. It enables cross-country comparisons by industries.

Organisation for Economic Cooperation and Development   The Organisation for Economic Cooperation and Development (OECD) is an organization of 30 industrial member countries with a commitment to democratic government and the market economy. It is best known for its publications, statistics, and research. It issues semiannual growth forecasts for its members and nonmembers China, India, Brazil, and the Russian Federation.

Overnight rate   The interest rate charged within the banking system (i.e., the interest rate charged by banks to other banks on loans that are due for repayment the following day. The Bank of Canada carries out monetary policy by raising and lowering its target for the overnight rate.

People's Bank of China   The People's Bank of China (PBOC or PBC) is China's central bank and is responsible for monetary policy in China.

Purchasing managers' index manufacturing survey   The Purchasing managers' index manufacturing survey is a composite indicator designed to provide an overall view of conditions in the manufacturing economy. It is based on monthly replies to questionnaires sent to purchasing executives in industrial companies. The data are collected by NTC Research and are available to subscribers only.

Purchasing managers' index services industry survey   The PMI service industry survey is a composite indicator designed to provide an overall view of conditions in the service economy. It is based on monthly replies to questionnaires sent to purchasing executives in service industry companies. The data are collected by NTC Research and are available to subscribers only.

Producer input price index (UK)   Input price index measures change in the prices of materials and fuels bought by U.K. manufacturers for processing.

Producer output price index (UK)   The output price index measures change in the prices of goods produced by UK manufacturers.

Purdah   Purdah describes what we call in the United States the blackout period—the time before and after Federal Reserve Open Market Committee (FOMC) meetings when committee members cannot comment on monetary policy.

Raw materials price index (Canada)   The raw materials price index (RMPI) reflects the prices paid by Canadian manufacturers for key raw materials. Many of these prices are set in a world market. Unlike the IPPI, the RMPI includes goods not produced in Canada. In the United Kingdom, it is called the producer input price index.

Remit   Remit is the name of the document or letter written by the Chancellor of the Exchequer that gives the Bank of England its inflation target.

Retail price index excluding mortgage interest payments (UK)   The retail price index excluding mortgage interest payments (RPIX) is a principal measure of consumer price inflation. It is defined as an average measure of change in the prices of goods and services bought for the purpose of consumption by the vast majority of households in the United Kingdom. Until January 2004, the Bank of England's inflation target was stated in terms of the RPIX. It was replaced with the consumer price index at that time to better conform with European Union standards.

Repo rate   The repo rate is the interest rate on securities repurchase agreements used by foreign central banks to influence domestic money markets.

Reserve Bank of Australia   The Reserve Bank of Australia (RBA) is responsible for monetary policy in Australia.

System of National Accounts (SNA)   A system of national accounting that enables nations to calculate the value and composition of national output and the distribution of incomes generated in its production using a similar format. It aids in the comparison between countries by providing a standard system of accounts for all to follow. Only the United States does not follow the SNA approach, but prefers its own system—National Income and Product Accounts (NIPA).

Tankan (Japan)   The Tankan is Japan's most widely watched business confidence indicator, surveying about 10,000 companies on their outlook for sales, profit, spending, and hiring. It is conducted by the Bank of Japan on a quarterly basis and is considered the most complete reading of economic performance in Japan.

Tertiary industry index (Japan)   The tertiary index measures activity in six industries: utilities, transport and telecommunications, wholesale and retail, finance and insurance, real estate, and services.

Unemployment rate   The unemployment rate measures the number of unemployed as a percentage of the labor force. In most countries, it is based on the International Labour Organisation definition of unemployment, which excludes job seekers that did any work during the month and covers those people who are looking for work and are available for work. In Germany, separate unemployment rates are calculated for East, West, and all of Germany. In the EMU, the rate reflects the aggregate rate for all member countries.

Unemployment rate (UK)   This measure of unemployment is based on the International Labour Organisation definition of unemployment, which excludes job seekers who did any work during the month and covers those people who are looking for work and are available for work.

Unemployment rate—claimant count (UK)   These data report on those who claim an unemployment-related benefit. The claimant count rate is the number of people claiming unemployment-related benefits as a proportion of claimants and jobs in each area.

Yield curve   The yield curve shows interest rate levels for different maturities. Typically, one looks at the Treasury yield curve by comparing interest rates for the 3-month bill, the 2-year note, the 3-year note, the5-year note, the 10-year note, and the 30-year bond.

ZEW Survey   The monthly survey, conducted by the Mannheim-based Center for European Economic Research (ZEW), asks German financial experts for their opinions on current economic conditions and the economic outlook for major industrial economies.

Bibliography

"A Brief Timeline of the People's Bank of China." *The Region*, Federal Reserve Bank of Minneapolis, December 2003. www.minneapolisfed.org/pubs/region/03-12/pboc.cfm.

"A Look at China's New Exchange Rate Regime." *FRBSF Economic Letter*, Federal Reserve Bank of San Francisco, September 9, 2005, Number 2005-23.

"A Standardized System of National Accounts." Office of European Economic Cooperation, National Accounts Studies. Paris, 1952.

Atkins, Ralph. "Comment and Analysis: Central Bankers Eye Norway's Clarity on Rates." *Financial Times*, May 26, 2006.

Bagehot, Walter. *Lombard Street*. New York: John Wiley & Sons, Inc., 1999.

Banister, Judith. "Manufacturing Employment in China." *Monthly Labor Review*, July 2005.

Bannock, Graham, and William Manser. *International Dictionary of Finance*, 4th edition. London: The Economist in Association with Profile Books Ltd. 2003.

Bekier, Matthias, Richard Huang and Gregory P. Wilson. "How to Fix China's Banking System." *The McKinsey Quarterly: The Online Journal of McKinsey & Co.* 2005, No. 1.

Berry, John. M. "Bank of Japan's Course Might Renew Deflation." *Bloomberg News*, November 4, 2005.

Blinder, Alan S. "Commentary: Inflation Targeting for the United States—Comments on Meyer." *Inflation Targeting: Problems and Opportunities*. Proceedings of a Conference Co-sponsored by the New York Association for Business Economics and the Canadian Consulate General in New York, February 2006.

Borio, Claudio, and Gianni Toniolo. "Central Bank Cooperation and the BIS: An Insider's Perspective." Fourth BIS Annual Conference, Past and Future of Central Bank Cooperation. Basel, Switzerland, June 2005.

"Brief History of National Accounts." Australian National Accounts: Concepts, Sources and Methods, 2000. http://abs.gov.au/AUSSTATS/abs.nsf/66f306f503e529a5ca25697e0017661f/6508c000a7de4a02ca2569a40006161-7!OpenDocument.

Chang, Chun. "Progress and Peril in China's Modern Economy." *The Region*, Federal Reserve Bank of Minneapolis, December 2003.

Chauvet, Marcelle, and Chengxuan Yu. "International Business Cycles: G7 and OECD Countries." *Economic Review*, Federal Reserve Bank of Atlanta, First Quarter 2006.

Dodge, David. "Inflation Targeting–a Canadian Perspective." Remarks to the National Association for Business Economics, Washington DC, March 21, 2005.

Economic Cycle Research Institute. Business Cycle Chronology. April 2006. www.businesscycle.com.

Gavin, William T. "Inflation Targeting." *Business Economics*, April 2004.

"Getting Japan's Measure." *The Economist*, March 31, 2005.

Gjedrem, Svein. "Experiences with Inflation Targeting in Norway and Other Countries." Speech at the Centre for Monetary Economics/Norwegian School of Management, Oslo, June 7, 2005.

Gramlich, Edward M. "The Politics of Inflation Targeting." Remarks at Euromoney Inflation Conference. Paris, May 26, 2005.

"Guide to Economic Indicators." *Economist*, 5th edition. New York: Bloomberg Press, 2003.

Leonard, Dick. *Guide to the European Union*, 8th edition. London: Profile Books, Ltd., 2002.

Levinson, Marc. *Guide to Financial Markets*, 3rd edition. London: *The Economist* in Association with Profile Books, Ltd., 2002.

Lomax, Rachel. "Inflation Targeting—Achievement and Challenges." Speech to the Bristol Society at the University of the West of England, Bristol, February 18, 2004.

Mead, Charles Ian, Karin E. Moses, and Brent R. Moulton. "The NIPAs and the System of National Accounts." *Survey of Current Business*, December 2004.

McGregor, Richard. "China economy larger than previously stated." *Financial Times*, December 13, 2005.

Meyer, Laurence H. *A Term at the Fed*. New York: HarperBusiness, 2004.

Meyer, Laurence H. "The Future of Money and Monetary Policy." Remarks at the Distinguished Lecture Program. Swarthmore College, Swarthmore, Pennsylvania, December 5, 2001.

Meyer, Laurence H. "Coming Soon: An Inflation Target at the Fed." *Inflation Targeting: Problems and Opportunities*. Proceedings of a Conference Co-sponsored by the New York Association for Business Economics and the Canadian Consulate General in New York, February 2006.

Meyer, Laurence H. "Inflation Targets and Inflation Targeting." Remarks to the University of California at San Diego Economics Roundtable, San Diego, California, July 12, 2001.

Meyer, Laurence H. "Remarks: The 2001 Homer Jones Memorial Lecture." Washington University, St. Louis, Missouri, March 28, 2001.

Munchau, Wolfgang. "The Beginning of the End for Inflation Targeting." *Financial Times*, June 5, 2006.

Murray, John. "Future Trends in Inflation Targeting: A Canadian Perspective." *Inflation Targeting: Problems and Opportunities*. Proceedings of a Conference Co-sponsored by the New York Association for Business Economics and the Canadian Consulate General in New York, February 2006.

Parker, George. "Eurozone Fairness in Question as Lithuania Denied." *Financial Times*, May 16, 2006.

Parker, George. "Slovenia Cleared to Join Eurozone in 2007." *Financial Times*, May 16, 2006.

Parker, Robert P. "Integration of U.S. Macroeconomic Accounts: A Progress Report." *Business Economics,* April 2005.

Picker, Anne D. "Euro Continues to be Market Focus." *Econoday,* January 12, 2004. www.econoday.com.

Picker, Anne D. "Bank of Japan vs the Government." *Econoday,* February 15, 2006. www.econoday.com.

Picker, Anne D. "Chain Weighted GDP Now Arriving at the EU." *Econoday,* July 19, 2005. www.econoday.com.

Picker, Anne D. "Oui or Non–EU Constitution on the Line." *Econoday,* May 11, 2005. www.econoday.com.

Picker, Anne D. "PBC Surprises." *Econoday,* November 3, 2004. www.econoday.com.

Picker, Anne D. "International Economic Indicators—the Good, the Bad and the Ugly." *Econoday,* August 31, 2004. www.econoday.com.

Picker, Anne D. "EU Constitution—Can 25 Members Agree?" *Econoday,* August 4, 2004. www.econoday.com.

Picker, Anne D. "Now There Are 25." *Econoday,* April 20, 2004. www.econoday.com.

Picker, Anne D. "Focus on China." *Econoday,* May 12, 2004. www.econoday.com.

Picker, Anne D. "EU Looks to the Future." *Econoday,* February 5, 2003. www.econoday.com.

Picker, Anne D. "Sore Time for the EMU." *Econoday,* September 18, 2002. www.econoday.com.

Picker, Anne D. "Spotlight on Japan." *Econoday,* April 10, 2002. www.econoday.com.

Picker, Anne D. "What Is Inflation Targeting?" *Econoday,* April 25, 2001. www.econoday.com.

Pollard, Patricia S. "A Look Inside Two Central Banks: The European Central Bank and the Federal Reserve." Federal Reserve Bank of St. Louis. *Review,* January/February 2003, pp. 11–30.

Roger, Scott, and Mark Stone. On Target? The International Experience with Achieving Inflation Targets. IMF Working Paper. Washington, DC, August 2005.

Svensson, Lars E. O. "The Instrument-Rate Projection under Inflation Targeting: The Norwegian Example." *Inflation Targeting: Problems and Opportunities.* Proceedings of a Conference Co-sponsored by the New York Association for Business Economics and the Canadian Consulate General in New York, February 2006.

Tainer, Evelina M. *Using Economic Indicators to Improve Investment Analysis,* 3rd edition. Hoboken, NJ: John Wiley & Sons, Inc., 2006.

Tett, Gillian. *Saving the Sun.* New York: HarperBusiness, 2003.

United Nations. A System of National Accounts and Supporting Tables, Studies in Methods, Series F, No. 2, UN, New York, 1953.

United Nations. "National Accounts: A Practical Introduction." New York: United Nations, 2003.

United Nations Statistical Office. A System of National Accounts, Studies in Methods, Series F, No. 2 Rev. 3, UN, New York, 1968.

United Nations Statistical Office, Provisional International Guidelines on the National and Sectoral Balance-sheet and Reconciliation Accounts of the System of National Accounts. Statistical Papers, Series M, No. 60, UN, New York, 1977.

Commission for the European Communities, International Monetary Fund, Organization for Economic Co-operation and Development, United Nations and World Bank, System of National Accounts 1993, Brussels/Luxembourg, New York, Paris, Washington DC, 1993.

White, William R. Is Price Stability Enough? BIS Working Papers, No 205. Basel, Switzerland, April 2006.

Wynne, Mark A. "The European System of Central Banks." Federal Reserve Bank of Dallas. *Economic Review*. Dallas, First Quarter 1999.

INDICATOR SOURCES BY COUNTRY

Australia

Australian Bureau of Statistics. "Australian National Accounts: Methods, Classifications, Concepts & Standards, 2000." www.abs.gov.au/AUSSTATS/abs@.nsf/DirClassManualsbyCatalogue/8AC0D9921051E17BCA2570B300807D36?OpenDocument.

Australian Bureau of Statistics. "Balance of Payments and International Investment Position, Australia, Concepts, Sources and Methods, 1998." www.abs.gov.au/AUSSTATS/abs@.nsf/DirClassManualsbyCatalogue/F0F9482037038946CA2570B300817354?OpenDocument.

Australian Bureau of Statistics. "Australian Consumer Price Index: Concepts, Sources and Methods, 2005." www.abs.gov.au/AUSSTATS/abs@.nsf/DirClassManualsbyCatalogue/DFC56A5A470ED1A9CA2570B400792923?OpenDocument.

Australian Bureau of Statistics. "International Merchandise Trade, Australia, Concepts, Sources and Methods, 2001." www.abs.gov.au/AUSSTATS/abs@.nsf/DirClassManualsbyCatalogue/71E55A18E58E2093CA2570B300831F57?OpenDocument.

Australian Bureau of Statistics. "Labour Statistics: Concepts, Sources and Methods, 2006." www.abs.gov.au/AUSSTATS/abs@.nsf/Latestproducts/6102.0.55.001Contents12006?opendocument&tabname=Summary&prodno=6102.0.55.001&issue=2006&num=&view=.

Australian Bureau of Statistics. "Methods, Classifications, Concepts & Standards." www.abs.gov.au/websitedbs/d3310114.nsf/Home/Methods,%20Classifications,%20Concepts%20&%20Standards.

Australian Bureau of Statistics. "Producer and International Trade Price Indexes, 1995." www.abs.gov.au/AUSSTATS/abs@.nsf/DirClassManualsbyCatalogue/162784BBD7C76796CA2570B4000FB740?OpenDocument.
Reserve Bank of Australia. "Currency Notes." www.rba.gov.au/CurrencyNotes/.
Reserve Bank of Australia. "Domestic Market Operations." www.rba.gov.au/DomesticMarketOperations/
Reserve Bank of Australia. "Financial System Stability." www.rba.gov.au/FinancialSystemStability/.
Reserve Bank of Australia. "Monetary Policy." www.rba.gov.au/MonetaryPolicy/.
Reserve Bank of Australia. "Payments System." www.rba.gov.au/PaymentsSystem/.
International Monetary Fund. Dissemination Standards Bulletin Board. Australia. http://dsbb.imf.org/Applications/web/sddscountrycategorylist/?strcode=AUS.

Canada

Bank of Canada. "About the Bank." www.bank-banque-canada.ca/en/about/about.html.
Bank of Canada. "Bank Notes." www.bank-banque-canada.ca/en/banknotes/index.html.
Bank of Canada. "Financial System." www.bank-banque-canada.ca/en/financial/financial_ system.html.
Bank of Canada. "Markets." www.bank-banque-canada.ca/en/markets/markets_sub.html.
Bank of Canada. "Monetary Policy." www.bank-banque-canada.ca/en/monetary/monetary_ main.html.

Canadian Indicators adapted from:

Consumer Price Index. Record number: 2301. Detailed information for April 2006. Data release—May 18, 2006. www.statcan.ca/cgi-bin/imdb/p2SV.pl?Function=getSurvey&SDDS=2301&lang=en&db=IMDB&dbg=f&adm=8&dis=2.
Industrial Product Price Index (IPPI). Record number: 2318. Detailed information for March 2006. Data release—May 1, 2006. www.statcan.ca/cgi-bin/imdb/p2SV.pl?Function=getSurvey&SDDS=2318&lang=en&db=IMDB&dbg=f&adm=8&dis=2
Raw Materials Price Index (RMPI). Record number: 2306. Detailed information for March 2006. Data release—May 1, 2006. www.statcan.ca/cgi-bin/imdb/p2SV.pl?Function=getSurvey&SDDS=2306&lang=en&db=IMDB&dbg=f&adm=8&dis=2.
National Income and Expenditure Accounts. Record number: 1901. Detailed information for fourth quarter 2005. Data release—February 28, 2006. www.statcan.ca/cgi-bin/imdb/p2SV.pl?Function=getSurvey&SDDS=1901&lang=en&db=IMDB&dbg=f&adm=8&dis=2.

Gross Domestic Product by Industry—National (Monthly). Record number: 1301. Detailed information for February 2006. Data release—April 28, 2006. www.statcan.ca/cgi-bin/imdb/p2SV.pl?Function=getSurvey&SDDS=1301& lang=en&db=IMDB&dbg=f&adm=8&dis=2.

Canadian International Merchandise Trade (Customs Basis). Record number: 2201. Detailed information for March 2006. Data release—May 12, 2006. www.statcan.ca/cgi-bin/imdb/p2SV.pl?Function=getSurvey&SDDS=2201& lang=en&db=IMDB&dbg=f&adm=8&dis=2

Canadian International Merchandise Trade (Balance of Payments Basis). Record number: 2202. Detailed information for March 2006. Data release—May 12, 2006. www.statcan.ca/cgi-bin/imdb/p2SV.pl?Function=getSurvey&SDDS= 2202&lang=en&db=IMDB&dbg=f&adm=8&dis=2.

Canada's Balance of International Payments. Record number: 1534. Detailed information for fourth quarter 2005. Data release—February 27, 2006. www.statcan .ca/cgi-bin/imdb/p2SV.pl?Function=getSurvey&SDDS=1534&lang=en&db= IMDB&dbg=f&adm=8&dis=2.

Monthly Survey of Manufacturing (MSM). Record number: 2101. Detailed information for March 2006. Data release—May 15, 2006. www.statcan.ca/cgi-bin/ imdb/p2SV.pl?Function=getSurvey&SDDS=2101&lang=en&db=IMDB&dbg= f&adm=8&dis=2.

Monthly Retail Trade Survey (Department Store Organizations). Record number: 2408. Detailed information for March 2006. Data release—May 19, 2006. www.statcan.ca/cgi-bin/imdb/p2SV.pl?Function=getSurvey&SDDS=2408& lang=en&db=IMDB&dbg=f&adm=8&dis=2.

Labour Force Survey (LFS). Record number: 3701. Detailed information for April 2006. Data release—May 5, 2006. www.statcan.ca/cgi-bin/imdb/p2SV.pl? Function=getSurvey&SDDS=3701&lang=en&db=IMDB&dbg=f&adm=8& dis=2.

Survey of Employment, Payrolls and Hours (SEPH). Record number: 2612. Detailed information for February 2006. Data release—April 28, 2006. www.statcan.ca/cgi-bin/imdb/p2SV.pl?Function=getSurvey&SDDS=2612& lang=en&db=IMDB&dbg=f&adm=8&dis=2.

"Canada's balance of international payments." *The Daily*, February 27, 2006. Statistics Canada.

"Canadian economic accounts." Fourth quarter 2005, December 2005 and annual 2005. *The Daily*, February 28, 2006. Statistics Canada.

"Gross domestic product by industry." February 2006. *The Daily*, April 28, 2006. Statistics Canada.

"Canadian international merchandise trade." March 2006. *The Daily*, May 12, 2006. Statistics Canada.

"Consumer Price Index." May 18, 2006. *The Daily*, April 2006. Statistics Canada.

"Industrial product and raw materials price indexes." March 2006. *The Daily*, May 1, 2006. Statistics Canada.

"Labour Force Survey." April 2006. *The Daily*, May 5, 2006. Statistics Canada.

"Monthly Survey of Manufacturing." March 2006. *The Daily*, May 15, 2006. Statistics Canada.

"Payroll employment, earnings and hours." January 2006 (preliminary). *The Daily*, March 29, 2006. Statistics Canada.

"Retail trade." March 2006. *The Daily*, May 19, 2006. Statistics Canada.

International Monetary Fund. Dissemination Standards Bulletin Board. Canada. http://dsbb.imf.org/Applications/web/sddscountrycategorylist/?strcode=CAN.

China

International Monetary Fund. GDDS. China. http://dsbb.imf.org/Applications/web/gdds/gddscountrycategorylist/?strcode=CHN.

National Bureau of Statistics of China. "Employment and Wages." www.stats.gov.cn/english/indicators/currentsurveysindicators/t20020424_18326.htm.

National Bureau of Statistics of China. "General Survey." April, 2002. www.stats.gov.cn/english/indicators/currentsurveysindicators/t20020419_17995.htm.

National Bureau of Statistics of China. "Investment and Fixed Assets." May, 2002. www.stats.gov.cn/english/indicators/currentsurveysindicators/t20020517_19812.htm.

National Bureau of Statistics of China. "National Accounts." April, 2002. www.stats.gov.cn/english/indicators/currentsurveysindicators/t20020419_17997.htm.

National Bureau of Statistics of China. "Production and the Consumption of Energy." May, 2002. www.stats.gov.cn/english/indicators/currentsurveysindicators/t20020517_19815.htm.

The People's Bank of China. "Introduction to the People's Bank of China." www.pbc.gov.cn/english/renhangjianjie/.

The People's Bank of China. "Monetary Policy." www.pbc.gov.cn/english/huobizhengce/.

EMU

European Central Bank. "The ECB." www.ecb.int/ecb/html/index.en.html.

European Central Bank. "ECB, ESCB and the Eurosystem." www.ecb.int/ecb/orga/escb/html/index.en.html.

European Central Bank. "European and Monetary Union." www.ecb.int/ecb/history/emu/html/index.en.html.

European Central Bank. "European Community." www.ecb.int/ecb/history/ec/html/index.en.html.

European Central Bank. "The Governing Council." www.ecb.int/ecb/orga/decisions/govc/html/index.en.html.

European Central Bank. "Monetary Policy." www.ecb.int/mopo/html/index.en.html.

Eurostat. "Annual National Accounts: Main Aggregates." March 2006. http://europa.eu.int/estatref/info/sdds/en/aggs/aggs_ sm.htm.

Eurostat. "Balance of Payments." July, 2005. http://europa.eu.int/estatref/info/sdds/en/bop/bop_ base.htm

Eurostat. "Balance of Payments." Eurostat Metadata in SDDS format: Base Page. http://europa.eu.int/estatref/info/sdds/en/bop/bop_ base.htm.

Eurostat. "Euroindicators—Business and Consumer Surveys." Special Data Dissemination Standard (SDDS), http://europa.eu.int/estatref/info/sdds/en/euroind/bs_ base.htm.

Eurostat. "European System of Accounts." http://forum.europa.eu.int/irc/dsis/nfaccount/info/data/esa95/en/titelen.htm.

Eurostat. "Euroindicators: National Accounts." Eurostat Metadata in SDDS format: Base Page. http://europa.eu.int/estatref/info/sdds/en/euroind/na_ base.htm.

Eurostat. "External trade Euro-Indicators." Eurostat Metadata in SDDS format: Base Page. http://europa.eu.int/estatref/info/sdds/en/euroind/et_ base.htm.

Eurostat. "Harmonised Indices of Consumer Prices (HICP)" February 2006. http://europa.eu.int/estatref/info/sdds/en/price/hicp_ base.htm.

Eurostat. "Harmonised Indices of Consumer Prices (HICP)." Eurostat Metadata in SDDS format: Base Page. http://europa.eu.int/estatref/info/sdds/en/price/hicp_ base.htm.

Eurostat. "Industry, Commerce and Services (European Business Trends). Eurostat Metadata in SDDS format: Base Page. http://europa.eu.int/estatref/info/sdds/en/ebt/is_ base.htm.

Eurostat. "Labour Market." Eurostat Metadata in SDDS format: Base Page. http://europa.eu.int/estatref/info/sdds/en/euroind/lm_ base.htm.

Eurostat. "The Eurostat Concepts and Definitions Database." http://forum.europa.eu.int/irc/dsis/coded/info/data/coded/en/Theme2.htm.

France

INSEE. "Industrial Product Price Indices." March 2003. www.insee.fr/en/indicateur/indic_conj/donnees/method_ idconj_ 25.pdf.

INSEE. "Unemployment and Jobs." July, 2004. www.insee.fr/en/indicateur/indic_conj/donnees/method_ idconj_ 16.pdf.

INSEE. "Household Consumption Expenditure in Manufactured Goods." May 2005. www.insee.fr/en/indicateur/indic_ conj/donnees/method_ idconj_ 19.pdf.

INSEE. "Industrial Production Index." January, 2004. www.insee.fr/en/indicateur/indic_conj/donnees/method_ idconj_ 10.pdf.

INSEE. "Consumer Price Index." www.insee.fr/en/indicateur/indic_conj/donnees/method_ idconj_ 29.pdf.

INSEE. "Quarterly National Accounts." August 2005. http://www.insee.fr/en/indicateur/indic_ conj/donnees/method_ idconj_ 26.pdf.

International Monetary Fund. Dissemination Standards Bulletin Board. France. http://dsbb.imf.org/Applications/web/sddscountrycategorylist/?strcode=FRA.

Germany

Federal Statistical Office. "Statistics from A to Z." www.destatis.de/presse/englisch/abisz/a_ bis_ z.htm.

Federal Statistical Office. "Foreign Trade Statistics." *Statistics from A to Z.* www.destatis.de/presse/englisch/abisz/aussenhandelsstatistik.htm.

"Harmonised Index of Consumer Prices." *Statistics from A to Z.* www.destatis.de/presse/englisch/abisz/Hvpi.htm.

Federal Statistical Office. "Index of Orders Received." *Statistics from A to Z.* www.destatis.de/presse/englisch/abisz/auftragseingangsindex.htm.

Federal Statistical Office. "Gross Domestic Product." *Statistics from A to Z.* www.destatis.de/presse/englisch/abisz/bip.htm.

Federal Statistical Office. "Retail Turnover." *Statistics from A to Z.* www.destatis.de/presse/englisch/abisz/einzelhandelsumsatz.htm.

Federal Statistical Office. "Index of Producer Prices for Industrial Products." *Statistics from A to Z*, www.destatis.de/presse/englisch/abisz/erzeugerpreise.htm.

"Ifo Business Climate Index." CES Ifo Group. www.cesifo-group.de/portal/page?_ pageid=36,1899103&_ dad=portal&_ schema=PORTAL.

International Monetary Fund. Dissemination Standards Bulletin Board. Germany. http://dsbb.imf.org/Applications/web/sddscountrycategorylist/?strcode=DEU.

"ZEW Indicator of Economic Sentiment." ZEW – Center for European Economic Research. www.zew.de/en/daszew/daszew.php3?mi=ZEW.

Japan

Bank of Japan. "About the Bank of Japan." www.boj.or.jp/en/about/index.htm.

Bank of Japan. "History of Japanese Currencies." www.imes.boj.or.jp/cm/english_ htmls/history.htm.

Bank of Japan. "Monetary Policy." www.boj.or.jp/en/theme/seisaku/index.htm.

Bank of Japan. "Organization." www.boj.or.jp/en/about/soshiki/index.htm.

International Monetary Fund. Dissemination Standards Bulletin Board. Japan. http://dsbb.imf.org/Applications/web/sddscountrycategorylist/?strcode=JPN.

"Guide to Official Statistics in Japan." Director General for Policy Planning (Statistical Standards), Ministry of Internal Affairs and Communication. www.stat.go.jp/english/index/official/inde2.htm#1.

"Short-term Economic Survey of Enterprises in Japan." Director General for Policy Planning (Statistical Standards), Ministry of Internal Affairs and Communication. www.stat.go.jp/english/index/official/211.htm#13.

"Corporate Goods Price Index." Director General for Policy Planning (Statistical Standards), Ministry of Internal Affairs and Communication. www.stat.go.jp/english/index/official/213.htm#8.

"Census of Commerce." Director General for Policy Planning (Statistical Standards), Ministry of Internal Affairs and Communication. "Census of Commerce." www.stat.go.jp/english/index/official/208.htm#1.

"Indices of Industrial Production, Producer's Shipments, Producer's Inventory of Finished Goods and Producer's Inventory Ratio of Finished Goods." Director General for Policy Planning (Statistical Standards), Ministry of Internal Affairs and Communication. www.stat.go.jp/english/index/official/206.htm#3.

"Indices of Tertiary Industry Activity." Director General for Policy Planning (Statistical Standards), Ministry of Internal Affairs and Communication. www.stat.go.jp/english/index/official/208.htm#9.

"Trade Statistics." Director General for Policy Planning (Statistical Standards), Ministry of Internal Affairs and Communication. www.stat.go.jp/english/index/official/208.htm#10.

"Monthly Labour Survey." Director General for Policy Planning (Statistical Standards), Ministry of Internal Affairs and Communication. www.stat.go.jp/english/index/official/203.htm#5.

"Family Income and Expenditure Survey." Director General for Policy Planning (Statistical Standards), Ministry of Internal Affairs and Communication. www.stat.go.jp/english/index/official/213.htm#2.

Italy

Italian data can be found at Istat (in Italian), Istituto Nazionale di Statistica. www.istat.it/.

International Monetary Fund. Dissemination Standards Bulletin Board. Italy. http://dsbb.imf.org/Applications/web/sddscountrycategorylist/?strcode=ITA.

United Kingdom

Bank of England. "Banknotes." www.bankofengland.co.uk/banknotes/index.htm.

Bank of England. "Financial Stability—the bank's role." www.bankofengland.co.uk/financialstability/index.htm.

Bank of England. "History." www.bankofengland.co.uk/about/history/index.htm.

Bank of England. "Markets." www.bankofengland.co.uk/markets/index.htm.

Bank of England. "Monetary Policy." www.bankofengland.co.uk/monetary-policy/index.htm.

Office for National Statistics. "GDP." www.statistics.gov.uk/CCI/nugget.asp?ID=56.

Office for National Statistics. "Retail Sales Index." www.statistics.gov.uk/CCI/nugget.asp?ID=122.

Office for National Statistics. "CPI." www.statistics.gov.uk/cci/nugget.asp?id=181.

Office for National Statistics. "RPI and Finding Data." www.statistics.gov.uk/cci/nugget.asp?id=21.

Office for National Statistics. "Labour Market Guide." www.statistics.gov.uk/about/data/guides/LabourMarket/default.asp.

Index